The Hidden Whisper

J.J. Lumsden

Published in 2010 by Bennion Kearny Limited.

ISBN: 978-0-9559114-1-5

Bennion Kearny Limited
6 Victory House
64 Trafalgar Road
Birmingham
B13 8BU

Acknowledgments

I would like to extend my heartfelt thanks to my friends and family for their support during the writing of this book. I would especially like to thank Charlotte Woodcock for her assistance and good humour. In turn, I am grateful to Claire Anderson, Paul Stevens, Danny Lopez and Ofelia Zepeda for their counsel and guidance in getting the book to where it is today.

This book is dedicated to the memory of Professor Robert L. Morris.

CHAPTER 1

Sunday Night.

Stale alcohol infused the room.

Welcome to Harry's Tavern.

Welcome indeed.

Harry's was large and dimly lit; a simple space with dark velour booths, some tables and chairs, and sticky acrylic carpet. Above the bar, a Guinness emblem shimmered in electric orange, whilst the crack of balls on a pool table resonated gloomily throughout.

Luke sat at the bar with Anita, another hostage to the storm that had closed Chicago's airspace. He propped himself up on his elbows and stirred his drink, as he did when going nowhere: little figures-of-eight turning in on themselves. The remnants of a steak sandwich sat on a plate nearby. She took frequent gulps of wine and manly drags from a low-grade cigarette. Every so often, her arm would stretch towards a black ceramic ashtray, eighteen inches away.

Anita put down her glass and continued: '...as I said, no sir, not for me. Just the thought makes my skin crawl.'

Luke narrowed his eyes.

'I'm not big into those sorts of things,' she went on. 'Mind you, I'm all right with spiders.'

'Yeah, I don't come across many spiders,' replied Luke softly.

Anita was not listening.

'I saw this documentary once,' she continued, 'about these mites somewhere in the jungle. Bolivia? Maybe Africa? They burrow into the skin, real difficult to get out. You ever come across anything like that in your work?'

'No, I don't tend to see many mites either,' he replied, 'just people.'

There was a delay as Anita reached for her packet of cigarettes. 'Well what sort of parasites do you work with then?' she asked sniffily.

Luke scratched his ear.

'Err. I'm a para-psychologist,' he said. 'I study the paranormal.'

It took a moment or two.

Then Anita's features softened and her eyes opened wide. She dropped her chin to reveal lipstick-marked teeth and a nicotine smile.

'Really?'

She sat up straight then swung around in her seat, knees brushing against Luke's thigh.

'Ghosts? Mind Readers? That sort of thing?' she asked excitedly.

'Well, to an extent. It's more the case-'

She cut across him sharply.

'-Honey. I've got one hell of a story for you.' She clicked her fingers at the barman and pointed out their glasses. 'Two more over here.'

Luke gazed across the room. The exit sign glowed icy neon blue.

CHAPTER 2

Previously.

'No-one told me at this age I'd spend so much time trying to pee,' sighed Jack.

He looked down at the toilet bowl and the lack of activity, then straight ahead at the bathroom wall. Finally, satisfied matters were unlikely to progress further, he flushed and adjusted the waistband on his pyjamas. Then he rinsed his hands and walked back into the bedroom.

Chloe was sitting up in bed, with her reading lamp on. Her head was cocked to one side, and her face radiated concern.

'Did I wake you?' asked Jack. 'I'm sorry. I thought I was being quiet. Go back to sleep.'

'Hush,' directed Chloe. 'Keep your voice down.'

Jack continued walking towards the bed. His eyebrows furrowed as he observed his wife. She shifted uncomfortably and there was little colour in her face.

'You gonna tell me what's going on?' he enquired gently.

She bit into her lower lip lightly before answering. 'I can hear a voice,' she said.

Jack had reached the foot of the bed. He cupped a hand around an ear. 'I don't hear anything,' he replied.

Chloe raised her forefinger to signal for patience. 'I hear a voice,' she repeated. Her breathing had become erratic, and it was a while before she spoke again. When she did, her tone was low and firm. 'There, right now,' she said. 'Can you not hear that?'

Jack looked away from her, towards the half-open door that led out of the bedroom, conscious not to make any sound of his own. For fifteen seconds they both remained still.

He shook his head. 'I know I'm a little deaf, but I still don't-'

'-Jack, there's someone in this house,' said Chloe with growing alarm. 'I can hear someone whispering.' As the inevitable conclusion drew near, her eyes grew wide. 'Which means there must be more than one of them.'

Jack ran his tongue over his teeth. Nervously, he asked if she could make out what was being said.

'No,' came the reply. 'I don't think it's English.' Chloe's nightgown was sleeveless and the hairs on each forearm stood upright.

Jack stood frozen for a moment, unsure how to proceed. Then he turned on his heels and made his way to a walk-in dressing room, lined with mirrored cupboards. On the left hand side, he slid open a door, then knelt down and pushed a stack of shoe boxes aside to reveal a safe. He began to turn the combination, clockwise first.

Chloe saw what he was doing. 'Jack, no,' she appealed. 'We're too old for that kind of thing.'

Jack opened the safe door, reached in and pulled out a white linen cloth, within which something heavy was wrapped. As he walked back into the bedroom, he opened up the cloth to reveal a matt black handgun. Holding it in his right hand, he dropped the magazine from the grip for inspection then pushed it back into place with a metallic clunk. He pulled back on the slider and chambered the first round.

'Jack, don't be ridiculous. You're almost seventy. Who knows how many of them might be downstairs? They might also be carrying guns. We need to call the police.'

Jack seemed unimpressed: 'Chloe, it's one o'clock in the morning. There are gonna be two guys on duty at the station, probably half asleep. By the time they send a patrol and it gets here, it might be too late.' He gripped the gun firmly, and his index finger came to rest against the trigger guard. Then his tone became belligerent: 'And I'll be damned - nobody makes us prisoners in our own home. Whoever's here shouldn't be.' There was a finality to his statement.

Jack began to move towards the bedroom door. Adrenaline was flowing and mild tremors caused his body to shiver. His complexion had turned ghostly pale as blood was drawn back to the core.

'Wait for me,' instructed Chloe, as she got out of bed and went to stand behind him. 'I'm not staying up here alone.'

Jack nodded and waited for her. Then they moved across the carpet together. Small, quiet steps, each one carefully placed.

At the side of the room, Jack cautiously opened the door wider, peered out, and satisfied himself that nobody waited in the hallway. Silver moonlight shone through a picture window and illuminated the landing. They paused as their eyes adjusted. There was no longer any noise in the house. It was very quiet.

At the top of the stairs where the landing overlooked the entrance hall, Jack glanced down below into the emptiness. Content that nobody lurked in the shadows, the couple began to descend the stairs. Jack led. Both hands were wrapped around the gun and the barrel was pointed at the ground in front of him. Chloe followed, one hand resting on her husband's shoulder.

As they reached the bottom, one step from the cool marble floor, Chloe reached out and stopped her husband: 'There. Again,' she whispered.

A low-level noise percolated down the hallway.

Ethereal.

Strange.

She strained her neck to look down the corridor. 'It's coming from the drawing room.' She pointed down the hall. 'They must be in the drawing room.'

It was thirty-five yards to the closed double doors and room beyond.

'You're sure?' checked Jack.

'Positive.'

He licked his lips. His hands shook, but he raised the gun perpendicular to his body, took the final step down and turned into the hallway.

Chloe had a change of heart. 'This is lunacy, Jack,' she murmured. 'Let's go back upstairs and call the police. Even if they take their time, it's surely the sensible option? If the burglars come into the bedroom, then you can shoot them there.'

But Jack had a look of determination in his eyes, and without hesitation began to edge down the hallway. Chloe released his shoulder and ducked down, so as to remain hidden behind the balustrade. Her fear grew more tangible and her stomach tightened. She watched Jack press his frame against the left-hand wall and feared she would throw up. His gun remained trained on the room twenty-five yards ahead.

He continued along his path.

With fifteen yards to go, he stopped and pushed against the door handle that led onto the garage. It was locked. He glanced to his right, down the corridor that led to the dining room and kitchen. Then he took a breath and continued.

Ten yards.

Chloe held her breath.

Five yards.

Jack reached the doorway and the bitter taste of bile hit the back of Chloe's throat. Slowly and carefully she watched him open one of the doors. He looked through the narrow gap cautiously then inched forwards keeping low. He disappeared from Chloe's line of sight, into the silence.

Time slowed to a standstill.

For an age, nothing happened.

Suddenly, a deafening blast reverberated down the hall, and muzzle flash lit the darkness between door and frame. Automatically, Chloe's hand rushed to cover her mouth.

She waited.

The drawing room lights came on.

And she continued to wait.

Eventually, the doors opened wide and Jack appeared. He was cast in silhouette with his arms by his side and the gun in his right hand.

'Jack, are you okay?' called out Chloe. 'What's happened?'

With puzzlement in his voice, he spoke: 'There's no-one here.'

'No-one?' Chloe seemed confused. 'But it was clear as day…'

'Not a soul,' added Jack. 'And what's more, everything's locked up tight. The doors, the windows, they're all bolted shut.'

Chloe began to walk carefully down the hallway.

'But it was definitely coming from…' she began.

Jack clicked the gun's safety into position. 'In the morning, we'll need to phone the carpenter,' he said sheepishly, 'I just put a hole in the patio door.'

CHAPTER 3

Monday morning.

The duty manager picked up the handset and dialled room 310. After several rings, a startled and clearly confused English voice answered with a disproportionately loud: 'Hello?!?'

'Morning Dr. Jackson. Jim at the front desk here.'

Jim? Front desk?

'Sir, this is your quarter-of-six wake-up call.'

There was no response. Luke was becoming conscious of the razor-edged pain drilling at the back of his skull.

'Sir? Are you there? This is your wake up call.'

Rustling.

'Erm, wake up call,' repeated Luke. 'What time is it?'

'Quarter-of-six.'

Huh?

'Well okay then. I hope you have a great day,' added Jim, and with a click the line went dead.

Luke had not slept well.

Having successfully extricated himself from Anita and the story of her dead Uncle Bill, Luke had returned to his hotel room to discover that alcohol and jet lag were not conducive to sleep. Much of the night was spent angrily watching the scarlet-red digits on his bedside clock grow big, and when sleep did take hold, his dreams were mashed and fleeting. A deserted railway station. An albino pigeon. A never ending search for Coach H.

Luke turned on the spot lamp directly above his bed and rubbed his eyes. He kicked off his sheets and following several ineffectual attempts, managed to clamber to his feet. Once there, he was uncertain what to do next, so he shambled across the spartan suite towards the window, rubbing the back of his head and yawning widely.

Standing there in his boxer shorts with magnificent bed hair, he pulled back the heavy curtains and looked out onto the hotel's car park. The storm that had grounded flights across the north-east had blown itself out during the night, but light drizzle remained, sustaining a shiny grey veneer on the concrete. He reached for the window's handle, opened it wide and inhaled deeply for a post-storm hit.

A porter was scurrying across the car park with a trolley. He happened to look up and see Luke breathing hard. Then Luke saw the porter and felt rather self-conscious. He raised his hand and gave an awkward thumbs-up but the porter put his head down and pretended not to see.

Although only in the room for a few hours, Luke had messed it up considerably. His suitcase was open and his clothes lay scattered across the floor, along with most of his hand luggage and all his travel documents. The television's remote control hung down the side of the bedside cabinet on an elasticised tether. Upon the small writing desk, a used teabag had been jammed into a cup, next to a white plastic kettle.

Luke breathed in heartily one last time then closed the window and re-crossed the room. He stopped at a chair to retrieve a mobile phone from his jacket pocket, and then slumped onto the bed. He turned it on and the phone awoke with a tinny electronic tune and the swirling animation of the manufacturer's logo. Luke looked at the bedside clock and counted out time zones on his fingers. He soon gave up.

She'll be awake.

He returned to the phone and worked at the keypad haphazardly. There was a short delay before the double ring of the British telephone system.

'Hello?' said the other end.

'Hi Baby…it's me,' he declared croakily.

'Hello *Me…*' came the reply, slow and sensual. 'You don't sound too hot.'

Luke covered the mouthpiece and tried to clear his throat. Something unwanted travelled upwards from inside his chest and he swallowed it back down with a grimace.

'Is that better?' he asked.

'A little. I picked up your barely coherent voicemail from last night. A little tipsy were we?'

'Tipsy?' asked Luke with mock indignation.

'Drinks on the flight?'

'No, I was good on the flight,' replied Luke slowly. 'Water only. There wasn't much to drink; the flight attendants were only handing out those miniature bottles of booze. Y'know – the ones for kids.'

'Yes. The child-sized bottles,' she replied dryly. 'And what about when you got off the plane?'

'That's a slightly different matter. Five hours of waiting in a crowded, sweaty airport came and went, so I might have bought a drink or two to help pass the time.' A smirk crossed his face. 'Then the flight was cancelled and we got bussed to this hotel. With nothing to do, I wandered to the bar next door.'

'And how's your brain function this morning?' she asked.

'The wheel's spinning,' he said stoically, 'but the hamster's gone missing.'

'Well,' said the voice reassuringly, 'make sure you get plenty of water. What time is it there?'

Luke checked the clock again; it had barely changed. 'Too early. Around ten to six.'

'And has the weather cleared?'

Unconsciously, he dipped his head to look at the clouds through the window. This prompted a new and unwelcome feeling of nausea. He bobbed back up slowly. 'Well it's stopped chucking it down, and the wind's died away. I'm sure we'll be flying again. Quite a storm.'

He tucked the phone under his chin and reached both arms towards the ceiling in an exaggerated stretch.

'And where are you now?' she enquired. 'You managed to find your own room didn't you?'

'Yes,' he replied sarcastically. 'My room, on my bed. Not for much longer though. They said they'll take us back to the airport around 6.30.'

'Only teasing. Remind me how long you're with your Grandparents for?'

'Just two days,' he replied. 'I left the phone number on the fridge door.'

'And any exciting plans for your time with them?'

'No, it's bound to be fairly quiet, just the three of us. Eagle Canyon isn't exactly a hotbed of excess.'

'And then on to the conference?'

'Yup.'

The questioning continued.

'And did you get your presentation finished?'

'I finished it on the plane. Although there was a minor crisis when the rat child sitting next to me spilled his diet coke everywhere, and it began to… lap around my laptop. I had the stewardess pack him in the overhead locker for the rest of the flight.'

Luke sat upright and in doing so noticed the pay-per-view box on top of the television flashing steadily.

Oh great.

He shifted tack swiftly. 'Anyway, enough about me. What's new at your end?'

At that particular moment, Luke's phone began to beep and he pulled it from his ear and viewed it with suspicion. 'This new phone of mine,' he said returning to the conversation, 'it's chirping.'

'Maybe it needs recharging?'

'Or it wants to be a bird?'

'Go plug in your charger.'

He glanced at the detritus across the room and groaned: 'I wouldn't know where to start. In fact, by the looks of it I might have tried to find it last night. Did I leave it at home?'

She ignored the question and spoke rapidly: 'Right then. The meeting in Brussels got rescheduled so I'm in the office at the moment, but off to Belgium tomorrow and back the following day. My sister is coming through Friday night to stay for the weekend-'

'-And how is the dreaded Mel?'

'She's okay. And please don't preface her name with dreaded every time.'

'Has she still got an opinion on everything?'

'Well you can be quite opinionated too. Need I remind you of your outburst at my office Christmas party?'

'Moving on…'

'Then, this Saturday I'm looking at tiles for the bathroom-'

'-Tiles for the bathroom?'

A hint of exasperation: 'Yes, new tiles for the bathroom. We've discussed this. More than once.'

'Oh yes,' said Luke feigning recollection.

'And before I forget – Dylan phoned. He asks that we make time on the 28th for a big party. He's finally sold his house and is going on his round the world trip.'

Tiles for the bathroom?

'Luke, we need to get him something. A leaving present. Any suggestions?'

'A map.'

'Very droll. Listen, give me a call when you get to your Grandparents? I'll be back at the flat around-'

The conversation ended abruptly.

'Hello?' said Luke. 'Amy?'

Silence.

He pulled the phone from his ear and looked at the now blank screen. With a sneer, he tossed it onto the bed behind him, and in doing so noticed the phone charger sitting proudly in one of his shoes.

He sighed.

With much effort, Luke made it to his feet and walked over to the anonymous ensuite bathroom. He pawed at a switch on the doorframe and a strip light flickered into life, bathing the cubicle in an eerie yellow fluorescence.

He leaned forward to place his hands either side of the wash basin. A jaundiced looking Luke Jackson gazed back obliquely.

Good Morning.

'You look rough,' he said aloud.

He pushed his face close to the mirror and examined a bloodshot eyeball carefully. Then he stuck out his tongue to scrutinize the coating of fur that had materialised overnight. Somewhat offended, he opened the cold tap and filled a cupped palm with water. He wiped it across his face and into his mass of hair.

As they stood there pondering developments, both Lukes rubbed their chins in unison. At a combined age of 68, their stubble had begun to turn grey.

CHAPTER 4

Previously.

Jack sat at the kitchen table with Pete, his youngest son.

His hands danced around him, as he expanded upon his theme: 'And if I thought that was bad, I only had to wait until I got to the fifteenth. It's become a nightmare. They've moved the tee. They've moved the flag. And the bunkers, pah!'

Pete smiled agreeably but looked bored.

'I don't know what they were thinking,' continued Jack. 'The bunkers are now tight on the dogleg. Damned near everyone ends up in the sand.'

Jack was midway through drawing out the fifteenth in the air with his fingers when Chloe walked in.

'Boys,' she said. 'Why don't we head down to the country club for some lunch?'

'Sounds good,' said Jack energetically. 'Pete do you want to phone Stephanie and find out if she's going to join us?'

'Sure,' replied Pete. 'She thought she'd be finished around one. Why don't I tell her to meet us there?'

'Why? Where is she?' asked Jack.

'She's taken Davy shopping. Ten-year-old boys appear to need new sneakers at least once a month.'

'Well, you're lucky you have only one child. Your Mother and I had three of you.'

'Right then, that's agreed,' said Chloe. 'Let me just go freshen up for a few minutes, and when I'm done, we'll be away.' She excused herself, and Jack raised his hands back into the air to continue his golf talk. When he finished, he looked at his son thoughtfully.

'You okay?' he asked. 'You seem quiet today. Not your usual force-of-nature self.'

Pete blew out his cheeks. 'Work's really busy. I'm finding it hard to switch off at the moment.'

Jack made no response. He just folded his hands, one into the other, and looked down at the table top. Pete pulled out his phone and flipped it open. As he began to dial, the calm was broken. A shriek pierced the house.

'What the hell was that?' said Jack.

'I… don't know,' stuttered Pete. 'It must be Mom.'

Both men were now on their feet and moving at speed into the hallway. They reached the bottom of the stairs as Chloe came rushing down. She looked gaunt and frightened.

'Chloe! Are you okay?!' shouted Jack. 'What's happened?'

There were tears in the corners of her eyes.

'Chloe! What's going on?'

She reached the bottom of the stairs and the safety of Jack's embrace. 'Up… upstairs,' she began to say. 'The guest bathroom. The one Davy's using.'

'What's upstairs?' asked Pete. Chloe did not reply.

Pete looked at his Father. 'Get her sat down,' he instructed authoritatively, 'I'll go see.'

He skirted past his Mother and moved up the stairs cautiously.

'Pete. Be careful,' called Chloe after him.

Jack held Chloe tight and she buried her face into his chest. He stroked her head to calm her.

'Oh sweetie,' he began. 'Let's get you sat down. C'mon, it's gonna be okay.'

With his arms around her shoulders Jack guided Chloe towards the kitchen. She breathed deeply trying to regain her composure. Jack steered her towards the nearest chair and sat her down.

'Let me get you a drink,' he announced, moving to a side cabinet laden with bottles. He grabbed a bottle of brandy, and a crystal tumbler then walked back to the table, pouring.

'Drink this,' he said, passing it to her.

She took a sip then inhaled robotically, purposefully trying to calm herself.

'Tell me what you just saw.'

She took another breath and another sip of brandy before talking.

'I went upstairs to get ready, and was adjusting a picture on the wall in the hallway that was squint. Then I looked down the corridor and noticed that the light in Davy's bathroom was on. So I went to switch it off.'

Jack nodded compassionately.

'I went into the bathroom. And when I was there, I looked over to the mirror.' She gulped. 'Across it, written in large red letters were the words: Leave Now.'

Chloe took another drink.

'Leave Now,' she repeated. 'Scrawled across the glass. Plain as day.'

Now, it was Jack's turn to look unhappy. He re-crossed the room and returned with a second glass into which he poured more brandy.

'I felt the hairs on the back of my neck standing up,' continued Chloe. 'Then I screamed and rushed down here.'

He drained his glass in one.

'This is getting out of control, Jack. If it's not one thing, it's another,' she continued. 'Things are getting worse and worse, and we need to do something about it.'

Jack looked pensive.

Chloe continued: 'My goodness, do you think it was blood? Leave Now written in blood? That's a fairly unequivocal message, don't you think?'

From outside the kitchen, the sound of approaching footsteps grew clear. Both Jack and Chloe looked over towards the door as Pete entered.

He looked pained, and crouched by his Mother's side, resting his hand on her knee.

'Mom?' he asked. 'You okay?'

She smiled weakly, as though reassuring herself. 'Yes. I'll be fine. It's just the shock.'

'You said the bathroom?'

She nodded.

'Davy's bathroom, right?'

'Yes. Davy's bathroom. Letters on the mirror.'

Pete stood back up, and ran his fingers across an eyebrow to wipe away sweat. He looked embarrassed.

'Why?' asked Chloe. 'What's in there? What did you see?'

'Umm, I'm not really sure how to put this.' He paused. 'But there's nothing there.'

CHAPTER 5

Monday mid-morning.

Chet Baker watched the passengers move through the jet bridge into the terminal building. A young mother with a cheerless, bad tempered child. A gaggle of businessmen talking hurriedly into their phones. A skater couple with piercings and matching spiky blue hair.

And bringing up the rear, a tall man dressed smartly in a dark suit and white shirt. He had a greenish tint and was plainly unprepared for the heat of Arizona.

Chet eased himself forward: 'Luke Jackson?' he asked hesitantly.

Luke smiled at him weakly. 'That's me,' he said.

'Hi, welcome to Tucson. I'm Chet Baker, a friend of your Grandmother. She sent me to collect you.'

They shook hands.

'You look a lot like her,' he added.

Like an 82 year-old woman?

'She couldn't make it, so I'm gonna run you over to the house,' continued Chet. He pointed at the directions board suspended from the ceiling. 'Baggage reclaim is downstairs.'

As they began to walk towards the escalator, Chet coughed self-consciously, 'I'm afraid I have some bad news.'

Thirty minutes later, both men stood in the airport car park. As the mercury rose under a cloudless Tucson sky, Chet fought with various pockets to locate his car park ticket, and a subdued Luke loaded his luggage into Chet's jalopy. The car was a muddy brown colour, because it was covered in dried brown mud.

Conversation to that point had been limited.

Chet was a smallish man with a tanned, friendly appearance, and thick round glasses that gave him a boggle-eyed look. He dressed like he knew no better, with a garish t-shirt from Acapulco tucked into khaki shorts and white socks pulled up to his knees. Sparkling clean tennis shoes completed the look.

'Here it is,' he exclaimed, holding the ticket up proudly.

Chet drove slowly down the expressway, the car's speed matching the atmosphere within.

'It's a hot one, huh?' he offered.

'Sure is,' confirmed Luke.

On either side of the road were expansive plains full of huge saguaro cacti with thick prickly fingers pointing to the heavens. As the car passed one, Luke recalled a story his Grandfather had told him several years earlier, detailing a redneck craze for blasting cacti with shotguns. In one case, however, the assailant had bagged the cactus from too close a range and the impact of the shotgun round cleaned out the middle of the plant. In a suitable act of revenge, the cactus then toppled onto its adversary, killing him.

They passed a road sign for Eagle Canyon and Luke searched for conversation. 'So, you live in Eagle Canyon?' he asked.

'Err yes,' replied Chet, happy to break the silence. 'Been there a while now. I was originally from Wisconsin. Milwaukee to be precise.'

'I see.'

Traffic was light.

A moment or two passed, then Chet spoke delicately, eager to keep some semblance of dialogue flowing: 'So, Luke, Your Grandma tells me you're a parapsychologist.'

'That's right,' replied Luke.

'Interesting.' Chet nodded and shuffled in his seat. He saw an opportunity, but trod carefully, as though asking for a first date. 'I had to look it up in the dictionary…not your everyday profession,' he ventured.

'It's a bit different.'

'You happy to discuss it?' enquired Chet before hastily adding: 'If not, feel free to tell this old buzzard to take a hike.'

Luke was happy for the conversation. 'I'm fine with it. What do you want to know?'

'Well,' Chet paused. 'What exactly do parapsychologists do?'

Luke had been here before many times, but did not mind the distraction: 'In simple terms, we study the paranormal. That includes things like ESP, mind-over-matter events, hauntings, Out of Body Experiences-'

An interruption.

'- And tell me. What's ESP?'[1]

'Extra Sensory Perception. When you pick up information psychically.'

'The sixth sense?'

'Yeah, if you like. A way of acquiring information, outside the five regular senses, or inference.'

Chet stared ahead as he listened, and then shook his head. 'Telepathy? That would be ESP?'

'That would be one type of ESP.'

Chet pointed a finger to his temple and chuckled: 'Not much in here young man.'

Luke smiled back kindly and tapped his forehead. 'Ditto,' he replied.

The car had been positioned in the middle lane of the freeway, and Luke took in the view. He glanced up towards the mountains in the east upon which a blue haze clung stubbornly. He looked out the side window as they passed a flattened snake, and then frontwards again as a black Corvette raced past.

Chet licked his lips nervously. 'You mind if I'm honest with you, Luke?' His tone was hushed, almost apologetic. 'I mean we've only just met and I don't want to seem rude.'

Luke opened his hands as though they were a book: 'By all means.'

'I have real problems with psychic stuff. I can't help but think of palm readers at the fairground, and superstition, and old wives tales. I mean, frankly, I can't help but think most of it's...bullshit.'

'Lots of people see things like you do,' replied Luke matter-of-factly, and Chet seemed pleased with the solidarity. 'But there's a big difference between dubious psychic hotlines, and what we do. Our research is rigorous and scientific; controlled experiments in research laboratories across the world, and most of the time with quite regular people.'[2]

'Really?'

'Yeah. One big question to answer is whether everyone has psychic abilities and to what degree, or just a select few.'[3]

'Sounds reasonable.' Chet paused. 'Presumably you get a hard time from the sceptics?'

'Less and less. Informed critics know we do a proper job, and that we have no agenda. We're not out to prove or disprove anything. Mind you, there are still some diehards out there who hate the idea of paranormal research, full-stop. They desperately try to talk away positive results.'[4]

A bug hit the windscreen, leaving green gumbo welded to the glass.

'How do they do that?'

Luke gave a half smile. 'Take your pick. Accusations of incompetence, or fraud, or poor methodologies.'[5]

'So you're incompetent?'

'Apparently so.'

'Maybe you're just plain crazy?'

'Bonkers.'

Both men giggled.

Chet switched the air-conditioner up a notch and was greeted with an unenthusiastic groan from the dashboard. In the road ahead, under the shade of some scrub, a coyote sat panting heavily. It fixed the car in tired scrutiny.

Chet summarised: 'So all you're really saying is, look at our experiments and our results, and if you can't find fault with them...'

Chet was thinking, and as he did so, the car hit a pothole that reverberated through the cabin. He pushed down on the indicator stalk, pulled the car into the inside lane and they cruised down the off-ramp for Eagle Canyon. And then, unexpectedly, he changed the conversation.

'What do you know about poltergeists?' he asked.

'Poltergeists?' queried Luke. 'Not exactly my main field of enquiry.'

'You ever been to a poltergeist...' he searched for the word, '...hotspot?'

'Umm.' Luke's face creased slightly as he tried to rekindle his memory. 'Yeah, a couple of years back. In North Wales. One of my colleagues was investigating, and he asked me to go with him.'

Chet steamrollered through the recollection: 'Luke, I've got these friends in town, Jack and Chloe.' He stopped himself. 'Oops, probably shouldn't have given their names out like that. Pretend you never heard that.'

'Heard what?'

Chet smiled. 'I like your style kid. Anyway, I have these friends. Good honest folk, known them for a long time. Not the sort of people who spook easy.'

Alarm bells began to ring in Luke's head.

Uh-oh.

Chet's hand went up and rubbed the corner of his brow. 'It seems they've been having unusual happenings at home.'

'What sort of happenings?'

Chet's tone changed. 'Poltergeist happenings. Only a few of us know about it. It's very hush hush.'

An uncomfortable silence hung in the cabin for several moments as Luke waited for Chet to elaborate. When he did not, Luke spoke up. 'Sometimes, things that appear to be one thing, don't turn out that way in the end.'

Chet dipped his head, as though offering his ear to Luke: 'What do you mean?'

'I mean, often there can be quite rational explanations.'

'Like?'

Luke took a moment to recall an example.

'I remember these two teenage brothers, based somewhere in the mid-west. It was the school holidays, but they were home alone as their Mother was out, and a storm was raging outside. Proper cats and dogs stuff.

They were bored out of their minds, so the younger brother suggested they make a ouija board, which after a great deal of convincing, the older brother finally agreed to. They found a sheet of glossy cardboard and drew the letters of the alphabet on it, along with the words "yes" and "no". They took an upturned shot glass from the kitchen to make a pointer. Then up in their room, they pulled the curtains shut, put a red cloth over the lampshade, lit some candles and swore each other to secrecy.'

Luke had Chet's attention.

'And they began. Around the table they sat, either side of the ouija board. They started off by asking if anyone was there, and got an affirmative reply. Then they asked important teenage questions, like which girls fancied them, and which girls didn't. And the shot glass moved around, spelling out names of someone or other.

Of course, each boy accused the other one of moving the pointer. And both swore they'd done no such thing. Anyway, they were enjoying themselves, they felt in charge, and after a while the older brother asks a fairly obvious question. Who's giving them this information? Who is this spirit presence with them?

"Who are you?" he demanded. "Who has joined us? Reveal yourself."

And the pointer started to move once again. Across the board, but this time sluggishly.

It moved to an S.

And the younger brother read it aloud.

Then an A.

Then a T.

And he went quiet.

Then an A.

Then an N.

S-A-T-A-N

Both boys looked at each other as their sense of humour went well and truly downriver. Again, both declared they weren't fixing the pointer, and were adamant they weren't screwing around. They asked who was there again, and got the same reply.

S-A-T-A-N

Now the older brother starts to lose his cool. He starts shouting and tries to order their conjured devil out of the house, to leave them alone. And the pointer responds.

It goes to NO.

Every time he demands it leave, it refuses. Three times in all. The kid starts to curse the devil. Strong stuff… he's effing and blinding. Suddenly the pointer stops moving. They wait in silence to see what happens next.

The house is still. All they can hear is the wind and rain battling the house outside, when suddenly there's a loud BANG, and the lamp with the red cloth goes out, leaving them in pitch blackness.'

Luke drew breath.

'Well, this is too much. This is out of control. The older brother sees his chance to peg it from the room and the house. He's closely followed by the younger boy, and they don't look back. They spend the next hour sitting at the bus station pondering their actions.

Eventually, they know they have to return home and when they do, they find a none-too-pleased Mother. She's standing on the porch with a scowl on her face and demands to know what the hell they'd been up to. They walk back into the hallway and there are shards of pottery all over the floor from a broken bowl, and glass from a wall mirror that's crashed to the floor.'

Luke stopped and looked at Chet.

'And…?' asked Chet.

'Well, the truth came out pretty quickly. It turned out the younger boy had thought up this brilliant scam to spook his brother. A practical joke to scare his brother stiff. He worked the pointer. He spelled out SATAN. He made the pointer shift to NO. And every time his brother asked him if he was doing it, he swore he was not.

Except, and here's the thing…the kid got caught up in the moment. As the atmosphere in the bedroom changed and his brother got more and more agitated, the younger brother's juices began to flow and he too began to get worried. He started to wonder if he had actually summoned up something bad, even in jest. He began to half believe the devil was actually there. When he had enough, he stopped the pointer, hoping everything would calm down; but then there was the loud bang and the lights went out and when his brother decided to cut his losses, the young boy decided that was pretty shrewd and followed him.'

'And what of the bang?' asked Chet.

'It was the fuse board. They lived in an old clapboard house and the driving rain got into it, causing a short circuit. When it did so, the circuits overloaded, there was a bang and the power was killed.'

'And the broken bowl and mirror?'

'The Mother returned to the house to find the front door wide open. In their hurry to escape, the boys hadn't stopped to close it. The wind must have blown in and caught various things – the bowl, the mirror, some plates on a dresser. There were leaves scattered throughout the downstairs. The whole event was a combination of things, an ill judged practical joke and other events that made the whole thing seem supernatural.'

Chet took a moment to mull the story over.

'Luke, I get your point,' he began. 'But this is different.'

'I'm sure it is-' said Luke.

But Chet cut across him: '-I don't think we can look for rain in the fuse board in this instance.' He peered across the cabin towards his passenger. 'If they were amenable to it, would you check the house out? Cast your eye over things? You don't need to launch a full scale investigation or anything. Just have a look. That's all. You wouldn't mind that would you?'

The asthmatic air conditioner was struggling, and Luke could feel a bead of sweat running down his cheek. A light film of moisture had also appeared on the old man's face that caused his glasses to slip down his nose. Chet pushed them back into position.

'They're not the sort of folk to get spooked,' added Chet. 'Strong headed. Sensible. But this is out of their league. I don't think they'd seek outside help, unless it somehow came to them. You know what I mean?'

'Lucky I'm here then,' murmured Luke.

'Luke, a couple of years after moving to Eagle Canyon, my wife Josie died. I'll be honest - I was lower than the belly of a snake, and these folks really helped me through a tough patch. It'd be good if I could help them out now. Now that they're in a spot of difficulty.'

Again his glasses slipped down his nose, and once more Chet pushed them back into place.

'Just have a look?' queried Luke.

'That's all I'm asking.'

Luke looked out of the window and ran his hand across his jaw. 'How long has it been going on for?' he asked without enthusiasm.

'A month or so. Maybe six weeks. To begin with, it seemed kind of a curiosity. No particular malice. But recently, things have turned far more sinister. They had an incident just three days ago.'

'What sort of incident?'

Chet became reticent. 'Y'know, I think I'd better let them explain it in person. I wouldn't want to screw things up by giving out duff information.'

He turned his head and looked at his passenger. 'What do you say Luke? Obviously, with matters at home as they are, I don't want to seem pushy or insensitive. We would work everything around you and your Grandma.'

Luke hesitated. Finally, after a prolonged silence, he spoke: 'Well, I guess I could meet up with them,' he said. 'See what I can do. But my first priority has to be with my Grandmother.'

'For sure.' Chet developed a broad grin. 'Excellent. Thanks Luke. Really good of you. Once I've dropped you off, I'll sort things out with my friends, and then I'll-'

He stopped mid sentence.

The car had swung into Hummingbird Lane.

From the driveway of number 4, a large black hearse was pulling away.

CHAPTER 6

Monday mid-morning (2).

The house did not seem to have changed much since Luke was last there. A low-rise with sun bleached paintwork and terracotta tiles. A front yard of potted plants and sugar-water bird feeders. A carport with yellow cat's claw around the support posts and a spider's nest in the rafters.

Luke stepped out of Chet's car and retrieved his luggage from the boot. Up the stone path that led from the kerb to the house, his Grandmother emerged from the shadow of the doorway. Her hands were clasped together in front of her, and Luke approached cautiously.

'Hi there,' he said gently.

Her voice was even. 'Luke, sweetheart. I'm so pleased you've made it,' she replied, beckoning him towards her. There was a thin smile on her lips, and she looked in the direction the hearse had just taken. 'Although I'm afraid you just missed Grandpa.'

They stepped back into the house and Luke dropped his bags, before delicately putting his arms around her.

They held each other, and the outside world faded.

In the carport, Chet stood aimlessly with his hands in his pockets before opting to inspect the rear tyres on Rebecca's car. Finally, Luke broke the clinch and Rebecca called out beyond him: 'Chet.'

'Yes Ma'am.'

'Thank you for going to the airport for me. I am really most appreciative. This morning has been so difficult.'

'That's okay. A pleasure. If there's anything else, just let me know.' He bowed his head: 'I'll be off then, leave you two alone.'

He gave a clandestine wink towards Luke, then clambered back into his car, and slammed the door shut. You could hear the car's rumble even when it was out of sight.

Rebecca turned her attention back to her Grandson: 'My,' she said, 'you seem bigger and more handsome than ever. It is so good to have you here. Come let's go inside.'

She drew Luke behind her, closed the front door and moved through the entrance hall towards the kitchen. A calendar was pinned to the wall and "Luke to stay" had been circled twice with a black felt marker.

At the stove in the kitchen, she lifted a kettle and swirled it to gauge its fullness.

'Tea?'

'Please.'

She lit a burner, and as the kettle began to wheeze into life, retrieved two mugs from a mug tree; one that read: 'Grumpy Old Man', the other: 'I Love Coffee'.

Rebecca placed them on the counter: 'Umm. In light of everything that's happened here, I hope you'll be able to stay on a bit longer than planned,' she said. 'Perhaps you could give the conference a miss this year. And stay for Arthur's funeral?'

Luke answered resolutely. 'Of course.'

A moment passed between the two of them, until Rebecca said, with a half sigh: 'It'll be funny being in this house all by myself. Arthur and I spent sixteen years here.'

Then she laughed. 'I remember back in Florida, when he told me he wanted to move. I was roasting a chicken and asked him where he had in mind. "Southern Arizona" he said straightaway. I was sure he must have been sick. I even found the thermometer and took his temperature. But he was insistent.'

'Why Arizona?'

It took a moment before Rebecca offered her explanation:

'Arizona is a long way from the ocean, Luke. I don't think Arthur could forgive it for taking your Father as it did. And after all those years your Grandfather spent studying it and looking after it. In the end he came to resent it.'

Number 4 Hummingbird Lane was a pleasant place to be. It had a large living room with a kitchen off the far end, three good sized bedrooms and a couple of bathrooms. In the living area, a dining space had been made, replete with an antique table, chairs and a sideboard. On the table, a lone candle burned. An overhead fan turned slowly above it, and on the breeze Luke picked out the faintest hint of vanilla.

The kettle began to whistle and Rebecca lifted it from the hob.

'Milk and sugar?' she asked, and Luke refocused.

'Just milk, thanks.'

The drinks were made in silence, and once Rebecca passed Luke his tea, she picked up her own mug and headed for the living room.

'I've left a message for your Aunt, telling her the news,' she said calmly over her shoulder, 'I left it with her publisher. They said she was somewhere south of Georgetown, in Guyana. They were going to leave word, asking her to phone here as soon as she could.'

'How is Aunt Sam? Is she writing another book?' enquired Luke.

'Updating the old one, I believe.'

Rebecca sat down on a sofa, kicked off her shoes and tucked her thin legs under herself. Wrapped up, she seemed small and fragile. She pushed a stray lock of hair behind her ear and Luke noticed how slender her wrists and how prominent her veins were.

'How is your Mother these days?' asked Rebecca.

'Not too bad.'

'She remarried, didn't she? How is that going?'

'Yes, about a year ago. Everything seems to be going well.'

'Do you think she would come to the funeral if I sent her an invitation?'

'I don't think so,' replied Luke, drawing his lips tight. 'I know she has a lot on, at the moment.'

Rebecca put her head down.

The living room had sandy yellow walls and a sea green carpet. Ancient sofas were arranged around a glass coffee table, upon which books had been stacked in ever decreasing size. Upon each seat, unique embroidered cushions had been placed: an eagle dressed in captain's uniform - piloting a jetliner; a lobster working over an engine - using its claw for a spanner.

'It's been a curious twenty-four hours,' stated Rebecca. She paused. 'Goodness me, that sounds like an understatement.'

There was another delay as she organised her comments in her mind. Luke took a sip of tea.

'Yesterday afternoon, your Grandfather and I were reading in bed, we had been out for lunch and wanted to rest up for your arrival. At six, I took your phone call from the airport saying you weren't coming through that night, and Arthur said he'd stay in bed a little longer. I went outside to do some gardening. It's too hot during the day you realise. I was out back, tending some plants when I stopped dead, with the queerest feeling.'

She gulped.

'I knew something terrible had happened to Arthur, so I put down my cutters and went back into the bedroom. I had this strange feeling of compulsion, but no sense of urgency. When I entered the bedroom, there he was, serenely propped up in bed, his book across his chest.'

Luke watched Rebecca's eyes darting this way and that, as she revisited the memory in her mind. 'I just went up and kissed him on the forehead, told him I loved him, and closed his eyelids.'

She glanced up, a remote look on her face. 'But it was such a strange feeling,' she repeated, '…in the garden.'

The two of them sat in silence.

And then, the hush was broken by a clock in the hallway striking the hour. Rebecca gazed towards the sound and noticed Luke's bags by the front door.

'Would you be a dear and move your luggage into the guestroom. I'm expecting Reverend Small in the next few minutes. We don't want him tripping over them.'

'Sure,' said Luke putting down his mug.

'I'm sure you can remember where you're staying. Same room as last time, second on the left,' she added.

Luke pushed on the bedroom handle and opened the door. The pale wallpaper with the red and gold piping was the same as ever, as was the cream carpet and sheepskin rug by the bed. The bedroom had its own distinct perfume: a mild mustiness mixed with sweet furniture polish and the essence of recently washed linen.

In the corner, a walnut desk had been positioned against the window, and a selection of photographs stood to attention. Luke put his bags by the bed, and walked over.

Many of the photos were new to him. Sepia tinged images of men in uniform bearing assured smiles. Photos taken at graduations. Babies cuddled in arms. At the back was a print of his Grandfather, standing with scuba equipment and waving to camera with a happy smile on his face. Luke picked it up and looked it over, his fingers running over the frame, as though decoding some message in braille.

Another photo caught his gaze.

It was Luke, as a boy, standing with his parents. There was a manic grin on his face and perspiration across his face, and in his arms he held a jet black rabbit whose eyes bulged large. He remembered back to when the picture was taken – the time when he fell out with his best friend over a schoolboy bet. Luke liberated the boy's rabbit and held it for ransom until his parents rightly insisted it was returned. But not before they took a picture for posterity. It was to mark Luke's descent into criminality, joked his Father.

It must have been the picture, for as he looked into his Father's eyes, the memories came crashing back.

The rocks, the boat, and crack from the hull. The masked concern on his Father's face. The coldness of the water. The boy in the charcoal sea buoyed in his orange lifejacket. His breathing - shallow and fast and anxious.

Luke put the picture down.

Back in the living room, his Grandmother was where he had left her. A diary had appeared and Rebecca held it open across her lap whilst her right hand clasped a fountain pen. She looked up.

'This feeling I had Luke.'

Luke retook his seat: 'Feeling?'

'The one outside. When, I knew something was wrong. My experience might be classified as psychic, would it not?'

Tread carefully, Luke.

'Possibly.'

Rebecca waited for some explanation, but Luke seemed disinclined to continue. She surveyed him closely: 'Would you like to expand on that?'

Luke seemed uneasy. 'Is this not a bit close to the bone?' he asked.

'Not for me,' replied Rebecca. 'Arthur and I knew a day like this would come. When one of us would depart. We faced our demons a long time ago. Besides, I cried my eyes out all last night. I won't get upset if we talk.'

As you wish.

Rebecca closed the diary and placed it on the coffee table.

'It might have been what's known as an intuitive impression,'[6] began Luke. 'And intuitive impressions account for maybe a quarter of spontaneous experiences.'[7]

‘And spontaneous experiences are common?’ she asked.

Luke puffed out his cheeks. ‘It’s been suggested that between 50 and 60% of the population think they have one during their lives.’[8]

‘That many?’ said Rebecca.

‘Apparently.’

Rebecca sat back in her seat and digested the information.

‘As you might imagine,’ continued Luke, ‘episodes tend to surround major life events. Death, accidents, marriages, illnesses.[9] Things that are personally meaningful.’

‘Well you can’t get more personally meaningful than the death of a husband of fifty years,’ stated Rebecca. ‘What about physical distance? Is that relevant? I mean, I was just out back, with Arthur no more than twenty yards away. What if I’d been further away?’

‘Distance doesn’t seem to be a hindrance. You get reports where people were separated by thousands of miles.’[10]

Luke picked up his mug, took another sip then held it between both hands as though warming them.

‘And what are people doing?’ asked Rebecca.

‘When?’

‘When these things happen?’

‘On the whole – not much. They might be sleeping or sitting down. Something with low physical activity.’[11]

‘And it’s normal to experience strange feelings?’

‘Yes and no. Sometimes people report hearing voices and seeing visions. They might even claim to smell something unusual.’

‘Sounds like hallucinations to me,’ interjected Rebecca.

‘Yup. That seems quite plausible,’ replied Luke. ‘The pertinent question, of course, is whether these hallucinations are conveying information. Information they couldn’t have gathered in a conventional way.’

Luke put his mug back onto the coffee table and continued:

‘When we talk about spontaneous ESP, the majority of cases - something like two-thirds - tend to occur during sleep and dreams.’[12]

‘Do people dream the future?’

‘They can do. In these dream episodes, around three quarters are precognitive,[13] with 50% coming to happen within 48 hours. And 80% within a month.’[14]

Rebecca nodded again. ‘Presumably, there have been experiments into dream ESP?’ she enquired.

‘Yup, a fair number.’[15]

Luke repositioned himself in his seat.

'The main problem with any spontaneous episode is working out whether something is genuinely paranormal,' he said. 'As human beings, we're not always terribly good at determining if events are coincidental or due to chance. Sometimes we link things causally, that are pretty dubious.'[16]

Rebecca looked contemplative: 'So many spontaneous things are just wishful thinking, or selective memory?'

'At least part of the time. You've also got to consider other factors, such as the person's honesty or motivation for recalling an experience. Can alleged events be corroborated?'

Rebecca pushed her feet out from underneath herself and rested them on the floor side by side.

'And as you might imagine,' continued Luke, 'symbolic experiences are especially problematic. People are notorious for finding patterns when there aren't any. We need to ask how valid an interpretation is. Imagine I dream that my house catches fire and I lose all my possessions. Then 3 days later it actually gets burgled, and I lose all my possessions. Was my dream precognitive? What if it does catch fire - 5 months later? What about 15 months later?'

Luke went on: 'And does an episode become self fulfilling? I see myself on holiday in the Caribbean, then go book a holiday for Jamaica. A sign? Or the spark that sends me to the travel agent?'

'Indeed.'

'It's one of the reasons why many researchers prefer to work in the laboratory. The important thing to remember is that if psi exists-'

'-Psi?'

'Yes, psi is often used as an umbrella term for the various paranormal actions someone might produce,' he explained. 'If psi exists, it must operate in the real world in some way, not just in the laboratory.'[17]

'Well I felt some connection with Arthur. Do you think he was trying to let me know what was happening, as he died?'

'It's possible. However - and this might seem a bit counter-intuitive - some evidence suggests it is the recipient who's actively seeking information.[18] That you are using your ESP to monitor your environment.'

'So Arthur didn't seek me out as he passed away? I was monitoring him? I realised that something was very wrong?'

'Yup.'

‘Wouldn’t that mean I’d spend a lot of time monitoring lots of people?’

‘Not necessarily. Just those you’re emotionally close to.[19] And it might be that this subconscious monitoring only becomes an accessible thought when something extraordinary happens. A life threatening event, for example.’

Rebecca took on a kind disposition. ‘So you believe in psi? In ESP?’

‘Well it appears to happen under controlled conditions, so yes. Although there are certain caveats-’

She interrupted: ‘-Do you think we can use it to communicate with the spirit world?’

Luke rubbed his eyes. ‘That’s a whole different question,’ he said. ‘It assumes there’s some form of post-mortem survival.’ He smiled. ‘Maybe a topic for later on.’

‘Bored with our chat?’ joked Rebecca.

‘No, I’m just feeling a bit wonky. Jet lag, I guess.’

And a stinking hangover.

‘Do you mind if I duck out and take a nap?’ he asked.

‘Not at all. Go ahead and have a rest. Reverend Small will be here any minute, anyway.’

Luke stood then walked over to Rebecca. He placed his hand on her shoulder: ‘Look, if there’s anything I can do…’

His sentence tailed away.

Rebecca lifted her arm to touch his hand. ‘I’ll let you know,’ she said.

Luke broke away, then stopped and turned back. ‘Oh, before I forget, Chet asked me to help him out. A friend of his is having some problem or other, and I might be of assistance. Now and then I may need to pop out, is that okay with you?’

She laughed: ‘I saw the little wink he gave you.’

‘Not so subtle, huh?’

‘I presume it’s some paranormal problem?’

Luke shrugged.

Rebecca looked him in the eyes: ‘Be careful, Luke. There are plenty of wonderful people here in the Canyon, but there are crazies as well. And some don’t need much of an excuse to turn mean. You don’t want to cross some old fart who has nothing better to do than make your life a misery.’

‘Point taken.’

‘Some people don’t have a lot happening in their lives. Fresh attention can be very stimulating, and well received.’

‘But Chet? He’s on the level?’

‘Chet’s a sweetie. But he can get a bit excitable.’

Luke took the information onboard and turned away. Rebecca remained on the sofa, and as he left, tears welled in her eyes. Despite her strong outward appearance, the pain ran hard and deep.

In the guestroom, Luke closed the door.

From the edge of the bed, he looked back towards the photo of his Grandfather. Then he undid the strap on his watch and placed it on the bedside table. He swung his legs off the ground and wearily lay back on the bed. As his head touched the pillow, he heard the doorbell ring.

CHAPTER 7

Eagle Canyon.

'You know, you're welcome to use my car,' said Rebecca.

'Thanks, but I think I'll just rent one. I wouldn't want to inconvenience you.'

And with that, Luke pulled shut the front door and started the short walk down the road to the rental agency.

Eagle Canyon was in the heart of the Sonora Desert, a 120,000 square mile expanse that spread from south-east California through south-west Arizona, down to Baja in Mexico, and across the western part of Sonora State.

The town was surrounded on all sides by an arid sandy landscape that was garnished with shrub, and scrub, and rock that had been flushed from the nearby mountains. Arroyos zigzagged hither and thither. Summer temperatures regularly exceeded 40 degrees centigrade.

It did not seem the most hospitable place to live.

Yet life had evolved. Life had flourished.

Hawks, Owls, Eagles.

Tortoises, Chuckwallas, and Lizards.

Dragonflies and Fire Ants and Stinkbugs.

Rats, Snakes, Scorpions and Cats.

There was colour. From the yellows of the Desert Marigold and Creosote Bush, to the lavender of Ironwood Trees. From the orange of the Desert Globemallow, and the red of the Chuparosa, to the blue of the Scorpionweed.

There were plants with whimsical names.

Devil's Claw, Ghost Flower and Fairy Duster.

Mesquite shrubs of Velvet, Screwbean and Honey.
Joshua Trees. Elephant Trees.
Tumbleweed.
And of course, there were cacti.
Saguaro and Fishhook and Barrel.
Prickly Pear and Beavertail and Organ Pipe.

The Canyon, as it was affectionately known, sprung from the desert in the mid-1960s. It was conceived as a retirement community, and town ordinances decreed that homeowners had to be fifty or older to own property. Under-eighteens were not welcome to live there at all. In the early days, there were fewer than a thousand residents but since then it had expanded substantially in population and size and become home to almost twenty thousand, most of whom lived on quiet suburban roads and in neat cul-de-sacs. Much like the indigenous animals, residents followed the desert's rhythm. As the temperatures rose, the pace slowed and people retreated into their air-conditioned sanctuaries. When temperatures were lower, first thing in the morning and in the early evening, they came out to tend gardens and sweep front yards, to stand on street corners gossiping, and take sedate strolls.

The Canyon had the usual assortment of supermarkets and shops, chain stores, restaurants and fast food outlets, although late night opening was rare and mostly unnecessary. There was an abundance of churches, which were nearly always full, and testament to one of the town's main concerns - mortality. No leaking roofs or empty collecting plates in these parishes. Less usual was the high number of pharmacies. Each street corner seemed to have a large ChemiFlex or Pharmastore on it - a corollary to the elderly nature of the place and the medical establishment's penchant for over-medication. Drugstores were big business. As was Viagra.

Few people walked any real distance. The combination of sprawl, old age and heat meant that town was almost entirely traversed by car. Many were large and expensive, and symptomatic of the wealth in the area. A lot seemed to drive themselves, although upon closer inspection there was usually a diminutive figure peering over the dashboard. A lot of vehicles had minor bumps and scrapes, a product of the reverse-til-you-touch ethos that was popular when manoeuvring.

Many of the Canyon's inhabitants had come from more Northerly parts of the United States - keen to downsize and unlock capital from pricier homes. There was a strong seasonal element to town, and whilst winters were busy, the summer exodus saw almost a third of residents leave for cooler climes. During winter, however, the place was full and the warm temperatures gave many opportunities for improving backhand volleys and iron shots.

Golf courses were abundant. Green oases contrasting decidedly with the desert's earthy hues. As popular as they were - the social clubs proved the main draw in town. With names like The Hacienda and Desert Pavilion, members could swim and play chess. They could delight in canasta, bridge and photography classes. They could learn to email Grandchildren thousands of miles away. In Eagle Canyon, you could reinvent yourself a hundred times over.

Luke walked towards the car rental office as an old gentleman in an electric wheelchair came the other way. He looked like a decanted turtle, and wore industrial strength sunglasses that could have doubled as welder's goggles. A green tartan rug lay across his lap, a tube was under his nose and an oxygen cylinder nestled beneath the seat.

'Afternoon!' the old man called out.

'Afternoon,' replied Luke.

The old man whirred past, and gave a spirited salute.

Luke smiled broadly. There was something about Eagle Canyon he really liked.

CHAPTER 8

Tuesday morning.

Luke awoke before dawn.

He had not fully drawn the curtains the night before and illumination from a street-lamp out front seeped into the room. Luke dressed to it then tiptoed through the house to the kitchen, mindful not to wake Rebecca. He boiled the kettle and made some tea, then went into the living room. He stood by the French doors that led to the back garden and gazed out. Under the moonlight, the plants had lost their form and were little more than abstract monochrome shapes. Spontaneously, he unbolted the door and slipped outside.

There were no clouds that night and straightaway he felt the cold burning in his lungs. Overhead, the cosmos was in full flow, and Luke sat on a little wall surrounding a flower bed to savour it. He scrunched up tight to stay warm, and kept his fingers wrapped tightly around his mug.

The evening before had been a low-key affair. Luke picked up his rental car without hindrance or fuss then stopped by the supermarket to buy groceries. Dinner was taken in front of the television, and Rebecca fell asleep on the sofa. Just after nine o'clock, she awoke, bade a tired goodnight and kissed Luke on the forehead. He stayed up and aimlessly surfed the channels before lassitude overcame him and he also headed for bed.

In the garden, the darkness began to lift and Luke's mind wandered. He thought back to the occasions when he had spent time with his Grandfather and regretted that they had never become close. He thought of his Grandmother and how strong she appeared to be, and how he wanted to help her as best he could. As this filtered through, the conversation he had with Chet on the journey from the airport came to mind.

The poltergeist.

He felt uneasy. This was neither the time nor the place to split his loyalties. Rebecca would need his support and should remain his priority. Embarking on a potential wild goose chase would be folly.

As he mulled developments over, the horizon grew lighter. The blackness had given way to an azure blue that began to stretch towards him. With an empty cup and the chill penetrating his body, Luke decided to go back into the house. He returned to the kitchen, but there was still no sign of Rebecca, so he emptied the dishwasher, swept the floor, and generally tried to be useful. Finally, as he was reduced to sharpening the kitchen knives, she popped her head around the door.

'Morning,' she said. 'I could have slept forever. Have you been up long?'

After breakfast, Rebecca and Luke sat in the living room reading. Every so often, the phone would ring and Rebecca would field a call of condolence. It was during one of these that the doorbell chimed. Rebecca put her hand over the receiver and waved at him.

'Luke darling,' she whispered, 'can you get that?'

So he did.

A large older woman in a green and red floral print dress met him. She sported closely cropped hair.

'Hi!' she said enthusiastically. 'You must be Luke.'

The woman seized Luke and embraced him a bear hug that pinned his arms to his side. 'I've heard a lot about you!' she declared. 'I'm Margaret. From next door.'

'Hello there,' he replied, trying to breathe.

Need air.

She broke the hold and gave him a friendly slap on the side of his face, then pushed him out of the way and bustled through the door.

Rebecca put down the receiver: 'Margaret,' she said.

Margaret's demeanour flipped instantly.

'Rebecca my dear,' she began sympathetically. 'Oh my sweet dear.'

She bowed her head.

Rebecca did not reply but smiled a thin lipped acknowledgement. Then she pointed at the telephone: 'That was the coroner,' she began. 'They're going to do the autopsy as soon as they can. I suppose that means I can go ahead and plan Arthur's funeral for this coming weekend. Assuming there are no complications.'

'Complications?' queried Margaret.

There was a glint in Rebecca's eye. 'Maybe they'll find arsenic in the old boy.'

Margaret rocked with laughter. When she regained her composure, she seemed perplexed: 'The weekend? Ooh, that seems quite soon. Will people get here in time? What if they have to travel?'

'Well, they'll either make it, or they won't,' replied Rebecca firmly.

'That's true. And will it be a burial or cremation?'

'Arthur never liked the idea of burial. He said he didn't want to be worm food.'

'So, a cremation then? At Rolling Pastures?' proposed Margaret with excitement rising in her voice. 'Oh Rebecca, it'll be perfect, a wonderful send off. We can have the choir sing his favourite hymns. We'll see if Harvey will play his trumpet. I'll help organise things.'

She looked at Luke, who remained by the front door, still recovering from this force of nature. 'And there's no doubt Arthur would have loved to have his Grandson present.'

Both women now stared at Luke, who looked bemused.

I reckon he'd prefer to be alive.

'God Rebecca,' continued Margaret. 'I still can't believe it. Such a shock.'

Margaret Atkins was a bulky but attractive woman with a striking moon face. She was famous in Eagle Canyon for her indefatigable optimism and had been married four times, with mixed success, producing five children. When her last husband had died three years back, Margaret decided there was no point trying to figure life out. She found a new freedom and rediscovered butter, cream and wine. As her waistline grew, so did her happiness.

'How are you bearing up?' she asked.

'Getting by,' replied Rebecca. 'Although, I have my moments. It's only just beginning to sink in, the fact that he's not around any more.'

Margaret's voice became less confident: 'I'm gonna miss him too.' She rifled through her handbag, and Luke half expected an enormous lace handkerchief to appear. Instead, she pulled out a crumpled pack of cigarettes.

'Heavens I need one of these,' she said.

Rebecca pointed towards the French doors that led out back and Margaret made her way there to spend a contented few minutes wedged in a chair, sitting in a silver fog, producing the occasional smoke ring.

Rebecca turned towards her Grandson: 'That's Margaret.'

'So I gather.'

'She lives next door.'

Rebecca dropped her voice: 'Her daughter has cancer and is having chemotherapy. Margaret shaved her head in support. She said they'd grow it back together.'

Rebecca got to her feet: 'Luke, perhaps you could do me a favour and run to the library for me? I've got some books due back. Not a major priority I appreciate, but it would be just one less hassle to deal with.'

'No problem.'

'And,' she glanced towards the garden, 'maybe you could take Margaret with you? I love her to bits but I'm not really in the mood for talking right now. She can be a bit…'

'Sure thing. I'll go get my jacket.'

So, some 15 minutes later, Luke found himself being chauffeured across town by Margaret in her small grey car, where the combination of weights between occupants and tired suspension, caused it to lean at a jaunty angle. Rebecca's library books were piled up on his lap.

The sun was strong that morning, and he pulled his visor down to keep the light from frying his retinas. Margaret had another cigarette jammed in the corner of her mouth and was busy trying to ignite it from the car's cigarette lighter: 'Your Grandma's told me all about you,' she said from the other corner. 'She's very proud.'

'I think all Grandmothers are proud,' Luke said benignly.

'You're right,' she grinned. 'Comes with the territory. I've got seven grandchildren and adore all of them. They're all fantastic. Even Eugene.' She stopped speaking and reconsidered. 'Yup, even Eugene,' she conceded.

Whoever Eugene was and whatever he had done, suddenly caused Margaret much merriment and she snorted with pleasure. Then for no apparent reason she stopped the car at a traffic light. It was still green.

'Both Rebecca and Arthur were talking the other night about your trip,' she said. 'I had them around for dinner you see. They seemed so excited to have you over, said you were on your way to a conference or something?'

The traffic light changed to red.

'Yes. Once I left here, I was meant to be heading for Hawaii.'

'A parapsychology conference in Hawaii?'

'Yup.'

'That sounds most agreeable. Y'know I find the paranormal fascinating, simply fascinating. I've read about it here and there and caught a few programmes on the television.' Again, she reconsidered her statement. 'Actually, I haven't watched much TV recently. In fact, not really for about five years.'

Margaret went on: 'A long time ago I remember watching a documentary on PBS. Do you know what PBS is? Public Broadcasting. Anyway, on this show, they were testing people for telepathy with those cards that have symbols on them. What are they called?'

Luke started to laugh.

'What gives?' asked Margaret.

'Everyone around here seems rather taken with parapsychology.'

'Honey, a fresh face and new topics of conversation in Eagle Canyon are hugely welcome,' Margaret confided. 'Most of the conversations in this place revolve around failing health, how awful modern movies are, and why our kids never get in touch.'

She tapped the top of the steering wheel: 'Anyway, the cards with the symbols.'

'You're talking about Zener cards.[20] Five symbols: circle, square, wavy lines, cross and star.'

'Yes, that rings a bell. People would try to guess what the next card was. Is that right?'

The traffic light changed back to green, and the car accelerated. Slowly.

'That's pretty much it,' said Luke. [21] [22]

'- It's a square!' squealed Margaret with delight.

O-kay.

Margaret calmed down: 'Anyway, as I recall, people were pretty successful at guessing the cards. Does that sound right?'

'Overall?' replied Luke. 'Yes, more often than they should be, if it was down to chance.'

Margaret took a final drag on her cigarette and squashed it into the ashtray.

'What sort of people were tested?' she asked.

'It varied. But a lot of the time, it was just normal people. Not necessarily those who claimed particular abilities.'

'But there have been star subjects, no?'

'A few.' Luke dredged his memory. 'One man called Hubert Pearce springs to mind. His success rate averaged over 30%, when he should have only got 20%.'

'That doesn't seem like a big difference,' said a disappointed Margaret.

'It's actually pretty spectacular,' replied Luke. 'In terms of odds, take a million, multiply it by a billion and you're still short.' [23] [24]

'And the results from these experiments, overall? Bottom line?'

'The card experiments? Overwhelmingly positive.'[25]

Margaret glanced across the cabin at Luke. 'Do you still use Zener cards?' she asked.

'No, not any more.'

'Oh that's a shame. They seemed quite romantic.'

'These days it's all computerised. We mainly use a procedure called the autoganzfeld.' [26]

Luke gave an involuntary little cough then continued.

'Basically you come into the lab and get placed in a cubicle on a nice comfy chair. Then we put halved ping-pong balls over each eye, shine a red light onto your face, and play you soothing "white noise" – a pleasant gentle whooshing sound - through headphones. This sensory calm is thought to be conducive for ESP.'

'What does ganzfeld mean?'

'It's German and means "whole field". It refers to the uniform sensory stimulation you receive.'

'I see.'

'In another part of the building, a person tries to telepathically transmit a randomly selected video clip to you. It's somewhat unclear whether this other person is really needed - you might be able to access the information directly. Anyway… back in your cubicle, you just let your mind wander, and verbalise the experience you're having.'

'That sounds fun,' said Margaret quite genuinely. She took on a theatrical air: 'I see a snow-topped mountain with a chalet and a lake…'

'Indeed. After 20 minutes or so, you take off the ping-pong balls and headphones, and a computer offers you four possible video clips.

The real one and three decoys. You simply choose which video clip most closely matched the experience you had in the chair.'

'So, I've got a one-in-four chance of matching my experience with the target clip if I guess?'

'That's right. Over the course of an experiment with all the participants tested, you'd expect to see a hit rate of 25% if people were simply guessing. If there was some sort of information transfer at work, something like ESP, we'd expect to see the hit rate improve.'

In front of Margaret and Luke, a black sign with Library printed in bold black letters appeared, and beneath it, an arrow pointed left. Margaret pulled her little car into the parking area and into the first available empty bay.

From where they parked, the library stood directly in front of them. It was a large concrete edifice with a pebble-dashed façade and thin clerestory windows. The entranceway was recessed in a u-shape, providing a modicum of shade out front, where wooden benches had been positioned beneath glass fronted notice boards. It was too hot to sit outside, and almost all the library users scurried to and from the building without stopping. One man, however, stood outside examining a poster on desert plants, curiously shaking his head. Eventually, a woman came along, chastised him, and ushered him inside.

Margaret left the car's engine and air conditioner running.

'So what's the bottom line? For this ganzfeld thing?'

Luke licked his lips.

'Overall? The average hit rate across experiments is around 35%, which corresponds to a likelihood of billions-to-one that the effect is due to chance.' [27]

'So it's unlikely the results were due to luck or chance or whatever you want to call it?' clarified Margaret.

'Precisely. Individual studies have achieved even stronger results. One from the late nineties used creative people as participants, and the hit rate went up to 47%.'[28]

'Creative people?'

'Yes. Artists, musicians and the like.'

'So you think ESP is real then?'

'I think we've reached a point after all this research where we can be pretty confident ESP exists.'

Margaret nodded in acknowledgement.

'In turn, there are a variety of factors that appear to boost success rates,' continued Luke, 'things like self-belief.[29] Anyway-'

He picked up the books from his lap.

'-I'd better return these.'

'Yes,' replied Margaret. 'There's a chute, a few yards inside the door on the left. Drop them in there. If you go to the counter, you'll be forever.'

He opened the door and stepped out into the desert heat. It struck like a breeze block.

'On the left,' repeated Margaret as he shut the door.

He made his way into the library. Inside the door, underneath a sign marked 'Returns' was a chute that led into a locked box. There was only one person in line, a short woman with pink highlights and gold earrings, opening a beach bag. She looked up to see Luke and seemed surprised.

'Good morning,' he said politely.

Soon after, he realised that may have been a mistake. Now Luke got the lowdown on all the woman's books. She would reach into her bag, produce one, and provide a little commentary. And then another, and another. Just when he thought the bag had to be empty, another would appear.

'Five good. Four average. Three terrible,' said the old lady summing up. And with that, she shuffled away.

Luke offloaded Rebecca's books then walked back out into the blazing parking lot where his eyes narrowed involuntarily into a squint. A young man raced past him towards a car three parking bays down. He jumped in, slammed the door shut and proceeded to grasp the steering wheel with both hands. The car must have been in the sun for some time. Almost instantaneously, he shrank back into his seat, with pain across his face.

Ouch.

Although the car did a good job of containing many of the man's profanities, the more ferocious ones found their way out into the open. This prompted a bout of neck craning and tut-ing from other library users nearby. 'Potty mouth!' shouted someone behind Luke.

Luke got back to Margaret's car and found her pressing various buttons on a large mobile phone.

'Get lost did we?' she asked, slipping the phone into her handbag. But before he could reply, she steamed ahead: 'That was Chet on the phone.'

'Oh you know Chet too?'

'Oh yes, everyone knows him,' she replied cryptically. 'He said he'd mentioned our friends with the "problem" to you. On the drive in from the airport.'

'Yes.'

'Y'know…' she lowered her voice, '…the poltergeist.'

Yes, I remember.

'You also know these people?' ventured Luke.

'I do. Chet and I are probably the only people outside the family who know about the situation.'

'So what did Chet say?'

'He's been on the phone to them. Apparently they'd be delighted if you could make some time to pop in.'

'Right. Well I'm sure in the next few days-'

'-So I phoned them and suggested we go over once we finished here. That okay with you?"

Margaret began to reverse from her parking bay.

'It's all terribly exciting,' she announced.

CHAPTER 9

Previously.

'You know, I'm not terribly happy about all this,' said Jack.

From the look on his face, he meant it.

'Daddy,' said Clarice with exasperation in her voice, 'I've explained this to you. It's all quite safe; there's no danger. I went through it with my medium a dozen times.'

'Well who exactly is this medium?'

'Daddy!'

'I don't want you girls getting into something you don't fully understand. Making the situation worse.'

Clarice turned to face her Father.

'Just relax,' she said. 'Everything will be fine.'

From behind her, Chloe spoke. 'It's worth a try,' she said half-heartedly.

'Okay, okay.' Jack shrugged his shoulders and conceded defeat. 'If you need me, I'll be in the kitchen for a while. Don't stay up all night.'

Clarice and Chloe stood alone in the dining room. It was large and evenly proportioned with a table that ran much of its length and at which a dozen people could sit in comfort. Along the walls, oil paintings depicting English country scenes had been hung over deep blue wallpaper, and at the far end, a dark wooden dresser monopolised the wall. Upon it, carefully polished silver plates and salvers had been placed, along with a pair of five-armed candlesticks holding brand new blood red candles.

Clarice pulled one of the dining chairs out from the table and placed a wicker bag on the seat.

'Shall we begin?' she asked.

Chloe looked on nervously. 'It's your show.'

Clarice leant down and opened the bag. From within it, she retrieved a small folded piece of black velvet, which she opened and spread over one end of the table.

She glanced at the chandelier, then at her Mother: 'Do you want to dim the lights?'

Chloe obliged and made her way to the dimmer switch. Slowly the brightness dropped and the dining room became sombre and eerie. Chloe went back to stand by her daughter.

'Are you sure you're happy to do this?' she checked.

'I wouldn't be here if I wasn't,' replied Clarice.

She dipped back into her bag and pulled out a leather jewellery box. The top was hinged and she opened it to reveal half-a-dozen small compartments, each capped with cotton wool. Slowly and methodically she removed the cotton wool from each section to unveil different coloured crystals and gemstones. None were very large. The biggest was the size of a quarter.

'Where did you get these?' asked Chloe.

'I ordered them. They arrived yesterday.'

'Are they expensive?'

Clarice seemed to be concentrating. 'Not particularly,' she replied.

'Well you must let me reimburse you,' said Chloe. 'I don't want you out of pocket.'

'Mom, seriously. It's no problem.'

'Clarice, I insist.'

'Well let's just see if they work first.'

Clarice took out the first crystal and placed it on the velvet cloth as it glistened in the mellow light. Then she took out the next one, and placed it close by. She continued, until all the stones were on the table, arranged in a circle.

'There,' said Clarice, 'the circle is formed.' She adjusted the position of the final blue crystal. 'I was told that we must now make our feelings known to the spirit. That we must be honest and sincere. That we must explain we don't want any further disharmony in this house.'

She reached towards her Mother and took her hand.

'Let's begin,' she said.

Jack sat in the kitchen poring over a holiday brochure for luxury cruises in Alaska. He flicked from page to page, but promises of glaciers and unspoilt wilderness did not hold his attention. His thoughts constantly meandered back to whatever was going on in the dining room, and he felt slightly queasy.

Twice, he got up and walked down the corridor to stand outside the dining room. The muffled voices from behind the door were not coherent, and despite the urge to enter he chose not to interrupt. Restless, he went into his study, to take his mind off matters.

Twenty or so minutes later, there was the sound of voices in the hallway, and Chloe came through to join him. She put her arm around his shoulder, and kissed him on the cheek.

'We're finished,' she said.

Jack looked at his watch. 'Thirty minutes. Is that how long these things are meant to take?'

'I don't think there's any fixed length of time. Clarice said we had to continue until things felt right.'

'And do they?'

Chloe looked thoughtful. 'I don't know,' she eventually said.

Then she sighed deeply. 'And I don't know what we'll do if this doesn't work.'

Jack gave a reassuring look: 'We'll cross that bridge when we come to it. Where is Clarice?'

'I sent her to bed. She seemed exhausted.'

'I didn't realise she was staying here. Who's looking after the kids?'

'They're at home. Doug is back from his business trip.'

'I see,' said Jack.

'I'm also pretty beat. I think I might head up. Can I rely on you to lock up?'

'Sure.'

'See you upstairs.'

Jack stayed in his study for another five minutes, looking through and organising a folder of papers he had opened. When he made his way out of the study, he stopped by the front door to check it was properly locked, then sauntered through to the dining room. His curiosity had been aroused. He entered and switched on the light. The lights were still set to dim.

On the table, the six gemstones and crystals had been left in place, and he went over to examine them. He wanted to pick one up but thought better of it, and stopped himself. Then he took a slow circuit of the room and made sure that everything was as it should be. Satisfied, he switched off the light, closed the door behind him and made his own way to bed.

Last to bed, first to rise.

Jack put on his dressing gown and went downstairs. He made some coffee and drank it in front of the breakfast news on the television in the kitchen. When he had finished he began to make his way upstairs to get showered and dressed, but in the hallway he stopped impetuously. He peered into the dining room. Everything seemed fine. The circle of crystals was still there. Nothing seemed out of place.

And then his focus shifted down to the other end of the room.

He stopped and stared.

'I'll be damned,' he said.

He crossed the room, stopping in front of the dresser, directly opposite one of the candlesticks.

'I'll be damned,' he said again.

There in front of him, stood five candles in their holders. All of them were new and unused. Long and red, with pristine white wicks. Except, the furthest candle was not new and unused. It was three inches shorter than the others, and the wick's tip had burned black.

CHAPTER 10

Tuesday mid-morning.

Margaret and Luke headed out of the library's parking lot then doubled back onto the main road that led to the centre of town. From behind them, someone blasted a car horn, but Margaret did not hear it.

'So, Chet hasn't filled you in on any of the details?' she confirmed.

'Not really,' answered Luke. 'He seemed wary of giving too much up, without getting their say-so.'

'Okay, well, permission granted. But before I go any further,' she paused, 'I'm sure I don't have to tell you…' Her sentence tailed off.

'Go on.'

'…that discretion is the better part of valour.'

'Of course,' Luke reassured her.

She grasped the steering wheel firmly with both hands: 'The people we're going to see are Jack and Chloe Monroe. They live over in the western side of town. Both Chet and I have known them for a long time. They've had these bizarre things happening at the house for just over a month now.'

Margaret's nose twitched: 'What's more, I really don't think they've gone doollally.'

Soon the broad highway with dispersed pockets of living, gave way to a more urban landscape. Margaret pointed her car down a road marked Claremont where a central reservation of manicured bushes and palm trees separated the traffic streams. Smart two and three storied buildings with restaurants, bookstores, realtors and boutiques lined up either side of the road, and cars were parked along its length.

'You've been to Eagle Canyon before, right?' checked Margaret.

'Just a fleeting visit a couple of years back, for two days.'

‘Did you come down here? To Claremont?’

Luke thought carefully. ‘Yeah I think so.’

‘Well, Jack Monroe can take the credit for Claremont.’

Margaret pulled over to the side of the road, and left the car’s indicator flashing, the metallic click punctuating the cabin like a metronome.

‘Once upon a time there was nothing here. Eagle Canyon was a dustbowl town with a few dozen houses out by the freeway. But come 1963, the Canyon, as we know and love it, was born. A bunch of developers based in Tucson and Phoenix bought up what was here, and half the surrounding desert. Their ambitious plan was to create a town, a retirement town, pretty much from scratch.’

Margaret’s arms pointed in all directions: ‘They divided up the plot and set about what they were good at. Some worked on infrastructure, others on housing, others on the more commercial stuff. It’s why so much of the Canyon exists in clusters - each builder worked their particular patch.’

Luke stared ahead as an old man hobbled down the street, resting heavily on his walking cane. He lifted the cane and pointed towards something in the distance, then resumed walking.

Margaret cancelled the flashing indicator.

‘Jack Monroe was a junior partner in this consortium but recognised that lots of people liked the idea of small-town America. A community with a Main Street, where you could slip into a soda shop, or next door to the five-and-dime. A place where people stop to chat. Not everyone wants to live in condos and development villages, or do their shopping in those massive malls. So he did some side deals and over time acquired the necessary land which he then named Claremont. I think it’s named after his Grandfather on his Momma’s side. Anyway, Main Street here is the heart of Claremont. It’s our equivalent of Beverly Hills.’

‘So this is where people aspire to live?’ asked Luke.

‘Oh yes. It took a while, and in the early days, his grand scheme didn’t look so hot. But he was in for the long haul, and when things went slack, he just took it easy. Slowly, as Eagle Canyon grew, more and more people, and more businesses came. Patience was the key. Many of our wealthier residents live around here. Sadly, over the years, the five and dimes gave way to shops selling leather handbags and designer wear, and the soda shops became fancy restaurants, but I guess that’s progress for you.’

Margaret glanced into her side mirror and edged the car back into the limited flow of traffic.

'So this is all his land?' asked Luke.

'It used to be. He sold most of it as he grew the neighbourhood.'

'So he's not short of a few bob?'

'A few bob?'

'He's got money.'

'Oh yes, but you wouldn't always know it. He can be pretty tight. But that's how the rich get richer,' trumpeted Margaret.

They continued down Main Street, and as they reached the bottom, Margaret spoke. 'So this was sold by Jack over the years, but this... this he still owns.'

She slowed the car and turned right into a street marked Hampton Row, Private. One hundred yards down the road, she turned once again, through an imposing metal gate.

The house was not visible from the road, and Margaret steered her way along a twisting driveway lined with carefully cultivated bushes and trees. 'It's more of a mini-ranch really,' she explained. 'Something like two and a half acres right in the centre of town. And the garden's lovely too. The grey water from the house is filtered somewhere along the way, and used to irrigate it. Very eco-friendly, huh?'

Margaret's eyebrows danced as she talked.

'How do you know the Monroe's?' queried Luke.

'Jack and my late husband were friends from way back. We used to see lots of each other. Less so these days, although Chloe and I still play bridge together every week.'

'And what are they like?'

'Jack's what you might call - charismatic. He used to be a real hard ass when the mood took him, but retirement has done him the world of good. He can be very charming and entertaining. Chloe's a grand old gal from a grand old family, and that comes through now and then. She's a little high strung, and can get a bit uppity sometimes.'

Margaret smiled at Luke. 'But then, can't we all?'

The house was now in front of them, and it was spectacular. It was built on a substantial scale with tall columns along the front, double size windows and a barn door of an entrance. It reminded Luke of a plantation house likely to be found in the deep south. Margaret pressed on up the drive and they cruised past the garaging, which seemed to take up one wing of the property. Then the driveway became a turning circle, part of which was covered by a portico.

'Very nice,' said Luke with understatement.

'Isn't it,' replied Margaret with pride in her voice. 'It's the best property in town.'

The stars and stripes hung proudly from a flagpole out front, and Margaret brought the car to a halt under the shade of the portico. She beeped her horn with ebullience and as she did so, an old black Labrador lying by the front door sat up, pointed his nose towards the car, and took staccato sniffs.

'We're here!' she said purposefully.

A man appeared at a window next to the front door, and gave a friendly wave.

'That's Jack,' said Margaret, before turning to Luke. 'This is gonna be great. I've never seen a parapsychologist in action.'

'Margaret, I'm not sure what you expect,' started Luke, 'but I'm only here to look and listen, and maybe, maybe, give some advice.'

'Shucks. No Latin incantations?'

'Nope. And no ectoplasm readings either.'

'I know Luke. I'm only teasing.'

As she finished talking, the front door was thrown open and Jack Monroe walked out to meet his guests, broad smile fixed in place and arms out wide.

The dog then decided to bark.

'Hush Freddie!' said Jack gesticulating at the animal, which paid him no attention.

Jack swooshed around to the driver's side of the car and helped Margaret out.

'Margie, hello. Good of you to come over at such short notice,' he said.

Luke made his own way out of the vehicle and walked round to where the others were holding hands. Jack turned his way breaking the connection with Margaret: 'Luke, is that right? Good of you to swing by.'

They shook hands.

'A pleasure,' said Luke.

Monroe was dressed more for yachting than anything else, in a designer polo shirt and navy-blue shorts. He wore light coloured loafers without socks, a copper bangle on one wrist and a sizeable gold watch on the other. He had a kindly face, bushy snow-owl eyebrows and a limited amount of hair on top. Sleek aluminium bifocals were tucked into his shirt's collar.

'Hush Freddie,' he repeated, and the dog lay back down. 'He's getting old now. Please, come on in.' He guided them out of the heat, and they entered a hallway of cool white walls and greyish marble. The air conditioning enveloped them.

'Let me see where Chloe is,' said Jack wringing his hands together nervously. He opened a swing door and shouted – 'Chloe, our guests are here.'

It swung back into position: 'She'll just be through. Margaret you look as lovely as ever.'

'Thank you Jack,' she replied demurely.

'Tell me, are you going to the Liebermans' party?'

'I am.'

'God, I hope it's not like last year's, that was all terribly unfortunate,' he groaned, and they shook their heads vigorously.

Did someone die? Did the Liebermans pass around a bowl of car keys?

The swing door opened and a tall elegant woman, dressed in a flowing white dress walked through. She smiled a perfect smile, and spoke warmly: 'Hi there, I'm Chloe Monroe. You must be Luke.'

Chloe extended her hand, palm down and knuckles up, as though Luke should kiss it. A large diamond and sapphire ring on her index finger figured prominently.

Luke shook her hand as best he could. From the side.

'Luke Jackson,' he disclosed.

Chloe turned to Margaret. 'And Margie. Hi there. God, what a couple of days. First Marcie, and now you must have heard about Denise Lawrence. They say it'll take 3-4 months for her to recover.'

Like her husband, wealth served Chloe well. The cosmetic surgery had been expertly done.

'Well, introductions over,' said Jack clapping his hands together. 'Why don't you go into the drawing room and get comfortable, and we'll bring everything through. Would you like tea or coffee? Something stronger perhaps? After all, it is almost lunch time. Luke, can I get you a beer, some wine, or perhaps a scotch?'

'A coffee will be fine thanks,' said Luke. Margaret wavered, but agreed to coffee in the end.

'Okay then. Go down the end of the hallway and make yourselves comfortable. What am I saying? Margie, you've been here enough times. Go. Chloe and I will be through shortly.'

Margaret led Luke down the corridor, and opened the door to the drawing room with élan. The room was big and could entertain sixty people in comfort. Bravely, it had been split into modern and traditional halves. At one end, large oil canvases with abstract strokes of purple and blue dominated, and a contemporary looking fireplace of dark stone drew the eye. Thin-legged Italian tables in chrome and glass sat beneath the paintings, and upon them rested family photographs and gold edged party invitations.

The other end of the room bore delicate watercolours and antique European furniture. A walnut tall boy stood next to a rosewood sideboard, whilst glass cabinets housed jade sculptures and intricate glasswork. Somehow the opposing styles complemented each other.

Margaret collapsed onto one of the sofas arranged by the tallboy and began to root through her handbag. Luke walked the room, looking things over. When he had completed a circuit, he strolled over to the patio doors and looked into the garden. He noticed that the patio doors seemed freshly painted.

'Should we telephone your Grandmother and tell her we're going to be out for a while?' enquired Margaret.

'No,' he replied. 'I doubt we'll be here too long. She'll be okay. Tell me, how long have Chloe and Jack been in this house for?'

'Oooh, I'm not sure we'll have to ask. Fifteen years maybe?'

At that point, Jack strode into the drawing room holding a tray of cups and saucers. Chloe followed with her own tray, upon which a sponge cake sat. Luke noticed Margaret's eyes grow slightly bigger.

'How long have you two been in this house?' asked Margaret, sitting up in her seat. 'Luke was just asking.'

'Coming up for twenty years,' replied Chloe. She took charge of passing out the cups, whilst Margaret cut the cake.

Jack called Luke over to one corner of the room and a Persian rug on the floor. 'You see this?' he said. 'I got it in Paris. It once belonged to the Shah of Iran.'

'Really?'

'Yup,' answered Jack before adding mischievously, 'or so the salesman claimed.'

Jack began to take Luke on a tour of the room. He took obvious pride in pointing out various elements of the Monroe collection, each with an accompanying story. They stopped next to a painting.

'Do you still collect art?' asked Luke.

'Well, now and then. Not as much as we used to, but that's mainly because we travel far less. We haven't been to Europe for a couple of years. We don't even go to New York as often as we should. Now this piece-'

Beneath the picture, Jack pointed to a sideboard with a striking Chinese statue of a horse.

'-Tang Dynasty. Got it in Hong Kong.'

'It's beautiful,' commented Luke.

'Isn't it? I had fun with customs on that one.' Jack glanced across the sideboard. 'Shame it's got to sit next to that damned clock.'

The clock in question was a cube of stainless steel with black mesh strips across the front edge. In its centre sat a conventional analogue face with coloured numbers. It did not match the other furniture.

'Well it's certainly unusual,' remarked Luke good-naturedly.

'Hmmm,' Jack gave a little shuffle on the spot and looked down at the floor, 'a birthday gift for Chloe, from our eldest son, Harris.' He licked his lips before adding grimly: 'He's an artist.'

'Coffee's ready,' said Chloe looking up.

She noticed the men looking at Harris's gift: 'Jack darling, I think it might be time to move that elsewhere.'

'Kids!' said Jack, 'it's one thing when you're ten years old and you paint a blue tomato…' His comment trailed away. 'You got any children, Luke?'

'No.'

'Planning any?'

'Not right now.'

'Don't bother. They're a pain in the ass.'

'Hey!' called out Chloe.

'What?' he laughed.

Jack patted Luke on the shoulder in a manly way, and the two men wandered over to the sofas. Luke sat next to Margaret on one side of the table. Jack sat next to Chloe on the other. Coffee and cake was distributed accordingly. Then everyone turned towards Luke.

Showtime.

'So erm, tell me about this problem you're having?' he said.

In the space of ten seconds, the atmosphere changed completely.

The good humour evaporated and Chloe tensed up visibly. Jack looked around the room furtively, almost ashamedly. The house seemed to go ominously quiet, as though it was holding its breath, waiting to see whether its secret would be spilled.

'I should make clear, before we start,' Luke continued, 'that I wouldn't call myself an expert on poltergeists or haunts by any means. And I'm not sure if I can really be of much help, in the short time I'm around.'

Jack licked his lips: 'That's okay, Chet mentioned the situation at home, and I want to start by saying that Chloe and I are really sorry to hear of your Grandfather's death. I only met him once or twice over the years, in passing. We understand entirely that you've got to be there for your Grandmother. First and foremost.'

There was a suitable period of contemplation.

Jack continued: 'And if there's anything we can do to help – with funeral arrangements or anything else, just let us know. As for this place, whatever you can do for us, no matter how limited you think it is, well I'm sure it will be of help.'

'That's very kind of you,' said Luke, bowing his head slightly.

'And this will remain confidential, won't it?' asked Chloe timidly.

'Of course.'

Jack moved forward onto the edge of the sofa: 'Well where do you think I should start?'

'Why don't you start at the beginning?' suggested Margaret beginning her assault on the cake.

CHAPTER 11

Tuesday mid-morning (2).

Jack removed his glasses and laid them on the coffee table. Then, he rested his elbows on his knees, and interlocked his fingers under his chin.

'It started last month,' he said. 'The night of the thirteenth to be precise. We'd gone for dinner at my daughter's house and returned here around ten. Everything seemed fine; nothing was out of place. Our housekeeper, Leya, normally leaves a nightcap in here for us, so I put some music on and we enjoyed a glass of brandy. The evening had been a rather turgid affair.'

Chloe wriggled in her seat with some discomfort as Jack continued: 'I was sitting where you are now Luke. I remember thinking how Chloe seemed agitated. She was restless. She said that something didn't feel right.'

Jack worked his gaze across the room towards two ceramic vases, on the mantelpiece above the stone fireplace.

'Anyway, I suggested that Chloe might have had some bad food or something. Around 10.45 we decided to hit the sack. I switched off the lights and we headed up.'

Luke leaned forward and picked up his coffee. Simultaneously Margaret leaned forward to return her plate to the table.

'Next morning I had an early round of golf scheduled, and woke up around six forty-five. I got dressed and came downstairs with Chloe still in bed, and grabbed a bowl of cereal in the kitchen. The doctor has got me eating lots of bran.'

Jack's eyes began to intensify.

'When, it came time to leave I couldn't find my car keys. I looked in the kitchen and the study, then I came in here to see if I'd put them down the night before. They were on the table here and as I picked them up, the phone began to ring.' Jack pointed over his shoulder at a black telephone on a table to the right of the sofas. 'I answered it, but there wasn't anyone on the end of the line. Wrong number most likely.'

As if on cue, the phone began to ring with a synthetic warble that reverberated around the room. Margaret sat back with a jolt.

Luke allowed himself a discreet smile.

Coincidence.

Jack looked uneasy but reached across to pull the handset from its cradle. 'Hello?' he said cautiously.

A delay.

'Oh, Hi Chet.'

He chuckled to release the tension.

'No nothing important…yes, they made it here. I'm just running through it now.'

Jack listened then looked at Luke: 'Chet says Hi.'

Luke nodded in reply.

Jack spoke back into the receiver: 'He says hello… Okay. Speak later.' He returned the handset then reverted to his previous position with elbows placed on knees.

'Where were we?' he enquired. 'Oh yes. I was sitting here, the phone had rung and I'd just hung up. Anyway, as I put the phone down I looked across the room towards the fireplace.'

He gazed back at the vases, and Luke followed his line of vision.

'And I noticed that the vases were out of place. They had swapped position!'

A sense of disappointment washed across Luke.

The two vases were no more than eighteen inches in height. They had been fired with dark glazes and were tapered at their upper ends. To Luke, they did not look like the sort of vases to get excited about.

Jack pointed across the room towards them: 'The one on the left was on the right, and the one on the right was on the left.'

'Quite bizarre,' said Chloe.

'I see,' commented Luke impassively. 'The vases had moved.'

'Yes,' replied Jack with incredulity. 'So I went upstairs and asked Chloe why she'd moved them? "Moved them? I haven't touched them," she said.

Chloe took over: 'I came down here to see what Jack was talking about.'

She held her hand to her neck. The fingers and thumb were split in a vee around her throat: 'I mean, how could vases just change place like that? I hadn't moved them, and no-one else would have?' She slowed her voice for emphasis: 'It was not possible.'

'And obviously you checked that nobody else had moved them without telling you?' confirmed Luke. 'I mean, your housekeeper, for example, when cleaning them or something?'

'No,' said Chloe firmly. 'Those vases are by a rather famous American sculptor. They're exceptionally precious. Almost priceless to me. There's a rule in the house that no-one, including Leya, is to touch them. It's an absolute.'

Jack rolled his eyes.

'If there was one thing in this house,' continued Chloe, 'one belonging or possession that carried a message I would notice-'

Jack interrupted: '-Chloe's very fond of those vases. She bought them a couple of years back, for a significant amount of money.'

'It's not the money Jack,' said Chloe. 'They are exquisite. The artist was a dear friend of my Mother's, and he made them for her as a gift. Unfortunately, they were sold by other members of my family many years ago. Getting them back was very important to me.'

Luke looked at the vases: 'I know it seems an obvious question, but from this distance they look quite similar. Any chance they'd been swapped before then, and you hadn't noticed?'

'No,' replied Chloe icily. 'It must have happened that night.'

Luke turned back: 'Did anything else seem out of the ordinary? Did your housekeeper notice anything strange?'

'No.' replied Jack. 'She put our brandies out and said everything was quite normal.'

Luke paused momentarily.

'And that night, when you were at your daughter's - the house was locked up?'

'Err. We think so,' said Jack. Hurriedly he added, 'but since then, we've always been extra careful to lock the house up iron-tight every evening. Even when we're here.'

Jack must have sensed Luke's disappointment in the episode of the moving vases, and quickly moved on. 'The vases were only the start,' he volunteered, 'I mean, a couple of vases swap position. Big deal, right?'

Chloe looked mortified.

‘It was only the beginning. Things really began to get creepy soon afterwards.’ Jack sat back in his seat. ‘About a week later, we were in bed asleep. It was two in the morning, and I woke up to go to the bathroom. It’s a fairly regular thing, at my age I seem to spend a great deal of time just standing there, waiting. And nothing happens for-’

‘-move it on, dear,’ said Chloe.

‘I had just finished in the bathroom, and gone back into the bedroom to find Chloe sat up in bed.’

Jack began to spell out what happened that night detail by detail.

‘So I got my gun out of the safe…’

He made gestures and gesticulations whenever he considered a feature particularly important.

‘…then we started to head down the stairs, it was clear the noise was coming from this drawing room…’

At that point Luke saw Chloe give a small involuntary shudder.

‘…and then, I switched the lights on and told Chloe that we’d better phone a carpenter…’

Luke glanced at the patio door.

‘The slug went into it, just above the handle,’ explained Jack.

Luke focused his question on the mysterious noise: ‘Can you tell me any more about it? Could you describe it?’

‘It was unusual,’ replied Chloe. ‘Low-pitched and repetitive, as though somebody was whispering something, but not in an effort to be particularly covert. Every twenty or so seconds, the same sound.’

‘Like a whisper?’ clarified Luke.

‘Yes. It’s a bit difficult to explain. Like a whisper at normal volume. It was still quite loud, just very low pitched.’

Silence descended upon the room.

‘As you probably noticed, there are coach bolts on the inside of the patio door,’ said Jack. ‘They were locked when I came in. And afterwards, I looked around the whole damned house. Everything was as it should be.’

‘And there was no obvious source for the noise? I mean like a radio or television?’

‘No,’ said Jack. ‘The stereo was switched off.’

Chloe could see that the story so far did not seem particularly remarkable, and she appealed to Luke: ‘I realise houses, especially big ones like this, do make noises, sometimes in the middle of the night,’ she said. ‘But this one was quite different. This one had purpose.’

‘Has it happened since?’ asked Luke.

'No, we only heard it the once.'

'And you're sure you both heard the same sound?'

'Well, my hearing isn't what it used to be,' began Jack. 'But I heard something. I just can't be sure what I heard. You know I was a little disoriented and it all happened kind of fast. Chloe heard it better.'

'It wasn't English,' added Chloe. She waited before adding dramatically: 'we have come to believe it may have been a Native American dialect.'

'Oh yes, what makes you say that?' queried Luke.

Jack elaborated. 'When we heard the noise, on top of the vases moving, we began to get a little concerned. So we mentioned matters to our youngest son, Pete. Unsurprisingly perhaps, he was pretty sceptical, but eventually offered to find out if there was any history to the house or site. You know… anything unusual in the past.'

'And what did he find?'

Jack and Chloe looked at each other. Then Jack ran his fingers around the bottom edge of his mouth.

'We believe that this house is built on an Indian burial ground,' he explained.

'Tell Luke about the car,' instructed Margaret.

'Right,' said Jack. 'About five days after we heard the weird noise, we had another event. I came down to take my car out one morning and went into the garage. There, right in front of me I found every single one of the tyres on my car were flat.'

'All of them?'

'Yup. Each and every one, valve caps still in place. And you know what? There was nothing wrong with them. I pumped them up with a little travel compressor I have, and took them round to our local garage. The mechanic took each one off and checked them proper; couldn't find a darned thing wrong. They've been right as rain ever since.'

'After that, we had all the locks changed in the house,' confided Chloe. 'But there was no suggestion that anyone had gained access that night, anyway.'

Jack had built up a head of steam: 'Moving on. About ten days ago, which is almost 4 weeks after everything began – we had the most worrying episode. My son Pete and his wife had come over for the weekend with their son. They were having some work done at their house, and wanted to get out of there for a couple of days. Chloe suggested we go to the country club for lunch…'

Luke took a long slow sip of coffee.

'…we heard Chloe scream…'

Chloe stiffened in her seat at the recollection.

'…so Pete rushed upstairs to see what was going on...'

Luke put the empty cup down.

'And then he came downstairs looking really confused. He checked which bathroom Chloe had seen the message in. "Davy's" she said. He explained there was nothing there.'

'The message on the mirror had disappeared?' said Luke.

'Yes, we all went back upstairs together and checked straight afterwards,' said Chloe.

'It had gone,' reiterated Margaret.

'Now I realise that someone might figure I had imagined it,' began Chloe.

Luke waited.

'-but I really don't think so. It seemed very real.'

Now it was Margaret's turn to move the story on: 'Tell Luke about the candle.'

'Ah yes, if we move to the most recent event,' said Jack, 'just three nights ago, a candle in our dining room somehow lit itself.'

Jack explained the ceremony, and how he had found the lone red candle the next morning. 'All the others were pristine,' he said.

'Where is this candle?' asked Luke. 'Have you still got it?'

'I had Leya get rid of it,' said Chloe. 'I didn't want it in the house.'

'And all the doors and windows were locked?'

Jack nodded before looking Luke straight in the eyes. 'Listen,' he said. 'I'm a pretty rational kind of guy. I'd never normally believe in spirits or spooks or ghouls. But if I'm being frank, I've never come across anything quite like this. I can't find a rational explanation.' Then he took a deep breath: 'I think there's something unnatural in this house.'

CHAPTER 12

Tuesday mid-morning (3).

Luke took a moment to collect his thoughts: 'Well it's certainly a most unusual situation,' he said without fuss.

'It really is,' replied Jack.

Luke sucked on his lower lip.

'Do you think we've gone crazy?' asked Chloe.

'Why would I think that?'

'Well it all seems a bit far fetched.'

Luke smiled sympathetically. 'Tell me. Why do you think all this has started up, now? After all, you said you've been in the house for a good many years.'

'Good question,' began Jack. 'I can't think of anything. Nothing concrete.'

'Okay, and what about less concrete ideas?'

'Harris,' blurted out Chloe.

'C'mon Chloe,' said Jack with irritation. 'You know what I think about that.'

'Jack, I don't believe it can be a coincidence.'

Reluctantly, Jack began to explain: 'Harris is our eldest son. He owed some money to an Indian fella and the two of them fell out. The gentleman made clear that unless he got paid, there would be… repercussions.'

'He used those words?'

'Or something very close.'

'And you think these repercussions are related to events in this house?'

'I do,' said Chloe outright.

'You don't think he was threatening to sue Harris, or alluding to physical violence?'

'No,' she replied categorically. 'Harris understood the threat. In the same way you'd recognize a gypsy's warning.'

'And when did Harris tell you about this?'

'A few weeks back. When my tyres went flat,' said Jack.

Luke seemed contemplative.

'And what was your response?' he finally asked.

Jack looked grim. 'I settled the debt,' he said.

'But the incidents didn't stop,' pointed out Margaret. 'The message on the mirror, the candle, they came afterwards, right?'

'Yes,' said Chloe glumly.

'I'm a little confused,' said Luke. 'Since it was Harris's debt, why would you become involved?'

'We may not be the Rockefellers, but in these parts the Monroe name has a certain cachet,' stated Jack sniffily. 'Maybe it's the case of, a plague on you…and your family.'

'So,' began Chloe. 'There you have it. Do you think the house is haunted? Have we got a poltergeist?'[30]

Luke collected his thoughts for a few seconds.

'It's hard to say at this stage,' he began, before leaning forward slightly. 'Haunts are place centred. Poltergeists are person centred.' He looked directly at Chloe. 'The prevailing view is that poltergeists can normally be attributed to a living person, on the premises, unconsciously generating paranormal activity.'

'A living person?' asked Jack. 'Not a spirit?'

'Not a spirit,' affirmed Luke. 'Haunts and poltergeists can take similar forms: strange noises such as loud banging or rapping sounds, weird smells, temperature changes, object movement.[31] Poltergeist activity tends to last anything from a few days to a couple of months, and often disappears as swiftly as it arises. Haunts can persevere for much longer.'

Margaret eyed up the cake once more then peered across the table at Luke's cup.

'More coffee?' she asked.

'Please,' he said passing his cup towards her. 'Typically, when investigating any case, various options need to be considered.'

Margaret poured.

'First up is deception or fraud,[32] which is reckoned to account for up to a quarter of incidents.'[33]

'You think this case is fraud?' asked Chloe, somewhat aggrieved.

'No, I'm just offering possibilities.'

Margaret passed his cup back.

'Next, are the events hallucinatory? Do we need to consider mental illness, or psychotic drugs?'

'We don't take drugs. And neither of us have any history of mental illness,' said Jack emphatically.

'Hallucinations can arise under different circumstances. When people are really tired, when the brain is under or over stimulated, or when subjected to repetitive stimulus. Certain ceremonies such as those found in voodoo, for example, take advantage of this. By beating out rhythms for hours at a time, people get wrapped up into what seems a mystical experience. They begin to report seeing and hearing, tasting and feeling things.'

'My voodoo days are behind me,' joked Jack nervously.

'Mine too,' said Luke with a wink. 'Hallucinations can also come about through practises such as fasting, which might explain why a lot of religious experiences seem to follow periods of abstinence.'

'Ah,' said Jack knowingly, but he did not go on.

Luke continued. 'The hallucination explanation seems unlikely when more than one person has the same experience. Hallucinations are private affairs. People often realise they're not real.'

Margaret repositioned herself on the sofa.

'But you think the noise we heard is genuine, don't you?' asked Chloe.

'The fact that you both claim to have heard it and that it came from a distinct room makes a conventional hallucination unlikely. It would not, however, rule out the notion of telepathic hallucination.'[34]

Luke ran his hand across the top of his head as though smoothing down hair.

'Next we need to think about misperception. Sometimes we see or hear something a bit odd, or ambiguous, and assign meaning to it. Factors such as mood state[35] may have part to play. Apart from the strange sound you heard, have you seen anything unusual? Aside from the message on the mirror, that is.'

'Like a ghost? An apparition?'[36] asked Jack.

'Anything you can think of,' replied Luke.

Jack and Chloe looked at each other. After a while they both shook their heads. 'No, I don't think so,' certified Chloe.

'Have either of you felt that there was someone in the house with you. Have you sensed a presence?'[37]

Chloe shook her head again: 'I can't say I have.'

'Me neither,' added Jack.

'Okay. We'll move on,' concluded Luke. 'There's also the possibility, especially with recurring haunts, that there's something special about the property, like unusual geomagnetic or electromagnetic fields. Power lines or electrical equipment might cause some of these. There's also the suggestion that some buildings with a high iron content in the stonework might create localised electromagnetic fields, and when people stand in them, there's some sort of field influence on the brain.'[38]

Jack raised his eyebrows.

'Anything unusual about the construction of this house or the land it's built on?' asked Luke.

'Well we're on a burial site,' said Chloe sarcastically.

Jack interjected: 'In terms of geology or building materials, there's nothing unusual with the house or the grounds, as far as I'm aware. Standard build for the time. I oversaw everything myself.'

'Go on, Luke,' said Margaret.

'The next suggestion is one that I touched on just now. That haunts and poltergeist events are some form of psychokinesis, or PK.'

'Psychokinesis?'

'Yes. Where your mind is able to influence things around you.' Luke pointed at Jack's coffee cup. 'Levitating that cup would be a good example.'[39]

Luke sat up in his seat.

'One explanation for poltergeist events is that they are due to RSPK - Recurrent Spontaneous Psychokinesis[40], and are caused by a living agent on the premises. In most cases, this is a troubled adolescent with suppressed anger or resentment towards an authoritarian parent or guardian. By causing things to move around and smash, whether doors, plates or mirrors, PK agents are able to vent their anger and frustrations. When the agent is removed from the premises, or counselled, the incidents stop.'

'I never knew that,' said Margaret.

'I should add of course,' continued Luke, 'that the RSPK theory cannot, and does not, seek to explain every poltergeist occurrence.'

'The agent doesn't realise they're the cause of the activity?' asked Margaret.

'No, it's a subconscious act.'

'And there are examples that back up this theory.'

'Sure. If I recall correctly, there was Michael Lessing from Seaford, Long Island,[41] and Arnold Brooks[42], a thirteen year old from Newark. There was Julio Vasquez[43] from Florida -'

'-Is there a gender effect?' interrupted Jack. 'Are boys more likely than girls to be agents?'

'For a while it was thought that girls were more likely to be responsible, but that view now seems less credible.'[44]

Luke returned to his previous explanation. 'Possibly the best known RSPK case surrounded a kid called Julio Vasquez, a 19 year old Cuban refugee who worked in a warehouse in Florida in the 1960s. The warehouse housed lots of tourist souvenirs, which were reported to move around and smash when nobody was nearby. The warehouse owner brought in magicians, the police, anyone who could work out what was going on. They couldn't uncover what was causing these disturbances and weren't able to find evidence of fraud. Even while the investigators were on the premises, incidents continued to take place, and in the end some 200 were recorded.'

Luke followed on: 'Because of the regularity of the outbreaks, and due to the fact that certain parts to the warehouse, such as particular shelves, seemed more "active" than others, researchers were able to set up target objects for the poltergeist to move. When it duly obliged, it turned out that the common factor was Julio – situated nearby – but unaware of his role. When Julio was removed from the premises, the disturbances stopped. Psychological analysis revealed a troubled kid – he had manifestations of anxiety, rebellion and anger stoked by a dysfunctional relationship with his stepmother, a woman who wanted Julio to move out of the family home.'[45]

'What about times when there's no obvious agent on the premises?' asked Margaret. 'I mean, some places have things happen even with different people on site?'

'Harder to explain perhaps, but there's evidence to suggest that psychokinesis can operate across time.[46] It may be that consciousness can generate effects even though the agent is not physically present.[47] We also need to bear in mind that some places get a reputation for ghostly activity, which then simply gets perpetuated. Maybe disturbances continue to happen, not because of psychic disturbances but due to conventional things like noisy plumbing or unusual draughts?'

Chloe jumped in: 'I notice you haven't mentioned spirits as a cause?' she said.

Luke nodded. 'Evidence that dead people might be the cause of these effects has proved notoriously hard to validate. After all, we're talking the survival hypothesis.'

'The survival hypothesis?'

'Yes. That we continue to live on, after bodily death.'

Jack seemed to be getting impatient: 'So, what do you think is happening here?' he asked robustly. 'In this house?'

Luke sighed: 'At the moment, I'm not sure. Tell me more about what your son dug up?'

Jack stood up and began to pace. 'Pete runs my old property development firm. He asked one of his staff to dig through the land records and history to the place.'

'And you hadn't looked into that before?'

Jack winced a little: 'When we first built here we did some cursory searches. To be honest, in those days we were less sensitive to the indigenous people. Let's just say, we might not have had the same regard as we do today.'

'I'm afraid I'm not familiar with this area's history,' began Luke. 'Which tribe comes from around here?'

'The Tohono O'odham.'[48]

Luke looked at Chloe: 'Since you think the sound you heard was Indian, do you think you could recall it? Presumably it would carry some meaning?'

Chloe shook her head: 'I couldn't. It was too quiet and I was too far away to get a really good listen.'

Luke bit on his lower lip gently. 'This might be an odd question, but… how do these incidents make you feel?'

Jack reiterated the query, as though it was some sort of trick question, 'how do we feel?'

'Yes.'

'Well uncomfortable, I guess,' stated Chloe. 'Scared even.'

Jack agreed: 'I don't like the idea of living on another man's grave.'

Luke let the moment pass. 'And if I can't be of much help in the next few days,' he said eventually, 'what do you think the longer term solution might be?'

'I don't know. We could get someone in?' suggested Jack. 'Bless the ground or something. Put the spirit at rest.'

'We could move out.' added Chloe.

'Or we could live with it.' Jack smiled at his wife. 'You fancy that, Chloe?'

From Chloe's subsequent expression, this did not seem likely.

At that point, Margaret made an effort to get up and clattered into the table, causing the cups and saucers to rattle.

'Ooh clumsy,' she said. 'Go on without me, I just need to go powder my nose.'

She picked up her handbag and left the room, and Luke waited until she was out of earshot: 'While it's just the three of us, I need you to be really candid. Can you think of anything personal that might have helped start the disturbances?'

'I don't get you,' said Jack.

'Well, I need to put this delicately,' he said. 'Do you think the incidents might serve some personal purpose? I once met a young woman who had recently been bereaved. One day, she was sitting in the garden thinking of her husband, when he appeared to sit down next to her. He told her he loved her, but that the mourning must end. She was to move on with her life, and he'd keep an eye on her and look after her. Later, she realised the whole experience was probably her unconscious trying to make sense of her loss, and prompting her to get on with her life.'

Jack and Chloe made no comment.

Finally Chloe spoke: 'I can't think of anything off hand.'

'Me neither,' added Jack. 'I can't think of any reason why we'd unconsciously want to leave here.'

Luke nodded. 'What do the other family members think you should do?' he asked.

'Well, I don't think Pete believes us, and to be frank Harris probably doesn't care,' said Chloe. 'But my daughter, Clarice, thinks we should move. She doesn't think we should further upset the spirit world. This is their space. But she's always been a bit…' Chloe searched for the word.

'Neurotic?' suggested Jack.

'Sensitive,' replied Chloe, smiling weakly.

'Luke,' said Jack. 'What can we do?'

'Well we're not going to jump to conclusions too quickly. First up, I'd like you to keep a diary. Include everything, from happenings in the house, to the comings and goings of visitors, to what mood you're in and how things are affecting you. Be honest and open in the diary.'

'Okay,' said Chloe.

'Jack, have you got a portable tape recorder?'

'Yes, somewhere. I'd have to dig it out.'

'Do that. Buy new batteries and a fresh tape, and keep it close to hand.'

'Do you think it can pick up this Indian whisper, even if we can't?' asked Chloe.[49] 'Like those photographs that seem to show ghosts, or something similar?'

'No. I was thinking if it happens again, you can capture it on tape.'

Luke stared at Jack: 'You said that when you got close to this room last time, the sound stopped. So don't keep the tape recorder in here.'

'Right.'

'And do make sure the tape is new.'

'Okay.'

'In the meantime, I'll do some of my own research. I'm only here a short time, but I'll do the best I can.'

Jack walked over and extended his right hand: 'Luke. Thanks so much. We really appreciate you taking the time to do this.'

Luke stood up and they shook hands as Margaret trundled back into the room.

'Are we finished?' she asked.

'For today,' replied Luke. He turned to face the Monroes head on. 'I might have a chat with your children, and your housekeeper, if that's all right? Get their takes.'

'You can speak to Leya, our housekeeper, here,' said Jack. 'She's got the day off, but will be back at work tomorrow. And I'll give you the kids' numbers now.' He crossed the room to a desk, opened the centre drawer and removed a notepad. Writing quickly, he jotted down relevant names and phone numbers. He walked back and handed Luke the paper: 'I'll give them a call when you leave here, so they know you'll be in touch.'

'Well, if we're all done, I guess I'd better run you home,' Margaret cheerily announced. Chloe got to her feet.

The four walked in silence from the living room back into the entrance hall.

‘Please pass on my condolences to your Grandmother,’ said Jack as they reached the front door. ‘There’s gonna be a tremendous amount of adjustment for her.’

‘I will. Thank you both very much for the coffee.’

Margaret chimed in: ‘Yes, thank you for the coffee. The cake was super. Chloe, I’ll see you at bridge.’

‘Looking forward to it.’

Luke led the way. He walked over to Margaret’s car and held open the driver’s door for her.

‘Ciao,’ called Jack from the house. He closed the front door as Margaret climbed in and Luke made his way to the passenger’s side.

‘So what do you think?’ asked Margaret, as she put on her seatbelt.

Luke raised his eyebrows: ‘You tell me.’

CHAPTER 13

Tuesday lunchtime.

'Don't be a stranger now,' exclaimed Margaret from the driver's window. Luke was halfway through the front door, but stopped and acknowledged her. When he went inside, Rebecca was in the kitchen: 'Luke Darling. Chet phoned, not more than ten minutes ago. He wanted to know if you'd join him for lunch. The Sunflower Café at eleven-thirty.

'Lunch?'

At eleven thirty?

'We eat early here,' explained Rebecca. 'You can't miss it, there's a big plastic sunflower on the wall out front.'

The plastic sunflower was not big, it was enormous, and Luke was sure he had found the right place. He went into the restaurant, and in the reception, a woman with a plastic name badge and a concerned look across her face, punched keys on a cash register: 'Take a seat, honey,' she said, without looking up. 'Wherever you see a space. A waitress will be right with you.'

'I'm looking for someone,' replied Luke scanning the room. 'Chet Baker.'

She pointed behind herself, but her eyes stayed fixed on the till: 'Table at the back.'

The Sunflower was busy and humid with plenty of hubbub. Uniformed waitresses scurried about with notebooks tucked into their apron strings and pencils behind their ears. Cooks toiled at hot plates in the open kitchen, shouting to be heard above each other and the extractor fans. 'Service!' someone called. 'Table twelve!' A busboy disconsolately mopped the green linoleum by the toilets.

At the back, Chet sat alone at a table, with his glasses perched high on his forehead. He was ensconced in a newspaper, which he held no more than three inches from his face.

'Chet,' said Luke loudly, trying to gain his attention.

Chet peered over the top of the newspaper: 'Luke, my boy,' he replied happily. 'You found this place okay?'

'Yeah. How are you today?'

'Just dandy.'

Luke took a seat and looked over the room. 'This is a regular haunt of yours?' he asked.

With a shake of the head, Chet's glasses fell from his forehead onto his nose: 'Yeah, I come here a few times a week. You want a coffee or anything, before you order? I just got one.'

'No, I'll wait.'

Chet placed his newspaper on the seat beside him then put his hands together. He looked as though he was about to take a confessional: 'How is everything at home? Is Rebecca doing all right?'

'She seems fine,' remarked Luke. 'She keeps her emotions pretty much in check.'

'Tough Lady,' said Chet admiringly. 'I'm sure she's hurting like mad, but she wouldn't want anyone to know that. And how are you doing?'

He seemed sincere.

'I'm okay.'

Chet nodded sagely then passed a laminated menu across the table. 'You hungry?'

'Well, it's a bit early, but I'm sure I can be persuaded,' said Luke patting his stomach. 'Any recommendations?'

Chet laughed.

'What's so funny?'

'The food's lousy.'

'Then why come here?'

Chet broke out a wicked lascivious grin: 'Have you seen the hot stuff by the coffee machine?' he asked.

Luke twisted in his seat to get a look across the room. The only thing next to the coffee machine was a waitress with a blue rinse and a low-cut top. He turned back and the grin was still there, Chet's eyes said: I told you so.

'Oh, what to choose, eh?' said Luke quickly returning to his menu.

Chet ordered a mushroom omelette, and Luke ordered a BLT.

They chatted casually for a while, about this and that, but mainly about Chet. Apart from the climate, one of the reasons he and his wife had moved to Arizona was to see more of their son, who had moved to California. He was in "computers or something" Chet informed, "doing really well", but was so busy that he could never find the time to come out to Arizona. Chet made a roundtrip every few months to see him.

It turned out Chet had been an accountant, although in his own words he was "not very good". 'If I could go back and do it all again, I think I should have chosen something more practical, more hands on,' he said.

After a while, Chet became hesitant.

'All this talk about me and my life. Here I am dominating the conversation. Tell me Luke, you got anything you really like doing? What do you get up to in your spare time?'

'Spare time? I can't remember the last time I had any,' replied Luke. 'I've just bought a place back home, and when I'm not doing home improvements, there always seems to be a wedding, or christening to go to.'

'Time of life,' said Chet. 'You're lucky it's not divorces and funerals yet.'

Luke looked perplexed: 'How many divorces have you been to?'

'Well you know what I mean,' said Chet. 'You got any hobbies, or outside interests?'

'Usual stuff I suppose. But, if I get a couple of days together, I try to go sailing.'

'Really?' enquired Chet. 'You got your own boat?'

'No, just a part share.'

'Hmmm, I went sailing a couple of times. Never really got the bug for it. I didn't get sea sick or anything. Just didn't enjoy it.'

The food arrived.

'One BLT, and one mushroom omelette,' announced the waitress. 'Can I get you guys anything else?'

'That'll be all, Alice,' replied Chet picking up his fork. He loaded it and went to take a bite: 'Luke, I enjoyed our conversation the other day. On the ride in from the airport. When I left you, I went home and had a look on the internet.'

'Uh-huh.'

'There are a lot of paranormal websites out there.'

'Yeah that's true,' replied Luke breezily.

'And a fair few sceptical ones as well.'

Luke summoned up a deep powerful voice: 'We are the great debunkers. We can explain everything. The things we can't explain are irrelevant, so don't ask.' He finished with a sweet smile on his face. 'Some of them are rather misinformed.'

'Well, how do you counter them?'

'We don't really bother.'

Chet looked slightly surprised. 'Why not?' he asked. 'Some of it seems quite convincing, y'know.'

'If it wasn't convincing, people wouldn't give it a second thought. Unfortunately, a lot of internet wisdom boils down to misplaced statements of "fact" and name calling. If people really want to learn about the paranormal they'd best go buy properly researched books.'

'I saw this one site,' continued Chet, 'that offered $100,000 if someone could provide a verified example of psychic functioning. It said no-one had ever come close.'

'I know the one you mean,' replied Luke. 'Read the small print.'

'Meaning?'

'They refuse to accept experimental evidence. Sure, they'll agree to test the crackpot who says he can teleport Napoleon from the fields of Waterloo, but try submitting lab data, and they just say no. The competition's closed to anything with any credibility. They've always got a get out.'

Luke reached for the A1 sauce, opened his sandwich and gave it a healthy dollop. Then he took a big bite from the middle.

Chet seemed satisfied with Luke's explanation. 'In all this talking, I never asked what you do,' he said.

'Me?' replied Luke, speaking from the corner of his mouth, trying to prevent his food from joining the table.

'Yes. Specifically, what type of research do you do?'

Luke chewed rapidly, and Chet obligingly waited.

He swallowed: 'I'm involved in pre-sentiment research.'[50]

Chet looked at him blankly. 'And what's that when it's at home?'

'Fundamentally, I look at how people respond to different types of photographs.'

Chet picked up the ketchup and squirted a large pool of it around the edge of his plate.

'People watch a computer screen and look at different pictures,' continued Luke. 'Pictures of plants or landscapes.'

Chet cut a piece of omelette and pushed it through the puddle of tomato sauce.

'At the same time, I measure their physiological response.[51] Whenever people are presented with a stimulus – whether it's a photo, or a noise, even an insult – there's a subsequent bodily response.'

'Okay so you're measuring a person's physiological reaction to the pictures,' clarified Chet.

'Yes. With emotionally neutral pictures, there's a small response just after the picture is flashed up onscreen; a pretty limited reaction. But what do you think happens if I suddenly show you something really emotive? Something gruesome perhaps?'

'I guess, there'd be a bigger response,' suggested Chet. 'Certainly bigger than when I'm looking at a picture of a plant.'

'That's right.'

'So what's paranormal about that?' Chet took another mouthful of food.

'Well, here's the interesting bit. What actually happens, is that people start responding to the emotive pictures, like a gruesome one, before they're presented on the computer screen.'

'Really?' said Chet with disbelief. Some omelette now tried to sneak out the corner of his mouth, but he pushed it back in with his thumb.

'Yup. Every so often the computer randomly throws in an image that makes you go "yikes", and from the physiological data, it's clear the person's response starts before the picture is shown.'

'That doesn't seem possible.'

'Everything's randomised, and people can't guess when these images are going to appear. Some kind of extrasensory mechanism seems most likely.'

'No subtle cues?'

'Nope.'

'Maybe the experimenter accidentally helps them out?'

'No. They're not even in the same room as the participant.'

'Wow,' said Chet. 'And when does this pre-response start?'

'It varies, depending on what sort of image you're showing. With violent images, for example, you see the response start about three seconds before presentation.'[52]

'That seems amazing. It's like people are preparing themselves in advance for something unpleasant?'

'Yup. And that makes good sense; if you knew I was going to do something unpleasant to you, you'd prepare for it.'

'Are you?'

'No, you're quite safe.'

Chet sat back in his seat, with a look of amazement and there was a break in the conversation.

'So that's what I do,' concluded Luke. He took another bite from his sandwich.

The two of them sat eating in silence for a minute then Chet changed the subject: 'So how did your meeting with Jack and Chloe go?' he asked.

'I'm not sure. I think they were a little disappointed that I didn't jump up and down, and get a proton backpack out of the car,' said Luke. 'Have you spoken to Jack?'

Chet put down his fork.

'Briefly,' he replied. 'They appreciate your help, honestly they do.'

Luke recalled the earlier meeting: 'I ran through various possible causes with them. I don't think they were terribly amused when the idea of mental illness as an explanation cropped up.'

Chet shrugged. 'Don't sweat it. Jack said you also discussed fraud.'

'Well, I'm afraid it does happen.'

'Oh I'm sure. All I can tell you is that if Jack and Chloe are making this up – it's completely out of character. They've never courted attention and are certainly not prone to making such fantastical claims.'

Luke wiped his mouth with a napkin, as a waitress slunk past, and peered into Chet's mug.

'More?' she asked.

'Yes please,' he beamed in reply.

She poured.

'And for you, sweetheart?'

Luke put his hand over the top of the mug. 'No thanks.'

She walked away.

'Well is there anything we can do?' asked Chet.

'We?' asked Luke. 'As in, the two of us?'

'Yes, I thought I could help. We could be a dynamic duo, as it were.'

'Wasn't that Batman and Robin?'

'I might be helpful,' said Chet.

Luke made no reply.

'And I squared it with Jack and Chloe,' added Chet.

Again. Silence.

'I'll keep out of your way, whenever you ask.'

Chet dropped his chin and opened his eyes puppy dog wide. Through his thick rimmed glasses, it was a disturbing sight.

'All right, stop that,' said Luke. 'If the Monroes are cool with it, I guess I am. But I hope your friendship won't compromise anything. I mean, you need to understand that whatever we discuss is confidential.'

A puzzled look crossed Chet's face.

'With any apparent poltergeist case, we look towards living agents as the source. We try to find out whether there are repressed psychological issues that manifest themselves in the disturbances,' explained Luke. 'Or what if we do find fraud? What if this is a cry for help?'

The puzzled look began to lift.

'Basically, I need you on my side,' remarked Luke.

'Of course.'

'Give me a heads up on anything you think relevant. In turn, our private discussions mustn't get back to Jack and Chloe.'

'Not a problem,' said Chet pulling an imaginary zipper across his mouth.

A few seconds later he unzipped it: 'So, it's a yes then?'

Luke paused for effect then nodded, and Chet banged his fist on the table in delight. 'So what can we do next?' he enquired. 'You got a plan, Batman?'

'Well Robin-' said Luke

'-I always preferred Spiderman,' interrupted Chet.

'Whatever makes you happy. We can't sit around kicking our heels, waiting for something new to happen, so let's start by getting as much background information as we can. Perhaps you could begin by looking into the property. Did Jack tell you the house is on Indian land?'

'Yes, he did.'

'Find out what actually went on there. Do we know who was buried there? Was it a site of worship? Did something bad happen? I understand that Jack's son has already looked into it.'

'Yes – Pete Monroe.'

Chet broke off as hotstuff walked past, and his eyes glued themselves to her rear.

'Still with me?' asked Luke.

'Hmmm?' replied Chet absentmindedly.

'Pete Monroe?'

'Oh yeah, I last saw him at Christmas. I'll get right on it.'

'And I wouldn't mind meeting the daughter.'

'Clarice.'

'She was staying at the house when the candle was found. Maybe she has some other information, or a different angle as to what went on.'

Chet nodded his head: 'Sweet kid. Always very charming to me. She lives somewhere between here and Tucson. I'll get her address for you.'

Chet took on a contemplative expression. 'You know Luke, I've had a think about this, and as I see it, there's only one common thread.'

'Chloe?' suggested Luke.

'That's right. Should we not focus on her?'

'Not yet,' replied Luke. 'Let's not form any preconceptions at this stage.'

Both men continued to munch their way through their food.

Chet took a final mouthful to finish his omelette, then placed his fork along the plate's edge. He reached into his pocket and produced a calling card: 'It'd probably be useful if you had this. I've just had them printed.'

Luke surveyed it as he finished his sandwich. 'Very smart,' he said.

'It's got my home number and my cell phone details. There's also an email address at the bottom.'

Luke slid it into his shirt pocket: 'I'd better give you my mobile phone number,' he said, taking a paper napkin from a dispenser, and writing a phone number across it. 'It's my British number, so try calling me at my Grandmother's first.'

Chet inspected the napkin closely, from a very short distance, before folding it in half and squishing it into a pocket.

'Try not to wipe your nose on it,' joked Luke.

'I'll try. You want anything else? Some more food? Dessert?'

'No, I think I'm okay.'

'You sure? How'd you enjoy the BLT?'

'It wasn't too bad.'

'The food poisoning normally takes a while to kick in.'

Chet sat back in his seat and held his hand in the air: 'Excuse me, Lorraine,' he called out. 'May I please have the check?' He turned back to Luke. 'This is on me, Son.'

CHAPTER 14

Tuesday afternoon.

Chet proved remarkably efficient. Less than thirty minutes after Luke got home from The Sunflower he was on the phone. 'I just got hold of Pete Monroe's secretary,' he said. 'We've got a meeting, today, at three o'clock in Tucson. Is that good with you?'

Luke checked his watch. 'Yeah fine. Do you want to ride in together from here, or what?'

Chet declined. 'I've got an appointment on the other side of Tucson around two-ish,' he said. 'You're welcome to come with me and wait; I don't think it'll take very long. Just seeing my Doctor.'

The idea did not appeal.

'No, don't worry. I'll make my own way there.'

'Okay, you got a pen? Let me give you Pete's address.'

Luke wrote it down on the cover of the local phone book, and agreed to meet Chet in the building's lobby.

As he hung up, Rebecca came out from her bedroom.

'That was Chet,' explained Luke. 'I've got to head into Tucson later. Is that okay with you?'

'Fine,' said Rebecca with a poker face. Luke sensed her mood and possible displeasure. 'Why don't we go out for dinner tonight?' he added quickly. 'It'd do us some good to get out of the house.'

She smiled. 'Yes. That's a lovely idea. I'll book a table. You like Mexican, don't you?'

'Absolutely.'

'Now where do you have to be, this afternoon?' she asked. 'There's a map in the bottom drawer in the kitchen. You'll want to avoid the roadworks.'

Luke arrived early.

The journey had been faster than Rebecca had predicted, and with the exception of some pickup trucks racing each other on the freeway, uneventful.

Monroe's office was in a steel and glass skyscraper in the heart of downtown. And downtown seemed very quiet that day. Luke parked on a meter in the road out front, and dropped a bunch of quarters into the slot. To begin with, he thought he would wait for Chet on the pavement, but that idea evaporated as the heat began to bite and perspiration flowed. Instead, he found refuge in the lobby, and the close embrace of the air conditioning.

A small number of people were making their way in and out of the building. Looking at a directory above the security desk, Luke observed the place was home to several dozen firms. Several had the deluge of surnames synonymous with the legal world, others were more non-descript; three letters with "international" or "holdings" tacked on the end. There was no clue as to what the businesses did. They could be arms dealers or bible wholesalers.

Chet arrived.

'Woo, right on time,' he said merrily. 'You find it okay?'

They walked over to the reception desk, where a large sign informed all guests to register. The security guards looked them over suspiciously, and not surprisingly, as Chet had changed his clothes since lunch and now wore a maroon t-shirt with *Come Get Some* above an arrow pointing at his groin. 'It amuses my Doctor,' he explained.

'Monroe Land Developments,' stated Luke.

'Sign here, please,' said the guard without emotion. 'Then, go around to your right. Take the elevator to the 14th floor.'

They moved across the lobby in unison. The squeak from Chet's sneakers contrasting sharply with the harder clip from Luke's shoes.

'Smart office block,' said Luke reaching for the elevator call button.

'Mmmm,' concurred Chet. 'Not quite Jack's style.'

Both men stood back to watch the luminescent information panels above each door. The lift closest to them began to descend.

'Pete moved the firm here a year or so back,' explained Chet. 'Something about increasing visibility or raising perceptions or whatever. A load of horse if you ask me.'

'Where was the firm located before here?'

'On an industrial estate a few miles outside the Canyon, between a plastics factory and a haulage contractor. It was a bit rough and tumble. I don't think Jack could have stomached the rent here. He tends to watch the pennies.'

Ping.

The chrome doors directly in front of them opened, and Chet waved Luke in.

Luke pressed the button marked 14: 'So Pete's the boss now?'

The doors closed silently.

'Yeah, Jack retired. Pete's been in charge for a couple of years.'

'Does Jack still own it?'

'No. He passed it over to the kids, in some sort of trust. I don't know the exact ins and outs. They keep things pretty quiet.'

The lift stopped at the sixth floor where a pimply youth entered. He had coloured biros lined up in the breast pocket of his shirt. There was no further conversation until he exited at the eighth.

'And what's Pete Monroe like?'

'He's all right, A little abrasive. A little volatile by some accounts. His father expects him to make his own way in the world and he tries a bit too hard. There was a hoo-ha last year when he tried to rush some planning permission through.'

'But he's making a success of the business?'

Chet made a huffing sound: 'Difficult to say. As I understand it, he's changed the focus of the company. There's still some local stuff, but he's mainly developing start-ups along the border for Mexicans or something. Jack doesn't really talk about it, at least not to me. As far as I know he's doing all right.'

Luke looked down at his shoes.

'Are Jack and Pete close?'

'Not especially.'

'Then why's he in charge?'

'Family, my boy. Family.'

Ping.

The doors parted and both men stepped out into an airy hallway of bleached wood and halogen uplighters. Three offices shared the fourteenth floor but ahead of them, a pair of glass doors had been wedged open, and a shiny brass plaque informed them that this was Monroe territory. They moved forward, up to an imposing raised desk, where a pretty receptionist wearing a sleek headset was busily reading from a file. She spoke in rapid fire Spanish and sounded irritated.

As she finished her conversation, Chet led the way.

'Hi there,' he said, resting his chin on the desktop. 'We're here to see Mr Monroe.'

She looked at Luke then flashed a short-lived and impersonal smile: 'May I say who's calling?'

'Yes. Chet Baker and Luke Jackson,' Chet replied, before adding unnecessarily - '*Doctor* Luke Jackson'

Her look suggested Luke's title couldn't have mattered less. Then she tapped into a keypad: 'Mr Monroe, Sir. I have Mr Chet Baker and Dr Luke Jackson here.'

Her scrutiny shifted between the two of them.

'Yes Sir.' There was a pause of a couple of seconds. 'I understand,' she said. She tapped another button on the keypad and pointed to her right: 'Down the corridor. Last office on the left.'

They followed her directions and the reception area soon spread out into a large open plan office, with a pathway that bisected the workspace. Three people worked quietly at computers or on drawings spread over draughtsman's tables. There were photographs on the walls of previous projects and at the furthest end of the room, scale models of developments were displayed proudly under glass canopies. Little cardboard houses with painted sponge trees and matchstick people enjoying their beautiful new homes.

At the very back of the room was a line of doorways, and as they got close they heard a raised voice.

'You might think it's no big deal, but it is to me. I don't give a damn how difficult you think it is! Get it done, or I'll find someone who will!'

A man scurried out of an office looking suitably chastised. Chet glanced at Luke and raised his eyebrows. Moments later Pete Monroe emerged from the very same office. He had his shirt sleeves rolled up and was red in the face. He noticed his guests, and threw a mental switch. Instantaneously, the charm began to flow.

'Chet,' he said in a relaxed southern drawl, 'good to see you. It's been a while.'

'Hey Pete. A long time. This is Luke.'

Pete casually focused on Luke: 'Howdy. I'm Peter Monroe.'

'Hello.'

They shook hands, with Pete squeezing a little too hard.

'Well, come on in Guys,' he said. 'This is a bit of surprise. When I came in this morning, I wasn't expecting to see you folks. Can I get you anything to drink? Coffee or a soda? Some tea? I know you Brits love your tea.'

For some reason, Luke half expected Pete to throw a manly punch to his stomach, and he tensed in anticipation. 'I'm okay thanks,' he replied courteously.

Chet shook his head to signify that he did not want a drink.

Peter Monroe had the corner office - the best on the floor. It had thick carpet, expensive wallpaper, and a view across the city. There was decisive oriental art on the walls, and on his desk sat a flatscreen computer monitor and a pair of telephones. The carpets had been cleaned recently and there was a wet dog smell to the room.

'How's business?' asked Chet.

'Yeah not bad.'

Pete sat down in a high-backed leather chair and ushered his guests to sit as well. 'We're busy at the moment trying to wrap up a deal, near Albuquerque. We've got some lovely condos, really classy sought-after stuff, coming up for sale… if either of you fancy a change of scenery.' He opened his palms like a book. 'Double digit returns. Really great.'

Snake oil.

At that point, the telephone nearest him bleeped, and he held his hand up to pause the conversation.

His tone was brusque and businesslike: 'Yes. What? Oh for Christ's sake. Phone her back. Tell her I'll be there as soon as I can, and then hold all my calls.'

He hung up.

'Guys, listen. One of my project leaders has just phoned in. There's some almighty screw up on a build down by the border. It's gonna need my immediate attention. Perhaps you'd like to reschedule?'

'If you can just give us ten minutes, that'll be fine,' responded Luke.

Pete thought for a few seconds then licked his lips.

'Okay, it'll have to be quick,' he said picking up a pen from the desk and twirling it across his fingers. Then, he made a pistol gesture and fired it at Luke: 'You got ten.'

Chet jumped in. 'As I mentioned on the phone, Luke here is looking into the problems your Ma and Pa are having at home. He thought you might have your own take, as you were there when the mirror episode happened.'

'Good of you to do this Luke,' said Pete as an aside.

Luke held his hands up to indicate no problem.

'Well,' Pete pivoted his seat around forming a right angle to the desk, 'my wife and I were at the house for the weekend. We were having some work done at our own place and thought it'd be simpler to stay at Dad's. She'd taken our little boy with her shopping, and I was sitting with Pops in the kitchen, talking about…golf, I think. My Mom was upstairs.'

Pete recounted the story, and never stopped twirling the pen.

'When we hear a scream…'

He swung the chair back, faced his guests – 'Leave Now, right across the mirror, she said'. It was a flat emotionless recollection and Pete seemed apathetic to the tale. When he had finished he opened his mouth wide and ran his tongue along his incisors. Then he placed the pen carefully onto the desk.

'And that's what happened,' he said.

'And there was nothing in the bathroom?' clarified Chet.

'Nada. Empty,' replied Pete. 'No sign of nothing. I looked behind the shower curtain and out the window. And then, to be thorough, I checked out the medicine cabinet, and the cupboard under the sink. There was nothing there.'

Pete leaned back in his seat.

'And then everyone went up together and looked?' asked Luke.

Pete placed his fingers behind his neck and tilted the chair back: 'Yup. We went up there and had another look with Dad and me paying special attention to the mirror. Whatever Mom thought she'd seen was not there. Nothing on the mirror, or on the tiles. Not a trace.'

Pete's gaze came to rest on Luke.

'How did your Mother react when you all went up to look?' asked Luke.

'She seemed pretty adamant as to what she'd seen.'

'And then what?' asked Chet.

'After that, the afternoon's a bit blurry. Mom stayed pretty riled up, and Dad did his best to calm her down. My wife and son got back to the house around thirty minutes later. Obviously we didn't go out for lunch. Davy didn't improve matters when he asked, a little too loudly, whether Grandma was going mad.'

Pete gave out an ugly snigger.

‘So, in your opinion, there was nothing untoward? Nothing at all?’ said Chet.

‘Forget opinion. How about fact?’ said Pete.

He looked across at his computer screen then idly nudged the mouse. ‘There’s nothing more I can add really.’

‘And what about the other happenings at the house?’ asked Luke.

‘Well, I wish I knew, but I was away for most of them so got everything second and third hand.’ Pete seemed disinterested. ‘Maybe age is catching up a little. No disrespect Chet, but our older friends do get things wrong.’

Chet did not react.

‘Your Father told me you’d had the land researched,’ said Luke.

‘Yes I have. Oh God, I wish I’d never done that. Maybe this craziness would have gone away.’

‘Why’s that?’

‘Well a couple of weird things happen and I make the mistake of offering to look into the site. When I do, it turns out they’re living on a burial site. Now they think the place must be haunted.’

‘You don’t buy into the ghost explanation?’ asked Chet.

‘I don’t really know,’ replied Pete. He looked like he could not care less: ‘Luke, you’re the expert, you tell me.’

‘I’m still open to suggestions.’

Pete huffed a little: ‘As you ask my opinion… I doubt if anything ghostly is going on. They’ve been there two decades after all. It’s got to be someone in the house, messing around.’

‘So your Mum or your Dad?’ suggested Luke.

‘Seems most likely. Better check if they’ve paid Leya the housekeeper this month. Maybe whoever’s responsible doesn’t even know what they’re doing?’

‘Surely you’d know if you let all four tyres down, on a car?’ proposed Chet.

‘That’s not what I mean. Maybe it’s some kind of autopilot, maybe we’ve got a sleepwalker? Hell maybe the culprit knows what they’re doing, and they’re just trying to mix things up a little.’

He leaned forward confidentially, and rested his right forearm along the edge of the desk: ‘I don’t buy in to the Indian spirit explanation, full stop. If I was a betting man, it’s one of two possibilities. Either Mom and Dad have pissed off Leya once too often. Or my Mother needs a bit of R and R.’

‘Why your Mother?’

'She's the one who saw the message in the mirror. Dad didn't. She's the one who was in the dining room with my sister, doing crackpot ceremonies.'

'Meaning you think she's responsible for the candle as well?' queried Chet.

'I'd imagine so.' He swung his chair back towards the view: 'Maybe she really doesn't know she's doing it. Maybe her inner voice is trying to tell us something.'

'And the vases?' added Chet.

Pete sighed deeply. 'Let me tell you about those damned vases. I have never come across anyone who obsesses over anything quite like she does with those wretched things. They once belonged to her Mother and were sold during hard times. No-one, and I mean no-one, is allowed to touch them. If there's one thing in that house that would send a message…'

'But what about your Father,' said Luke. 'He says he heard the strange sound in the living room. How would your Mother do that?'

Pete's face took on a look of insouciance.

'Shoot, I don't know. Maybe it wasn't a voice they heard. Perhaps it was a TV or the air conditioner? Maybe he didn't actually hear it. He's just backing Mom up. His hearing's not that great, y'know.'

There was silence.

'Tell me some more about the history of the site,' directed Luke.

Pete pushed down his lower lip: 'I got one of my staff to look through things. I've got the report around here somewhere.' He began to search a desk drawer, and then all the others. Eventually he gave up: 'Sorry fellas, I must have taken it home. I don't like leaving family stuff in the office. How about I dig it out, and send it along for you. You got a fax machine? It's only a couple of pages.'

'I've got one,' replied Chet.

Pete nodded and picked up his pen.

'No, no. I have a card.' Chet stood and reached into his back pocket and from his wallet pulled out another calling card: 'There you are. The fax number is at the bottom.'

He passed the card to Pete who put it next to his telephones with barely a glance.

Chet nudged Luke, 'I'm gonna need more of those, at this rate.'

Luke spoke: 'If it's gonna be a hassle Pete. Why don't we print another copy now, or speak with whoever wrote the report. Presumably he's in the office?'

'Ah, problemo there Luke,' replied Pete. 'His Grandfather's ill. I put him on compassionate leave, and he left for Hawaii a few days ago.'

'Hawaii?' said Chet. 'Luke's meant to be in Hawaii right now.'

'Really? Which island?'

'Umm, Maui.'

'Beautiful. Really beautiful.' said Pete, his head bobbing up and down in approval. 'You should try to go back there sometime in the future.'

'I'm sure I will.'

Pete looked up at a clock on the wall and sucked his teeth.

'You said ten minutes guys, and you've had it. To recap. I don't believe in this spirit crap. Even if the house is on a sacred site – big deal. We've lived there twenty years, and it's only now that stuff starts to happen. Why? It's gotta be psychological. Mom and Dad's expectations are just making everything seem supernatural.'

Pete shook his head, and twirled his fingers around his temples to emphasise how crazy he thought it was.

'Well, what do you think the solution is?' enquired Luke.

'In what respect?'

'Well, whatever's happening can't continue.'

'Yeah that's true. I don't know. Maybe they should take a long vacation or something. Get Mom some counselling. Or leave the house; let some other schmo deal with our unwanted guest.'

He flashed a wide grin.

'Guys, I'm gonna have to dash,' he said standing up. 'If there's anything more, give me a ring.'

He paused for a moment then looked Luke deep in the eyes. His tone hardened. 'You know you probably think I'm a little casual about this, but deep down I am genuinely concerned. I don't want my parents worrying themselves into early graves.'

Luke doubted his sincerity.

And with that, Pete put his hands in his pockets, and walked around the desk.

'Chet, Luke. I appreciate your help. Like I say, get in touch if you need anything more.'

'Well, thanks for your time,' said Luke politely.

Pete walked to the door then held it open.

'See you later, fellas,' he said.

Chet and Luke stood by the elevator.

When it arrived, they entered, and turned to face the doors. The receptionist glanced up briefly from her work to eyeball them, and Chet gave her a sneaky wave just before the doors closed fully.

At the tenth floor he spoke. 'Short but sweet, huh? Pete seems to have made his mind up.'

'It seems that way,' said Luke.

Ping.

The elevator door slid open and both men headed for the street.

CHAPTER 15

Tuesday evening.

Leave a message at the tone.

'Hi Amy, it's me. I've made it to Arizona. Umm, my plans have changed as we've had some bad news here. My Grandfather... he passed away two nights ago when I was grounded by that storm out east. I didn't call earlier. I knew you were away.'

Unexpectedly, Luke could feel emotion building in his belly, and a tightening around his diaphragm. He forced it away.

'So I'm going stay for the next few days,' he went on, 'until the funeral. Obviously, I'll be a no-show at the conference. I'll phone and let the organisers know, when I get a moment.'

He shifted the phone to his other ear. 'Anyway, give me a bell when it's convenient. You can reach me on my mobile - I've found the charger. I love you, baby.'

He hung up, and without thinking, his hand lingered on the handset.

It was nine o'clock and Luke found himself in the living room, with the modest offerings of the television for company. The restaurant dinner had never happened. Upon his return from Tucson, Rebecca asked whether they could take a rain check. She did not feel up to it she said.

Instead, Luke fetched some takeaway food from a nearby Mexican restaurant, and the two of them ate burritos in front of the news. He attempted to engage her in conversation but it proved futile. She excused herself straight after dinner, which pleased Luke as her dark mood was contagious. There was melancholy in the air and it had begun to make Luke feel brittle and dispirited.

He needed to get out of the house.

He left a note on the hallway table in case Rebecca awoke. Then he slipped outside. The night air was balmy and the sweet aroma of freshly cut grass hung heavily on a light breeze. He stopped to enjoy it.

Take pleasure in the small things, he recalled.

Life is the small things.

Luke got into his car, and started it up. He watched the instrument needles slowly arc into position as the engine fired then settled into its deep bass thrum. It seemed like the only sound in the neighbourhood. He flicked at the stalk for the headlights. Up ahead, a cat with fiery eyes darted out of the road, pausing briefly to scowl down the road. Luke engaged Drive.

Hummingbird Lane ran parallel with Abrego Boulevard, the main artery between the eastern part of Eagle Canyon and the newer western part. Luke cruised aimlessly down it for a while, unsure of where to go or what to do. He passed a petrol station and a convenience store where a man pulled down stout shutters with a thump and clang. He sat at a red traffic light for an age but no other vehicle passed through the junction. Later he found himself on the freeway that had carried him in from the airport.

'You are now leaving Eagle Canyon.'

He read the sign aloud.

Traffic was minimal, just a set of headlights in his rear view mirror that never got closer, and the occasional big rig going the other way towards the border. The significance of driving an empty highway through an empty desert did not escape him, and he gave a knowing sigh.

He needed something to occupy his attention. Any distraction would do. An exit for La Costa, a small town off the highway, came and went followed by one for Copper Mountain, with its mine museum promising "fun for the whole family".

The next road sign proclaimed "Chicken City" ahead, and Luke's thoughts turned to images of chickens and skyscrapers and busy urban hustle. Predictably, it turned out to be a fast food restaurant.

Just as he considered turning back, a wide roadside hoarding boomed into view. "The Silver Dollar Casino – 3 miles" was emblazoned across it in red.

A sanctuary.

The Silver Dollar was built on reservation land by a consortium of businessmen from the local indigenous community. The lack of any immediate competition allowed for a low key and conventional approach to gaming, and the casino eschewed the gaudy razzmatazz of Las Vegas, which was only an hour's flight away. There were no laser displays or live crocodiles or bonza showgirls.

The casino building itself was a large triple storey box, constructed of sandstone and glass, with an entrance on each face. It could have been plucked straight from any number of business parks. To jazz up the venue, the owners had built a large replica tepee at one end, which was occasionally used for floor shows, and gaming tournaments. Overlooking the freeway was a billboard with an Indian character in full head dress, drawn in coloured lights. The lights flashed on and off so that his expression alternated between scowls and smiles. Children sometimes commented that the sign frightened them.

Luke let his car glide down the freeway's off ramp then found a space at the rear of the car park. Another car followed down the ramp, but disappeared around the far side of the casino. Luke began his stroll across the tarmac towards the casino entrance. As he neared, he picked out the growing sound of gaming: the dissonant hum of coins and bells, bleeps and metal-on-metal. He went inside.

Arranged in symmetrical rows ahead of him were the fruit machines and one-armed bandits, all competing greedily for attention. Some promised jackpots of six figures, others were more circumspect - offering 50 bucks for a nickel's play. In front of them, people were perched on stools. They reached into plastic buckets they had filled with tokens before rhythmically pulling handles and pressing buttons. Few displayed any outward emotion. When the buckets had been emptied, they would trudge away and substitutes hovering in the wings would take over in expectation of a payout.

Black plastic spheres hung from the ceiling, behind which the eyes of the casino watched for cheats and staff on the take. Somewhere, hidden in a backroom, a bank of hard drives whirred patiently and relentlessly, and surveillance operatives scrutinised video monitors. As with most casinos, there were no clocks on the walls to distract the players.

Behind the fruit machines, separated by low level screens, were the card tables and roulette wheels. There were two dozen tables, with varying bet limits, and the busiest tables started at a dollar. Between the tables walked the pit bosses with clipboards and walkie-talkies in hand, and in the background lurked sturdily built men in blazers with filament-thin earpieces. Luke passed one of them who straightened self-consciously before evaluating the newcomer carefully.

Luke quite liked casinos, they appealed to the psychologist in him. The elderly lady with the look of steely determination. The man in the baseball cap with sweat on his upper lip and eyes that would not settle. The young couple quarrelling quietly, trying to avoid outside attention.

He found a bar where a waitress was giving the lone barman an order. 'Three whiskies. On the rocks,' she said indifferently.

The barman pulled three tumblers from under the counter and scooped ice from a chest. Then he ran a bottle containing a chestnut coloured liquid over them. He did not stop pouring as he moved between glasses.

When he was finished, he moved down the bar towards Luke. 'What can I get you?' he asked benignly, tossing a paper coaster on to the bar top.

'Just a virgin-mary, thanks.'

'Coming right up. You like it spicy?'

'I do.'

The bartender set to work and Luke twisted on his heels to look around. Some video screens to his right were showing sports from around the world, and one man sat with a newspaper spread open on the table in front of him, avidly watching a horse race from somewhere in Asia. At the other end of the bar, a large woman in a red skirt and black cardigan sat on a stool. She did not look up from the bar top.

Luke's drink arrived.

'That'll be four bucks.'

Luke pulled a five dollar bill from his pocket. 'Keep the change,' he said before adding: 'You haven't got any nuts, have you?'

The barman found a bowl of pistachios.

Luke pointed at the woman. 'You know her?' he asked.

'Sure.'

'Is she a regular?'

'I wouldn't call her a regular. She comes in now and then. Another lonely heart. One of life's lost souls. You're not interested, are you buddy?'

The woman stared at the empty glass in front of her.

'What's she drinking?' asked Luke.

'Vodka tonics,' replied the Barman.

'See if she'd like one.'

The barman walked down the far end of the bar and spoke with the woman, who looked mildly surprised that someone wanted to buy her a drink. But she accepted, and looked over to see who her kind benefactor was. Her face dropped when she saw Luke, but she got off her stool and walked over. It was Margaret.

'You seem to have caught me in a moment of weakness,' she said.

'That's okay,' said Luke. 'We all have them.'

She made no effort to be cheerful and the bonhomie of their earlier meeting had disappeared. 'I come out here maybe once a month and have a few drinks,' she explained. 'My husband and I used to love the tables. He was a connoisseur of blackjack you know.'

Luke invited her to take a seat.

'Thank you,' she replied. 'You're seeing a side not many people see. I hope you're not disappointed.'

Luke took a sip of his drink, and looked straight ahead.

'Not at all,' he said kindly.

Maybe it was the vodka, or maybe it was the company, but Margaret slowly began to open up. She spoke of her husband, his death and how much she missed him. Then of her daughter with cancer. Luke bought her another drink, and the Margaret who had hugged him in Rebecca's front hall slowly began to emerge. She even reached a point where she began to laugh, and Luke suggested they take a stroll around the casino.

They stopped initially at a craps table where a big man in a small hat prepared to roll his dice. There was a large stack of onyx coloured chips on the green baize in front of him, and the watching group waited, chatting nervously.

He kissed the knuckles on his right hand and rolled the dice, bouncing them off the backboard.

A two and a three.

'You like to gamble?' asked Margaret.

'I don't like the odds,' replied Luke without elaboration.

The croupier passed the dice back to the man in the hat. Once again, he kissed his knuckles, but as he pulled back his arm, he stopped and spoke to them, under his breath.

He rolled again.

A five and a two.

The man's shoulders slumped.

He turned to the crowd with his hands in the air.

'The dice weren't listening,' he joked. 'Or maybe I don't speak dice well enough.' One of bystanders patted him on the back.

Margaret nudged Luke in the ribs. 'Something you'd know about, presumably?'

'Speaking to dice?'

'No silly. Whether they can be influenced?'

'Oh right,' replied Luke.

'Well?' prompted Margaret.

'Umm... Well... Dice used to be a popular method of measuring psychokinesis, or mind-over-matter effects,'[53] he began. 'Researchers wanted to know whether volition, or intention, could make certain faces show up more often than expected.'

They stepped away from the craps table.

'And?' prompted Margaret.

'It seemed it could... but only to a small degree.'[54] [55]

'Cool, let's go break the bank,' said Margaret looping her arm through Luke's.

'A small degree,' Luke repeated. 'And the house margin, in a place like this, is bigger than that.'[56]

'So I can't go down the casino and win a fortune?'

'I wouldn't have thought so.'

'Rats.'

Luke was enjoying Margaret's company and his maudlin mood had lifted. They continued their stroll quite contentedly.

'And there were problems with dice experiments,' continued Luke. 'Problems like bias to contend with.'[57]

'We're talking loaded dice, here?'

'Not quite. It's just that dice, even high quality ones, aren't perfectly random. Having said that - when biases were specifically taken into account - the effect, albeit slight, remained.'[58]

Luke and Margaret stopped next to a roulette table, where Margaret's arm remained looped through Luke's. 'These people will all think I've found me a toy boy,' she said, giggling to herself.

'Or I've got a sugar mama,' laughed Luke.

The minimum bet was $5, and with each seat occupied, the table was awash with chips. 'Place your bets,' instructed the croupier before spinning the wheel. He pushed the ball anti-clockwise and as its momentum slowed, he called 'No more Bets.'

'That's George Lewis,' said Margaret under her breath. She pointed at a bald man watching the wheel earnestly and counting his chips.

'Who's he?' asked Luke.

'He lives in the Canyon. There's a good story about him, although I don't know if it's true. You see, George's wife succumbed to Alzheimer's a few years back and it hit him hard. He watched her regress to pretty much being an infant, and decided that he would never let that happen to him. According to those in the know, George took out a contract on his own life with some assassin from across the border. Every three months, there's a telephone call from this gentleman to ascertain George's mental state. He's under strict instructions to end things if he thinks George is no longer with it.'

'Well, that is forward planning,' said Luke.

'It has been said that the two men have developed such a keen friendship during their phone conversations, that George is having him up for Thanksgiving.'

Margaret let out a laugh: 'I doubt it's true,' she said. 'But it makes a good story.'

They continued their walk.

'So how do you measure psychokinesis these days?' she asked.

'Ah,' said Luke knowingly, 'nowadays we ask people to influence Random Event Generators. Devices which use quantum level events, such as electron movement in semi-conductors, as their source of randomness.'[59]

'Honey, you'd better keep this simple,' advised Margaret.

They moved to another table where the ball on the roulette wheel began to run slow. It slid down the wall, striking the compartments between the numbers and bouncing around. There was a final clackety-clack before it came to a rest. Thirty-five. Red.

'Think of Random Event Generators as perfectly balanced coins which generate the equivalent of many heads and tails every second.

‘Okay.’

‘Basically, in any given trial, a participant is asked to produce a specific outcome.’

‘-More heads please,’ interrupted Margaret.

‘Or more tails. It depends.’

The croupier had cleared the losing bets from the table, and was paying out the winners. A man got up to leave the table and his seat was taken right away.

‘We know Random Event Generators should behave in line with the laws of probability. Experimental measurements show us that they do so – they behave randomly when no-one attempts to influence them. But when people try to influence these machines through consciousness – the randomness diminishes and devices take on a low level of bias.’

‘That’s all very well, but it doesn’t sound very exciting. Can’t you get people to levitate things?’ suggested Margaret.

‘It might not be exciting, and to the naked eye you won’t even see the effect,’ conceded Luke, ‘but it’s a sensible way to test psychokinesis. REGs simply shouldn’t take on order because someone wills them to.’

‘Couldn’t something else be responsible for the results? Electrical fields or temperature, perhaps?’

‘It’s unlikely. Experimenters spend a lot of time running control trials before, during and after experiments to check that it is volition and not electromagnetic radiation or humidity or anything else that accounts for positive results.’

Luke continued: ‘No. in the end, we find it’s the link between a participant’s intention and the REG’s output that persists. It would appear that some sort of mind-over-matter mechanism is the best explanation for the REG’s anomalous behaviour.’

Luke and Margaret began a slow circuit of the gaming area. They passed and settled briefly behind a group of players at a blackjack table. The dealer was young and pretty, and in front of her a man tapped the table with his middle finger. He flirted as she dealt another card.

‘So peoples’ minds are able to influence these devices. Are the results the same as when you used dice?’

‘Overall, they’re not too dissimilar to the dice results. When people try to bring about one outcome over another, they succeed, to a small but consistent degree.’[60]

‘So aren’t the results just statistical… aberrations?’

‘They are statistical aberrations in an absolute sense, but they are consistent and replicable, and that shouldn’t be the case. The universe is built around statistical predictability. If it wasn’t, we wouldn’t be here discussing this.’

‘And you’ve got any explanations for what’s going on? Y’know in terms of theory?’

‘A few,’[61] said Luke. ‘But I’m sure you don’t want to hear them now.’

Margaret smiled to indicate Luke was correct and they walked back to the bar.

‘So how’s it going with the poltergeist?’ she asked.

‘Slowly,’ replied Luke. ‘I’ll need to find out some more about the area’s history and things like Indian burial customs.’

‘I know a little about that,’ said Margaret. ‘I’ve always been a bit of a history nerd.’

‘Really? What can you tell me?’

‘The local people are the Tohono O’odham – “desert people”. Previously they were known as the Papago Indians, or “bean eaters”. No-one’s entirely sure where they originated from. Most people reckon they’re descendants of the Hohokam, who were ancient farmers in the region.’

Luke listened carefully, as Margaret continued: ‘The O’odham say that people and for that matter spirits, come from the centre of the earth via a secret cave in the Baboquivari mountains. You can see the mountains from the highway. The peak there is known as I’itoi, or elder brother. Historically, they lived on what might be called ranches and were quite isolated from each other. A village might have a couple of hundred people but be spread over many miles. Often, in the summer they’d move to a summer village, so that when the rains came they could farm better.’

‘Were they an aggressive people?’

‘No not at all. In fact, they never fought the white settlers, only The Apache. And that’s because they were fed up with Apache raids stealing their animals.’

‘You’re a font of knowledge, Margaret.’

‘Well, you pick up bits here and there. The people lived throughout this region, if you take even a short walk through the desert you’re bound to find arrow heads or some sort of remnant from their past.’

‘What did they do when someone died?’

‘They’d wrap the body in a cotton cloth and then bury it in the ground with rocks and branches on top, or seal them in a cave. They’d place the dead person’s favourite possessions alongside and some food for the journey to the spirit world. Ghosts and spirits are a major part of their mythology.’ She looked at Luke purposefully. ‘And who’s to say they’re wrong?’ she asked.

The casino crowd was beginning to thin out, and some tables had emptied entirely. Luke looked at his watch: ‘Margaret, it’s been really nice but it’s getting late, I think I might head home. You need a lift back to the Canyon?’

‘I’m okay. I think I might stay a little longer.’

‘You’re not driving, are you?’

‘No. I’ve got a cab booked,’ she replied. ‘Adieu, dear boy. Good luck with the rest of the investigation. I’ll probably see you next at the funeral. Rebecca seems to have everything under control.’

Luke hugged Margaret and said goodnight.

On his way out, he paused to tie a shoelace and when he stood up, he found himself facing an empty blackjack table where the dealer waited patiently with cards fanned out on the table in front. The minimum bet was $10. Luke reached into his pocket and retrieved a ten dollar bill, which he held between his fingers. The dealer raised his eyebrows expectantly, but Luke thought better of it. He shook his head at the dealer apologetically then slid the money back into his pocket and headed out into the night.

CHAPTER 16

Tuesday evening (2).

Luke exited the casino building, and noticed how the temperature in the car park had dropped. His car was at the back of the lot, and he sauntered towards it with his hands in his pockets and his jacket collar turned up. In the distance, he clocked another vehicle next to his with two young men sitting on its bonnet. They sat in silence and scrutinised him as he approached.

Luke got to within fifteen feet when one of them – a tall man with five o'clock shadow and a checked shirt, slid off the car onto his feet and slowly made his way around to the driver's door of Luke's vehicle.

'Evening lads,' said Luke calmly. 'Everything okay?'

The man leant back against the door, and pulled his foot up so it was flat against the bodywork. The parking lot's sodium lamps bathed the scene in a ghoulish orange light.

'Wouldn't it be?' replied the man tersely.

There was ten feet between them, and Luke slowed to a halt. The other individual, who was smaller but broader and athletic looking, began to skulk around the back of the car to join his comrade.

Confrontation began to brew.

Oh bollocks.

'Is this yours?' asked the tall man, patting the roof.

Luke surveyed them closely.

'You looking to buy it?' he answered.

There was no reply.

'Looks like a rental to me,' said the taller man. 'I doubt they'd appreciate you selling it.'

The strangers exchanged laughs as though some dirty joke had been made. Luke remembered there was a green sticker from the car rental company on the rear bumper.

The smaller stockier man broke eye contact with Luke and began to prowl the length of the car, flexing his neck from side to side.

'So what you doing round here? Bit of gaming?' asked the tall man lazily. He seemed content where he was, propped up against the driver's door.

'Something like that,' replied Luke.

'Were you lucky? You make a few bucks?'

'Nope. It wasn't my night.'

The smaller man continued to walk parallel to the rental car, taking long steady looks around the parking lot.

The taller individual spoke again: 'You look nervous, amigo.'

'I do?' replied Luke. He glanced over his shoulder casually. The casino door was fifty yards away. There was no-one else about.

'Yup.' There was a nasty sneer on the man's face. 'Mind you, I'd be pretty worried if I were you.'

Luke remained silent. This was not how he wanted his evening to end. The short man continued to rove, and as he doubled back towards the stand-off, he chimed in to the conversation: 'Luis,' he said to his friend, 'I don't like this guy.'

Luis concurred with a snort. The small man stopped scanning the car park, and gave a nod to his partner who pushed himself away from the car and started to move towards Luke, who instinctively began to back away.

Do something.

Luke broke into a broad smile.

The men stopped in their tracks. 'What's so funny?' asked Luis.

'You know what I like about you?' asked Luke jovially.

'What?' replied Luis seemingly confused.

Luke took his time to reply. 'Absolutely nothing,' he said. Then he took his hands out of his pockets and started to roll up his sleeves. 'Why don't you piss off and let me get to my car?'

The two men seemed taken aback, but quickly recovered their cool. There was no time for Luke to bolt.

The small man tapped his partner's chest with the back of his hand. 'Looks like our friend has a pair,' he said calmly.

Hit and Run.

'You must be real stupid,' said the smaller man. He opened and closed his fists, curling his fingers tight.

'That's the way I like it,' said Luke.

Both men started to laugh again.

'And I think you may have overestimated yourself,' said one of them.

Both men had now made fists, and they split apart to pincer Luke between them. One to the left, one to the right.

Luke began to back away more quickly, realising this was his only opportunity to break for safety.

But he did not.

From the corner of his eye he noticed an imminent intervention.

In silhouette against the orange sodium lights, a car was moving towards them. On its roof, in shadow, was the telltale light-rack of a police cruiser. It had pulled into the car park, and was slinking towards them with headlights off.

Luke put his hands up to signal he did not want to fight.

'Boys,' he said, 'maybe I was being a little hasty.'

'Uh-huh,' grunted Luis.

'You don't want to get into this now, surely?'

'Oh,' said the smaller man sarcastically. 'Suddenly you're not so brave, huh?'

Luke put his hands in the air.

'I have so much more to live for,' he added. 'I just taught a monkey to type, and he's producing some good stuff.'

The tall man looked puzzled: 'You still think this is funny?' he asked.

The smaller man began to get angry. He had had enough and started to close down the distance between Luke and himself, pulling his fists up to a boxer's guard. Luke did likewise and backed away further, and at that exact point the patrol car's red and blue strobe lights fired into action. There was a blip from the siren and all three men froze. The patrol car pulled up and a policeman stepped out.

'Stay where you are!' he said assertively. From the corner of his eye, Luke noticed the patrolman's hand resting on the butt of his gun.

Luke jumped straight in. 'Evening officer,' he replied. 'Good to see you. I'm having a bit of trouble getting to my car.'

The men tried to look innocent.

'Nothing happening here,' said the taller man.

'Quiet!' said the cop as he pulled out his flashlight, and shone it over the three of them.

'Which is your car?' he asked Luke gruffly.

'That one.' Luke pointed, and the beam of light followed.

It swung back into Luke's face, and three questions came out rat-a-tat.

'Where you from, Sir?'

'From Britain. Just visiting.'

'Your name?'

'Luke Jackson.'

'Where you staying?'

'In Eagle Canyon…with family.'

There was a pause and the policeman turned his attention towards the other two. 'And where's your car?' he asked.

'Umm. On the other side there,' said the taller man, pointing.

The cop cogitated then spoke: 'Were you causing this gentleman any difficulty?'

'No officer, we were just making our way past him, to the casino.'

'It didn't look like that from where I was. Why don't you just let him pass and then come join me over here, so I can take some details.'

Grudgingly the men rejoined one another and began to walk towards the patrol car.

'You have a good evening now, Sir,' said the police officer. 'Enjoy your stay in Arizona.'

'Thank you,' replied Luke. He made his way past the men and with his back to the policeman, puckered up a sly kiss for Luis. 'Some other time perhaps,' he whispered.

Luis did not respond.

At the car, Luke took his time. He opened the driver's door and carefully got in. He started the engine then backed out of the parking space. He made a mental note of the license plate belonging to Luis and his friend. Then he headed out onto the freeway.

The drive back to the house was slow, as Luke tried to dissipate the discomfort from the car park encounter. He could feel a nervous tingle throughout his body, and with the driver's window down, he filled the cabin with cold desert air to calm himself.

Back in the hallway of his Grandmother's house, he picked up the note he had written. He read it once then scrunched it up into a ball. It was 23.30.

CHAPTER 17

Wednesday morning.

'It's another hot one, with a high in the mid-nineties and no sign of rain. I'm Jerome Maxwell and you're listening to KWZN. The home of great new music.'

As the station jingle played, Luke checked the yellow post-it note he had stuck to his Grandmother's map.

18 The Palms, off Lipton Avenue, 11 a.m.

He killed the radio and pushed the gear lever into park.

Luke looked out the window. Across the road a row of modern town houses had been built, and a "to let" sign had been staked onto the small patch of garden outside number twelve. A woman with an attaché case was kicking it absent-mindedly as she talked into her mobile phone. Luke got out of his car to cross the street and the woman watched him approach. Then she turned her back and walked up to the front door.

He made his way to number 18, where a banged up blue car was parked in the driveway. It had a butterfly lying on its bonnet, bathing in the day's sunshine. Luke peered into the car's cabin. A selection of fast food wrappers, empty drinks cans and cigarette cartons were dispersed throughout, and the ashtray was full.

He walked up to the front door and rang the bell.

Nothing.

He rang it again, this time placing his ear against the door, listening for a sound.

Knock Knock.

A stirring.

Knock Knock.

A grunt, then a rustling from behind the door and the strong armed clunk of a dead bolt sliding back. A bleary eyed man in board shorts and a t-shirt answered the door.

'Yo,' it said.

'Yo,' replied Luke.

There was a momentary delay before it lifted its shirt to reveal a gym hardened abdomen, which it scratched lazily. Then it took a deep yawn with its mouth wide open.

'What can I do for you, Man?'

The smell of spent tobacco began to creep out from the house.

'I'm Luke Jackson. I'm hoping you're Harris Monroe.'

'You're Luke Jackson?'

The man searched for familiarity in the name.

He found it: 'Oh yeah, Mr Baker told me you were coming around this morning.' He stooped slightly and gazed towards the sky. 'What time is it?'

Luke lifted his wrist and pulled back his shirt cuff to reveal a watch: 'Eleven,' he replied.

Harris began to rub his shoulder. 'Oh right, well come on in.'

Luke delayed. 'If this is a bad time, I can always come back.'

'No, it's cool. I was just having a bit of a lie-in. It's time I got up anyway.'

He pulled the door fully open.

Chet's biography of Harris Monroe, delivered over the phone, was short: 'Jack and Chloe's eldest child. A class one screw-up. Dropped out of not one, but two colleges.' After some prompting he added: 'It's been said he's getting his act together, finding some sort of future as an artist.'

Luke walked into the house and into dimness. Wooden blinds had been closed at the back of the property and they kept most of the mid-morning sunlight from entering. As his eyes began to readjust Luke turned to engage his host but there was no-one there, so he backtracked towards the front door and the kitchen close by. In the kitchen, Harris was picking through the fridge.

'You want a drink or anything?' asked Harris.

'Yeah, cheers. Whatever's easiest.'

Harris pushed the door wide and pulled out a can from the middle shelf.

He held it up for Luke to see: 'Is diet okay for you?'

'That'll be fine.'

Harris placed it on the side then returned to his ferreting. Finally, he retrieved a bottle of pink lemonade.

'Oh Man. I need this,' he explained.

'Big night out?' asked Luke.

Harris stretched out his reply. 'Ooooh yeaaaah,' he purred.

A tumbler was located in a nearby cupboard and Harris pushed it into the ice dispenser on the freezer door. It broke the peace with a ferocious grinding. Then he poured Luke's drink and passed the glass over.

Luke figured his host to be in his late thirties or early forties. He looked like a Californian surfer with blonde highlights and a carefully graded goatee around his chin.

Harris cracked the screw top on his bottle of lemonade and drained half of it in one action. Then he picked up a crumpled pack of cigarettes and shook it next to his ear to judge how many remained. It made no sound.

'Your parents tell me you're an artist,' said Luke eager to get on with things.

'Yup,' came the assured response. 'Kinda new to it though. Only been doing it for a year or so.' He crushed the cigarette pack into a ball and threw it towards the sink.

'What sort of art do you do? Do you paint?' asked Luke.

'I sculpt. To be honest, I've never had much of a talent for painting, never had the technical skill. I'm better when I get my hands dirty.' He scrutinised Luke briefly: 'I've got a little studio upstairs if you're interested.'

'Absolutely.'

'Then follow me.'

Harris placed his lemonade on the kitchen top and padded into the corridor and up a staircase.

'It doesn't look like much, but it does me fine,' he said.

Harris's studio was small and chaotic. There was a metal table and swivel chair in the middle, upon which drawings were stacked next to pencils and catalogues. Lined up against the skirting board were cardboard boxes filled with bits and pieces, odds and ends.

'Ingredients,' explained Harris as he made his way through the room. Against the far wall, something as tall and wide as a man had been covered with a sheet. With a magician's flourish Harris pulled away the cover. He revealed a mannequin, or what had once been a mannequin. Its body had been drilled with hundreds of perforations before being painted black and augmented with charred wood and torn fabric. On its head, a fencing mask had replaced the face.

Harris's hand dipped into its ribs and Luke heard the click of a switch. Behind the mask, lights illuminated and a face appeared.

It glowered menacingly at Luke, like a malevolent sentinel with bright blue eyes.

'It's a new one. I only finished it a couple of days back,' explained Harris. 'As you can see, I'm not the traditional type of sculptor. I prefer to work with opposites. I juxtapose natural and man made materials. Wood, metal, textiles, electronics.'

Harris pointed at the catalogues on the table: 'I've just begun to build my own circuitry. Well, I'm still learning.'

He held his hand up to the mannequin's face. 'It changes expression every so often. Archetypes if you like. One minute it might be anger, the next – sadness or happiness or bemusement. You never know what it's gonna be.'

'Very good,' said Luke. 'How much would you sell something like this for?'

Harris blew out his cheeks: 'I won't sell this one. I think I'll hang on to it. But some of my other pieces have made $900. I've got a dealer downtown.'

Luke walked over and looked at it closely: 'Did you have any formal training?' he asked.

'A little. I took some art classes at college but most of it just comes from the heart. I work at something until I think it's any good. If it doesn't work out, I junk it.'

'And what are you working on now?'

'I like this theme of natural and artificial, and seeing as you asked I'll tell you. I'm building a giant spider.'

Luke turned towards Harris.

'It's gonna be big,' continued Harris. 'Six feet in diameter. It'll lift its front legs, hiss and bare its fangs when people sidle up to it. Can you imagine the looks on their faces?'

Both men moved over to the table, and Harris pulled some blueprints from a pile to show Luke the spider's outline.

Luke was intrigued. 'Where is it now?' he asked.

'On the other side of town. It's still in the early stages but I know a dude who's handy with a welder's torch, and it'll look heaps better if he does the precision stuff. I'm designing the mechanism, and I've lined up a buddy of mine who'll help finish it off. We'll have to bolt it together at his place. As you can see, not a great deal of room to work here.'

Harris had evolved from the scratch and sniff simian that had answered the front door, to someone animated and engaging. As he talked, Luke could pick out the smell of beer and cigarettes on his breath.

'I saw the clock you gave your Mother for her birthday.'

'Oh yeah. The clock.' A flicker of amusement crossed Harris's face. 'I don't think she digs it too much, it's not really her style. A bit too avant-garde. But I wanted her to have something I'd made. I haven't always been the easiest of sons.'

He leaned back and hit the mannequin's switch. Its recently acquired expression of sadness faded away.

'Anyway, that's that,' he continued. 'Why don't you go back downstairs? I'm just gonna take a moment to clean up and put on some clothes.'

Luke made his way back to the ground floor and into the living room. Everything about the house said bachelor; from the large entertainment centre to the leather seating and the lack of anything remotely homely. Between the TV and sofas, a low slung table was stocked with empty beer cans, magazines and remote controls. In the corner, a lilac dress shirt had been slung over a potted plant.

Luke waited on the sofa, sipping at his drink. Five minutes later a newly revitalised Harris appeared, holding a towel to his mouth. He wore golf pants and a black T-shirt and smelled of cologne. He tossed his towel onto the floor.

'How long are you around for?' he asked.

'Probably a week or so. I only arrived on Monday morning,' answered Luke.

'Staying in Tucson?'

'No, up in the Canyon.'

Harris screwed up his face dismissively: 'Eagle Canyon - pah. God's waiting room. If you wanna do something in Tucson, you let me know, I'll hook you up - a few drinks, some cool clubs,' he said. He changed the subject abruptly: 'Anyway, what's the house call for?'

'It's about the happenings at your parents' place.'

'I realise that. What in particular?'

‘Your Mother reckons there may be some link between events there, and the altercation you had with your Indian friend.’

Harris took a long hard look at Luke then walked back to the kitchen. He retrieved his lemonade and a fresh pack of cigarettes from on top of the microwave. He unwrapped the cellophane as he mooched back into the living room. Then he sat cross-legged on the floor and lit up.

‘Well, there’s not a great deal to say,’ he began. ‘Firstly the man in question is not a friend of mine. More like an acquaintance. I owed him some money, couldn’t pay him straight away, then things started to get a bit weird.’

The tobacco burned fiery orange.

‘Did you owe him a lot of money?’

‘It wasn’t nickel and dime stuff. Enough to get excited over.’ Harris held the burning cigarette between two fingers while his thumb played at an eyebrow.

‘And he didn’t threaten you with violence or anything like that?’

‘No. He’s not the sort.’

‘So what exactly happened?’ asked Luke.

‘It wasn’t very subtle. He said his people had ways of getting what they want. He said the ancestors saw to it.’

‘That was the word he used? Ancestors?’

Harris nodded.

‘And what did you take that to mean?’

‘When Indians speak of ancestors, you can be sure they’re not talking about a Grandmother in St Louis. The insinuation was pretty self evident. I’ve never really believed in curses or the evil eye, or stuff like that but weird shit started up straightaway.’

Luke frowned. ‘What sort of weird shit?’ he asked.

Harris shrugged: ‘I don’t want to get into that, if it’s okay. Put it this way - I’ve seen plenty of crazy things in life, especially with some of the people from round here. But my eyes were truly opened on this occasion.’

Luke drained the remainder of his diet coke. ‘When did it all start?’ he asked.

‘A couple of months ago.’

‘Do you know the date?’

‘Not off hand. I remember the guy asking for his money and me telling him he’d have to chill until I got it together. He tried getting hold of me a few times after that, but fortunately he only has my cell number. He doesn't know where I live and I'm not in the phone book. Then one day I pick up a message on my voicemail, and he's saying "the time has come". Payback.'

'Did you mention it to anyone?'

'At the time? No, I didn't really fear the mumbo jumbo stuff. I only told my sister when I heard about the happenings at Dad's place. She told me about Mom and Dad, and I thought I'd better go have a chat with them.'

Luke knotted his eyebrows. 'Yeah, I don't really get that. If there is a link, how come it's your parents who end up with problems?'

'I don't know,' replied Harris. 'Maybe it's all connected in some funny way.'

He took a lengthy drag from his cigarette and a swig from his lemonade. 'Maybe it's coincidence,' he said flatly.

Luke contemplated this last comment. 'So you spoke to your sister then went round to your Mother and Father's?'

'Yeah, quite recently. Told Mom and Dad the whole story.'

'And?'

'Oh Man…' He took another drag. '….I got both barrels from my Mom. She can lay it on pretty thick.'

Harris leaned over and dropped the cigarette into an old beer can that loitered on the coffee table. There was a sizzle as it hit the dregs in the bottom.

'Did they tell you that the night I was at the house explaining things, was the night my Dad's car got nailed?' enquired Harris.

'No.'

'Yup, I was there. They didn't mention it?'

Luke shook his head.

'Oh well, my visits tend not to be publicised. Out of sight, out of mind – isn't that right? Anyway, I went round there to explain what was happening, and after my Mom's tirades, had a few beers to relieve the stress.'

Harris stopped himself. 'It's a bit stuffy in here,' he commented. He got up and moved to the windows where he pulled open the blinds illuminating the numerous dust sprites floating in the room. Then he went over to a panel on the wall and adjusted the air conditioning.

'Before I know it, I've creamed a six pack, and Mom tells me I'm not to drive home. She didn't want me on another DUI. She actually took my car keys out of my jacket pocket, which is how I ended up spending the night there. I came down in the morning and found the two of them looking a little pale. Dad showed me the car - tyres flat as the proverbial. Then he went and got his chequebook.'

'He just paid off your debt, like that?'

Harris raised his eyebrows.

'But there's been no apparent let up at the house since,' added Luke.

'Apparently not,' said Harris deadpan. He fixed Luke in the eye.

Luke continued: 'And when you were staying there that night, you didn't hear anything out of the ordinary? Or see anything odd?'

'How could I? I must have been drunk.'

'Well maybe you woke up in the middle of the night?'

'Maybe. But then again I might have been too drunk to know.'

He smiled slyly, and Luke understood clearly enough.

Harris broke off eye contact: 'Look, that night aside, I don't know what the hell is happening there. But it's got nothing to do with me. Maybe they've disturbed something. It wouldn't necessarily surprise me. Dad must have pissed off a good few people in his time.'

As Harris offered this information, he stretched out his legs.

'And how would you describe your relationship with your parents,' asked Luke.

Harris seemed amused. 'My relationship with my parents? Is it amateur psychology hour? Should I speak of a neglected childhood, or not getting the affection I craved?'

'No, I was just interested,' replied Luke nonchalantly. 'If you feel uncomfortable…'

The last comment appeared to annoy Harris: 'Strained,' he replied gruffly. 'Our relationship is strained. We don't have much in common. They think I'm bad news. The black sheep of the family.' He shrugged. 'I think they're dysfunctional.'

'But they bailed you out, didn't they? They must care a fair amount to do that.'

'More self preservation than altruism,' scoffed Harris.

'Do you see them often?'

'Not really. Maybe three times in the last twelve months. Christmas, my Mom's birthday get-together, and the time most recently.'

Harris was beginning to lose interest in the conversation, and began to fiddle.

'Your Mother. How would you describe her?'

'Pretty uptight.'

‘And your Father?’

‘Equally.’

The conversation had become fleeting and uncomfortable and Luke twisted his empty glass in his fingers as he thought things over: ‘And you don’t know of anything that’s happened recently? Anything that might be relevant? Anything that might have put pressure on them?’

Harris spoke again: ‘Is this stuff really relevant?’

‘It might be.’

‘Look, you ask why shit goes on at home, I honestly don’t know. Maybe it’s bad karma. Maybe it’s because the house is on a burial site. You think of that?’

‘Sure.’ Luke smiled.

‘Whatever the cause, I’m sure they’ll cope.’

‘I’m sure they will, but you realise it’s quite upsetting for them.’

‘Yeah, no doubt,’ replied Harris without feeling.

He got to his feet.

‘Luke, my main Man. I don’t think I can do much more for you. I’ve told you everything I know and I’ve got a bunch of other stuff to be getting on with. Sleeping in has kind of put me behind for the day. Do you mind if we finish up, here?’

‘Okay,’ said Luke reluctantly. He waited for a moment: ‘I know this might seem a bit out there, but do you think I could speak with the man you owed the money to? I’d just be interested-’

The response was flat and immovable: ‘-No. That won’t be happening.’

‘Oh, that seems a shame. After all, he might-’

‘-That’s the way it is.’ There was a hint of menace in Harris’s tone. ‘I’ve stopped all dealings with him. He was bad news.’

‘And that’s final?’ said Luke, pushing his luck.

‘Final,’ said Harris impatiently.

‘Okay, fair enough. I guess if there’s anything else, I could give you a call. Or if you think of something, you could contact me.’

‘Of course,’ said Harris attempting to sound conciliatory. ‘You’ve got my number?’

‘I do. Your Father passed it on.’ Luke got up, holding his glass. A few ice cubes swirled around the base.

‘Just leave that on the table,’ directed Harris.

They walked back towards the front of the house. Luke opened the door and stepped outside. He turned to say goodbye.

‘It was good to meet you. Thanks for your help,’ he said.

‘No probs. Take it easy, dude,’ replied Harris. He flicked the door with his finger tips and it slammed shut.

CHAPTER 18

Wednesday morning (2).

Luke stood in the road fumbling for the phone in his pocket as it vibrated angrily. A light breeze had picked up from the west, and warm air blew meekly into his face.

He found the phone and retrieved it.

'Hello?'

A delay in the connection: 'Lukie, it's me.' There was wariness in the voice.

'Amy,' he replied sweetly.

'I got your message. I'm really, I'm so sorry about your Grandfather.'

'Thanks Baby.'

'It's just horrible when something like this happens. Especially when it springs up out of the blue.'

Luke crossed the road to his car.

'Is this a convenient time?' asked Amy. 'I tried the house first, but there was no answer. Are you out and about? Would you prefer it if I called you when you got home?'

'No, it's okay. I'm in Tucson. Just hold on one sec, while I get out of the sun.'

Luke dropped the phone from his ear and patted down his trouser pockets, looking for his car key. He found it and the car's alarm growled as he unlocked the door.

'Still there?' he asked, raising the phone back to his ear.

'Yeah I'm here,' she replied.

'So how was Brussels?'

'Oh, average. Busy.'

Luke left the door open for a moment, trying to dissipate the mass of heat that had consolidated in the cabin. Then he climbed into the driver's seat and started the engine. He cranked the air conditioner to full.

'Forget Brussels,' said Amy. 'Tell me what happened with your Granddad.'

'Well it's not all that clear at the moment, they haven't completed the post-mortem. I got to the Canyon on Monday morning to find a hearse outside the house. My Grandmother told me he had passed away the evening before.'

'And it wasn't expected? He wasn't ill?'

'No, not as far as I know.'

'God!' exclaimed Amy, the words acting as a release. 'It seems so sudden. You were talking about him and your Grandmother just three days ago, at the breakfast table.'

'I know.'

'Still at least it was fast. What's the cliché? He would have wanted it that way?'

'You know, I doubt it,' replied Luke. 'He could be a cantankerous old sod. I'm sure he would have loved a long and protracted battle against something truly nasty. Something he could get his teeth into.'

Luke nestled back into his seat and rested his head against the window.

'Do you know what time he died at?' questioned Amy.

'Around seven.'

'And, just out of interest, where were you at that particular moment?'

'I guess I was in that bar, with a strange woman called Anita.'

'Have I got a love rival?'

'Err…no.'

Amy chuckled.

'When's the funeral?' she asked.

'In a couple of days. We're hoping my Aunt Samantha can come through. A decent family showing would be good.'

'Do you want me to come out and join you?' said Amy. 'I'm more than happy to do so.'

'No. There's no need. It'll just be more expense. There's no point flying thousands of miles to attend a funeral.'

'Screw the money, Luke,' she replied categorically. 'I'll be there if you want me to be there.'

'No, don't worry.'

'Are you sure?'

'Baby. Honestly.'

The line went quiet, and in the silence matters were settled.

'I've sent some flowers,' said Amy.

'Thank you, they'll be appreciated.'

Amy murmured an acknowledgement. 'It's a shame you won't make the conference,' she said. 'I know you were looking forward to it. Maybe you can email your presentation through and get someone else to present it?'

'It won't matter. There's a formal paper in the conference proceedings.'

The air-conditioning had come fully on-stream and cold air blasted from the dashboard's vents.

'Is there much for you to do there?' enquired Amy. 'I mean, can you help out your Grandmother much?'

'Not really. She seems to have most bases covered. She's pretty self-sufficient. If I offer, she just declines it.'

'Just be there for her if she needs you, I guess,' instructed Amy.

'I will.'

Luke shifted the phone to his other ear. A ring of moisture had formed on the earpiece, and he wiped it off with the side of his hand.

'So what are you doing in Tucson?'

'Y'know, I'm not entirely sure how this has happened, but I've got roped into investigating a poltergeist,' said Luke.

'You what?'

'A poltergeist,' he repeated.

Luke could almost hear the gears grinding in Amy's mind.

'Is that entirely wise?' she asked with clear consternation.

'Well I didn't really want to get involved.'

'You've been in Eagle Canyon for two days. How on earth have you got mixed up with a poltergeist?'

'It started on my ride in from the airport and, well, here I am.'

He set the air conditioner down a notch and explained the situation: 'This retired couple in Eagle Canyon, well everyone's retired there… anyway this couple - they've had a few things happen in the house…'

It took a couple of minutes to bring Amy up to speed, and when he finished, Amy commented with a non-descript 'Mmmm' from the back of her throat. Although formless, the noise sounded judgmental.

'I see. And you're sitting outside Harris's house? Where does he fit in?'

'He's the eldest son of the Monroe couple. I had a few questions for him.'

'Like what?'

Luke lifted his head as a car with blacked out windows turned in at the head of the street and slowed by the curb. It waited for a moment then executed a u-turn.

'Luke, you still there?'

'Yes, I'm here.'

'And…?' Amy asked.

'And? Oh Harris, yeah. Turns out he owed an Indian guy some money. There's the suggestion that everything might be related to this.'

Amy did not respond.

'It also transpires that he was staying at his parents' house, on the night that the tyres went flat,' continued Luke.

'The tyres went flat?'

'Yup. All four of them on his Dad's Cadillac. Honestly, you couldn't make this stuff up. Anyway, it was useful to meet him.' Luke cleared his throat. 'I'm sure he let the tyres down.'

'Really?' said Amy sceptically. 'Why would he want to scare his Mum and Dad like that?'

'I don't think they get on terribly well. Maybe he saw an opportunity for some payback, or maybe he did it to wheedle some cash out of them. They've got a few quid by the looks of it. He probably heard what was going on at the house and saw an opportunity.'

'Explain.'

'Harris hears that strange things are happening at the house from his sister. He turns up with some cock and bull story about an Indian guy he owes money to. And when he's staying at the house, the tyres go down on the car. Bingo. A sign from the spirit world to pay up.'

'C'mon, that's just too scooby-doo,' exclaimed Amy with indignation. 'Surely his parents didn't buy it?'

'Well they were pretty spooked anyway. So they wrote him a cheque and paid him off, hoping it all would end.'

'And did it?'

'Of course not.'

'You're sure he let the tyres down?'

'Yeah. He had this gloating manner about him. It was like he wanted me to know he was behind it – making clear he pulled a fast one and got away with it.'

'Why car tyres?'

'I suppose it's quieter than smashing the crockery. A finger nail in the valve is sufficient. It certainly makes a statement.'

'So you think he just wanted to mess with them?'

'I'm not sure of his motivation. Maybe he wanted to mess with them. Maybe he wanted to make some money. Or both.'

'Huh,' stated Amy.

'I suspect Harris is a diversion from the bigger picture. As far as I know, he wasn't around for any of the other incidents. The vases moving, the candles, the whisper from the living room.'

'Whisper?'

Luke explained.

When he had finished, he mentioned how the house was built on an Indian burial site.

'Oh this gets better and better,' said Amy.

'Well, that's what I've been told.'

'And these things that have happened around the house, y'know apart from the tyres, you think they're real?'

'I just can't tell. I'm getting everything second hand.'

'Maybe you've got a real life haunt?' said Amy.

Luke looked out of his side window towards number 18, and saw the curtains twitch.

'I think Harris is watching me,' he declared.

'He's probably wondering why you're still there. Do something,' she said. 'Shake the tree a little, he deserves it. He's a big meanie.'

'A big meanie?'

'Technical term.' Amy laughed.

'I doubt he's particularly scared by my being here, in all honesty,' said Luke.

'So what else can you do now?' asked Amy.

'After here, I'm off to see another of the Monroe kids – the daughter this time. I want to get a handle on the family dynamic-'

Amy took her opportunity: '-In case the root cause is unconscious PK? See I do listen to you sometimes.'

'You listen to me?' came Luke's reply. 'When?'

Amy ignored the comment. 'Listen I'd better stop tying you up like this. It must be costing a bomb. Good luck with everything. Please pass on my condolences to your Grandmother. And tell me if the flowers don't turn up.'

'I will do.'

'Good bye Luke. I love you, baby.'

'I love you too.'

A strained electronic screech passed down the line and she was gone.

Although she had only waved him off seventy-two hours earlier, it felt like much longer and he missed her. She had dropped him at the airport and presented him with a going away bag, as though he was a child leaving a birthday party. A mini pack of smarties, a bouncy rubber ball and a paperback for the flight. She always looked out for Luke.

Luke's phone rang once more, disrupting his solitude.

'Hello?' he said.

'Luke, my boy.'

'Hello Chet.'

'Isn't this amazing, I've just called you on your British cell and all the technical do-da has beamed me straight back to Arizona. Just a couple of miles down the road.'

'Yes,' replied Luke. 'Amazing.'

'I was just wondering how the meeting with Harris went.'

'I've literally just walked out of there,' said Luke. 'Have you got some tracking device on me?'

'No,' replied Chet matter-of-factly. 'How would I fix a tracking device to you? Hell I wouldn't even know where to buy one.'

Sigh.

Chet spoke again: 'So how'd it go?'

'It went okay.'

'Anything new?'

'Not as yet,' replied Luke.

'Well keep me up to speed,' said Chet. 'Oh, I spoke with Margaret. She says she saw you at the Silver Dollar last night.'

'That's right. I had a bit of fun in the car park afterwards though. A couple of lads looking for some trouble.'

'Punks? Nothing too serious I hope.'

'Nah,' said Luke. 'Listen, I'm just on my way to see Clarice. Why don't I speak to you when I get home?'

'Okay. That would be good. You have my numbers.'

'I do,' answered Luke with self-restraint. 'And Chet, whilst I remember it, has Peter Monroe faxed that land history through yet?'

'Hold on. My fax machine is in the kitchen. I'll go have a look.'

'No… hold on…' Luke tried to stop him, but it was too late and he listened to the swooshing sound of Chet's slippers padding through his house. A long twenty seconds later, he came back on the line: 'No. Nothing here Luke. I'll give his office a call and push him along.'

'If you would.'

'Yes sir,' said Chet. 'What do they say, over the pond in Britain? Cheerio?'

'That's right. Speak later.'

CHAPTER 19

Wednesday afternoon.

Luke sat on an old chesterfield and took in its soft leather aroma.

'Please make yourself comfortable in the den,' Clarice had instructed. 'I'll be with you as soon as I sort out this problem.'

He drummed his fingers over a thigh and surveyed the room. It was dominated by a big screen television and video game console. A number of DVDs and game discs were stacked on the carpet close by. Children's art efforts had been tacked to the walls, and in between them an incongruous picture caught Luke's attention. It was the sort beloved by white collar America - the staged family photograph. The husband stood at the back of the group with his hand on the seated wife's shoulder. Two boys with matching haircuts, shirts and ties sat on the floor. They all wore curious smiles as though a bad odour had suddenly entered the photographer's studio and caught them unawares.

Coming rapidly into earshot, Luke heard the whoop-whoop of synthesised sirens. He swivelled in his seat to check out the hallway behind him, and watched as a battered red toy car lurched across the polished wooden floor, closely followed by a police car with flashing lights on its roof. The sirens had been replaced by the sound of screeching tyres, and their source was a young boy, aged nine or ten, who came skidding across the ground behind them. He was the younger of the two boys in the photograph. He stopped and looked at Luke, then abandoned the chase and scooped up both cars.

He walked into the den. 'Who are you?' he asked abruptly.

'I'm Luke.'

'What ya doin' here?'

'I'm here to see your Mum.'

'Mum?' The kid spoke the word slowly, as though rolling it in his mouth. 'You speak funny.'

'I do my best.'

The kid walked around the chesterfield and stood between Luke and the television set: 'I'm Kyle,' he said confidently, 'this is my house.'

Then he plonked himself down on the floor, dropping each car nose first: 'Where are you from?'

'Britain,' replied Luke.

'Oh.' The kid scrunched his face up with a look of disgust. 'Britain sucks.'

Luke shrugged.

Kyle pointed at his video game console. 'You wanna play a game?' he asked.

'No thanks,' replied Luke.

'Oh.'

There was silence in the room.

Kyle's forefinger began to play at his left nostril and eager to curtail the boy's enthusiasm for whatever lurked there, Luke pointed at the toys. 'Cool cars,' he ventured.

'Yup,' replied Kyle, dropping his hand and resting it on the roof of the red car. 'I've got a bunch of them upstairs, but these are my favourite. The police car makes real police car noises. There are buttons on the fender.'

'I know. I just heard them.'

'The police car was chasing this red one. The man was wanted for murder,' said Kyle coldly. 'I'm gonna be a cop when I'm older and catch all the bad guys. Do you get Homicide in England?'

'Do we get murder?' asked Luke.

'No stoopid. "Homicide". The TV programme.'

Luke shrugged again.

'It's my favourite show,' added Kyle.

A piercing call from some distant part of the house penetrated the room: 'Kyle. You be nice to our guest!'

Kyle rolled his eyes. 'Yes Mom,' he shouted back. He turned back towards Luke. 'Do you know the Queen of England?'

'Do I know her?' asked Luke. 'Of course I do. She's a close personal friend. We had tea only last week.'

'No way!' exclaimed the boy. 'You're kidding.'

'That's right,' replied Luke.

Kyle looked very confused.

'Ever had any run-ins with the law, yourself?' enquired Luke.

Kyle thought carefully. 'No, but my Dad has,' he said proudly. 'And of course Uncle Harris has.'

'Oh yeah? I met your Uncle Harris earlier today.'

'Last month, he was here to see Mom. He was swearing and Mom had to tell him off... because there were children present.' An unsightly look crossed Kyle's face.

'What was he saying?' asked Luke.

'He used the f-word.'

'Ah,' said Luke. 'Falafel.'

Kyle seemed even more baffled.

'He was telling Mom about a speeding ticket he'd got. He swore real loud and was cussing the cop.'

'Would you bust Uncle Harris for speeding?'

'No, not Uncle Harris. Umm, well maybe, if it was my job.' Kyle seemed unsure. 'It's not good to speed. As Mom told him, he'll wreck his car one day, probably around Grandpa's where old people have slow reactions.'

Clarice walked in and spoke with her son: 'Kyle, honey. Mommy and Mr Jackson need some adult time. Would you please go play elsewhere.'

Kyle dawdled.

'Now!' she barked, gesturing towards the hallway.

Clarice had the look of a woman who was not having a good day. Exasperation seemed to ooze from every pore as she blew her cheeks out and dropped onto the sofa next to Luke's. She had dark hair that she had pulled back into a pony tail, a light complexion that highlighted the freckles across her nose and beautiful green eyes.

'Tough day?' asked Luke.

'It's been, so...' she let out a muffled scream, 'aaagh!'

He gave what he hoped was a look of support.

'My husband's out of town and we have this big party coming up that I'm trying to organise. The caterer has gone AWOL, half the guests haven't replied, and-' she checked herself '-anyway, it's not your problem.'

Clarice flicked some lint off the chair's arm. 'Now, where's my hospitality gone, can I get you something to drink?' she asked with a flirtatious smile.

'No. I'm okay thanks.'

She rotated her head and neck, as though releasing stress. 'You met Kyle. I do hope he behaved appropriately. He's going through a difficult stage right now.'

'He was very diplomatic,' replied Luke.

'Good,' said Clarice.

'And I appreciate you seeing me at such short notice.'

'That's quite all right.'

Clarice raised her hands towards her temples and began to massage slowly. 'So let me get this straight. You're in Eagle Canyon for a few days, and my parents want you to exorcise their house?'

Luke was not sure whether she was joking or annoyed.

Clarice zoned in straight away. With a deep breath, she pulled one hand from her temple and pressed it flat against the top of her chest. 'I'm a very psychic person, Luke,' she stated earnestly. 'Very sensitive. And there are some really bad energies in that house.'

He said nothing.

'When I walked through the front door, I could feel the forces at work. They made the hairs on the back of my neck stand up.'

She blinked a couple of times rapidly.

Her hand remained pressed to her chest. 'The house used to be a wonderful place to go to. It had a really good feel to it, but it's all changed now. I hope you'll be able to do something.'

Luke did not interrupt, and Clarice ran her hand across the side of her forehead, clearing some stray hairs: 'When I first heard about the vases, I had my suspicions.'

'Meaning what?'

She pressed a finger against her lips conspiratorially.

'Let's just say I've never warmed to Leya, the housekeeper.' Clarice hesitated. 'But then, with all the other things happening, I began to have my doubts she was responsible. I went to consult my medium. She told me there was an angry spirit in the house.'

'Did she say why?'

'No. She suggested we try to placate it, that we demonstrate we meant it no harm. I ended up going over to the house with a selection of crystals. I tried to cleanse the place with positive energy.'

'I heard about that. How did you know what to do?'

'The actual ceremony itself was a little off the cuff, but my medium gave me some general pointers,' said Clarice sincerely. 'Luke, I think we're dealing with very powerful forces, and with the message on the mirror I think we've reached a critical mass. No disrespect to you, but I think we need a powerful medium or healer, not a psychologist.'

She frowned, and worry lines appeared.

'Well, as I'm here anyway,' said Luke.

Clarice let out a contemplative sigh that echoed around the room: 'You say you saw Harris earlier, so I presume you're aware of his predicament.'

'Yes.'

'He plays it down a bit, but I know it was a far more unpleasant affair than he lets on. My Mother is sure he's to blame.'

Luke narrowed his eyes.

'I'm less convinced,' added Clarice. 'I think we need to look at things from a wider perspective. From time to time, lessons need to be learned. Things happen for a reason. We face these trials and tribulations in order to emerge on the other side, wiser and stronger.' She stopped and fixed her green eyes directly onto Luke's. 'Maybe the spirit is here to teach my Mother and Father a lesson.'

'This is some sort of learning experience?'

'Yes. The universe's way of opening their eyes.' She hesitated. 'Maybe we should think of it as karma.'

'And why would they need to be taught a lesson?'

'You don't become a successful property developer without a certain ruthlessness,' she confided.

'Your brother said much the same thing.'

'It's no great secret that Dad was pretty fierce in his business dealings. He is self made after all. Sometimes, he was pretty fierce with us.'

'So, your parents should take their medicine? Live with whatever's going on at home?'

'Not necessarily. I think we should leave our guest in peace certainly. After all, it's been there longer than we have. If Mom and Dad are uncomfortable, we can get them out of there. Perhaps that's the purpose of this spirit? He wants them to go out, and do something worthwhile. When they've done so, it will then go away.'

There was an intense look across Clarice's face. 'Although my medium couldn't explain why the spirit was angry, she did say the reasons would become apparent. I think she meant there's more to come.'

She smiled weakly.

‘This medium of yours,’ began Luke, ‘do you see her often?’

‘I consult with her regularly. She’s very accurate.’

Clarice surveyed Luke carefully, and scratched briefly at the top of her scalp. ‘You believe in mediums?’ she asked. It was as much a statement as a question.

Luke chose his words carefully and spoke slowly: ‘If ESP is real, then it probably operates in the real world in some way. In turn, there may be certain people who can access extra sensory information more easily than others.’ He paused. ‘It’s just that I come across plenty of charlatans, and believe me it’s not all that difficult to give the impression you’re psychic. Especially if someone wants to believe.’

Clarice gave him a patronising look.

‘Well, *my* medium is excellent,’ she said sharply.

‘I’m sure she is,’ replied Luke.

Clarice backed down a little and gave Luke a sideways glance. ‘These fakes… how do they… appear psychic?’ she enquired.

Luke quickly got into his stride. ‘There are lots of different ways, maybe a dozen main techniques,’[62] he began. ‘When used in a polished, professional way they can provide a very powerful experience.’

Luke put his head down as though he was concentrating hard: ‘I’m seeing your eldest son, at a desk at his school. He’s got his head in his books and he’s working hard. Outside, the building says Billimore? No…Phillimore. Does that make sense? Phillimore Secondary School. He’s a bright kid, gets some of the best grades in class. His teachers are really pleased with his work.’

Clarice looked puzzled: ‘How’d you know about Josh?’

‘The bumper sticker on your car outside,’ replied Luke with a smile. ‘It says - my child is an honour roll student at Phillimore Secondary.’

‘Oh,’ said Clarice. ‘Neat party trick.’

‘Psychic reading is about establishing credibility. You can look at a person and draw inferences pretty quickly. Age, sex, accent, they’re all relevant. Even apparently minor things like holes in belts, or worn heels on shoes.’

‘Holes in belts?’

‘Yup, it suggests weight change.’

‘And the shoes?’

‘A heavily worn right heel might indicate someone does a lot of driving. The point to remember is that the client wants something from the interaction; they're the ones who've come for answers. They won't want to sit in silence, so the psychic can fish around and gauge whether they're on track or not. Vocal cues, body language, eye blinks, dilated pupils, the client leaning forward. Even the little nods and tics people give out.'

Luke spoke slowly: 'I know I'm sitting here discussing all this rather dryly, and you're probably somewhat unconvinced but I can promise you, under the right circumstances, it's easy to make things look genuine and create a very powerful experience for the client.'

Clarice smiled: 'Very interesting,' she said. 'I still think my psychic is genuine.'

'Fair enough,' conceded Luke.

'I guess you're sceptical of auras, and Kirlian photography[63] as well?' said Clarice.

'Well,' began Luke, 'I'm satisfied that Kirlian photography doesn't unearth paranormal properties. You take an object, place it in a high voltage field, and capture its electrical discharge on film.'

'And auras? My psychic doesn't run a million volts through me as far as I'm aware.'

Luke laughed. 'No, I suspect not. Some have suggested that certain cases of aura reading might be a form of synaesthesia.[64]

'Which is what?'

'It's when your senses get mixed up. For example, words might prompt tastes, or sounds might trigger smells. Seeing auras may well be a function of how you feel towards a person. If you like them and feel happy, you see a certain colour. If you get a bad feeling, some other colour might appear.'

Clarice pursed her lips, and interrupted.

'Well, I'm sure it's all terribly scientific and I know you guys think you've got all the answers, but I personally doubt it,' she said.

'I'm only offering potential explanations for certain paranormal phenomena,' countered Luke. 'They're not definitive and they don't automatically exclude alternatives.'

Clarice was looking for an out, and glanced at her watch: 'Christ, is that the time? I have to go to the florists. We seem to have got a little off track. Back to the problem at my parents' house. What do you plan to do next?'

'Keep gathering more information,' said Luke. 'Have a good look around the house. Of course, there's no guarantee that we'll get any closer to resolving things before I leave.'

‘Well, whether you believe me or not, I’m convinced we’re dealing with a living spirit here, and I’d prefer to see Mom and Dad out of the house for a while. It’d probably be safer.’

‘There’s no suggestion they’re in any physical danger, is there?’ queried Luke.

‘For now at least,’ responded Clarice.

There was an almighty thump from upstairs that shook the ceiling.

‘What is that child up to now?’ shouted Clarice.

They both stood up.

‘Why don’t I just see myself out?’ suggested Luke.

Another crash.

‘Thanks,’ said Clarice as a lump of plaster dropped from the ceiling. ‘Kyle!’

CHAPTER 20

Wednesday afternoon (2).

On his way back from meeting Clarice, Luke stopped at Eagle Canyon's library. He wanted more information on the Tohono O'odham but the librarian was talkative and slow, and everything took twice as long as it should have. In the end, there was little useful information to be gleaned from the books they dug out and Luke left the library frustrated.

Back at Rebecca's, leafcutter ants shimmied across the path in convoy, and Luke stepped over them carefully. The snarling heat and time in the library, had given him a rich headache deep within one side of his head. As he unlocked the front door, he heard a call from the coolness inside: 'Luke?'

'Hello?'

'I'm in the dining room.'

He dropped his keys in the bowl by the front door and walked towards the voice. Rebecca was alone, with a cup of tea in front of her, apparently pondering life. There was a second teacup on the other side of the table, with tea stains along the lip.

'Do we have a guest?' asked Luke, looking at the empty place.

'Reverend Small again,' came the reply. 'You just missed him, he had to rush off. He got a phone call.'

She lifted her hand and gestured for Luke to sit.

'He was here to discuss the funeral. We've agreed this coming Saturday,' she continued.

'I see,' said Luke sliding into the seat nearest him. 'Does that mean the post mortem has been carried out?'

'Indeed. The coroner rang through earlier,' replied Rebecca. 'It was a heart attack.'

She pointed at the pot in the middle of the table. 'Would you care for some tea? There is a spare cup on the sideboard behind you, and quite a few cookies left.'

Luke leaned across and retrieved a cup. A strategically placed photograph of his Grandparents arm in arm and with carefree smiles caught his eye. It had not been there earlier that day.

He passed the cup to Rebecca who poured out the now tepid liquid.

'So, with the Reverend here I presume we're looking at some sort of religious service?' said Luke.

'Yes, there will be a service at the crematorium. It's only a couple of blocks from here. Midday.'

'And the reception afterwards?'

'The Madison Hotel. They're used to these sorts of things. They do everything very nicely.'

She passed him back his cup.

'It never struck me that Grandpa was particularly religious,' offered Luke quietly.

'Well, things with your Grandfather were never simple. It's true that he was not a religious man per se. But he believed in a God. It was just religion that he was not fond of.'

Luke took a sip. The tea had stewed and tasted grim.

'He could get quite excitable on the subject,' added Rebecca. 'You got him started on religion at your peril. He could talk for hours. He never particularly liked being told what to do, or how to lead his life.'

She stopped and giggled to herself: 'One morning I came in to find him watching a particularly self-righteous televangelist. We get them over here. Arthur was pacing in front of the television having this conversation with himself, and I was in the kitchen when I heard a crashing and came back out. Arthur had thrown the remote control into the television screen.'

The smile on her face slid away: 'What really upset him was the divisiveness. The politics of "my side is better than yours".'

She placed her cup on the table.

'Silly question then,' pointed out Luke. 'Why the church service?'

'Hedging his bets,' said Rebecca half-jokingly. 'No, seriously, he communed with his God, on his terms. Reverend Small understands that.'

‘So the Reverend is not your typical old school preacher? Fire and brimstone and all that.’

‘No, not at all. In fact, he has come out and said he doesn’t believe in literal interpretations of the bible, which is a brave thing to do in a God fearing town like this. People take the bible pretty seriously. We hear rumours every so often that the church elders are plotting to oust him but he’s been in the Canyon for a long time and he’s popular, especially with those who prefer their religion progressive and inclusive.’

Rebecca adjusted the spoon that lay to the side of her saucer.

‘He said he’s going to retire next year, and I’m sure we’re bound to get some rabble rouser to knock us into line, to get us back on-message.’

‘I imagine if you’re a man of the cloth, it’s probably quite nice working in Eagle Canyon? Lots of interest in your work,’ suggested Luke.

‘Oh, you’re quite right. Big congregations. Plenty of coffee mornings. And the occasional death bed confession.’

‘Not many weddings though?’

‘You’d be surprised. There’s a wedding coming up next month. He’s 92, she’s 85. They act like teenagers.’

‘What about Christenings?’

Rebecca smiled: ‘No, the baby business is a little slower.’

Luke picked up a cookie and crunched down on it.

‘Oh before I forget,’ said Rebecca, ‘your Aunt Samantha will be joining us for the funeral. She telephoned earlier to say she had found a connecting flight and should be arriving tomorrow morning.’

Heaven help us.

‘Do you want me to go to the airport and collect her?’ offered Luke.

Rebecca thought for a moment.

‘No, I think I’d prefer to collect her. It could be a little emotional,’ she replied firmly. ‘And whilst we’re on the subject - I’ve told her, so I’m going to tell you - I want you to be nice to each other.’

Luke crunched down on his biscuit once more and chewed determinedly.

That afternoon Rebecca went out to visit friends whilst Luke stayed in. He reviewed the notes he had taken at the library but little in the way of fresh insight emerged. Then he began an epic search throughout the house for aspirin to soothe his headache. It was unsuccessful, so he returned to the sofa to lie down and watch a documentary on polar bears. And a bad science fiction movie.

When the movie ended around six, he phoned Chet to offer a rundown of his meetings with Harris and Clarice. He briefly mentioned his theory that Harris was behind the flattened tyres but Chet made little comment. After finishing the phone call, Luke dialled the Monroe household and spoke with Chloe. They arranged for him to go over the next morning. Jack came on the line briefly to tell Luke that he had found his tape recorder.

'I'm very conscientious. I even take it with me into the bathroom when I'm doing my business,' he said.

'Please don't record that,' replied Luke.

Rebecca returned around 6.30 with groceries. 'There's more in the car Luke,' she said. 'Would you bring them in for me?'

So he did as asked and they met up in the kitchen to empty their respective brown paper bags.

'What have you been up to this afternoon?' enquired Rebecca.

'Not much, just lounging in front of the TV.'

'Anything good on?' She pulled out a bag of potatoes.

'Bit of a mix. A documentary on polar bear cubs and some naff sci-fi film.'

'Polar bear cubs? You big softie,' she teased.

Luke removed a can of chopped tomatoes.

'I haven't asked how all your work for Chet is going?' she continued.

'Not too bad. Nothing much to say at this point.'

'I see.' She did not press on. 'Well, how about some lamb chops tonight? Does that sound good?'

'It really does,' answered Luke enthusiastically.

'There are some beers in the fridge. Why don't you take one and go relax next door. You deserve a break after watching all that television.'

Luke was pleased that Rebecca's mood had lightened since the night before.

When Rebecca called through from the kitchen to say dinner was ready, Luke could sense a change in atmosphere. At the table, she asked that they hold hands and take a moment to think of Arthur and Luke duly obliged. When she had finished, she placed her napkin across her lap and indicated for her Grandson begin.

Her tone seemed lifeless: 'I've been in a reflective mood all day,' she said. 'Not surprising I suppose.'

Luke kept his head down and cut into his lamb chop.

'I keep wondering whether Arthur's up there, looking down on us.'

He loaded his fork.

'I was wondering whether we were any closer to understanding what happens at death. Whether there's something else out there?' she continued.

He began to chew. Discussions on life and death with a recently bereaved Grandmother would not be easy. Luke played it safe: 'I don't think anyone really knows.' He looked at his Grandmother. Her knife and fork lay on the place mat and her defocused gaze was aimed at the photo on the sideboard.

'Perhaps Arthur and your Father are side by side watching over us now?' suggested Rebecca.

'Perhaps,' replied Luke truthfully.

'Isn't there some evidence for survival? You hear examples of people and tunnels of light after all.'

Tread carefully.

'You do,' responded Luke gently. 'But in reality they are near death experiences.[65] And as no-one actually dies, I don't think it proves or disproves survival.'

'But they were dead, for a short period.'

'Their hearts had stopped, sure. But full-on death doesn't occur until the brain dies from oxygen starvation, and that can take ten minutes. It seems plausible that consciousness might continue to operate for a period, even when the heart stops.'

'A near death experience is a product of oxygen deprivation?' asked Rebecca.

'That's one possibility,' replied Luke. 'It could also be some sort of hardwired response, a psychological reaction to dying which tries to make things as comforting as possible. Then again, maybe it is some glimpse of survival. We simply don't know.'

He dabbed at his mouth with his napkin.

'The tunnel of light thing,' said Rebecca. 'I read somewhere that it's the re-experiencing of birth.'[66]

'Yeah, that explanation's been knocked on the head pretty soundly.'[67]

'Okay then,' began Rebecca. 'If we're looking for proof, why don't we try to contact the dead? Get information that could only be passed on from someone beyond the grave. Something foolproof and unambiguous.'

Finally, she began to work at her plate.

'That seems logical,' replied Luke. 'It's just that kind of approach hasn't been very successful.[68] Plus there's no guaranteeing that information comes from the other world.'

'Why not?'

'Because whatever information is offered as "proof" could come from a number of sources.'

'All right Luke,' Rebecca said, 'for argument's sake, I go see a psychic who tells me something about Arthur that only Arthur and I could ever have known. Something that she could never have guessed in a million years. Something personal to the two of us, and us alone. Does that not prove she's communicating with Arthur? That he's providing her with information.'

'Well it doesn't disprove it, but who's to say this psychic isn't picking up information from you via telepathy? You prime the psychic with information you know to be true, because you want to believe Granddad is out there.'

Luke stopped himself: 'Did that come out harshly?' he asked.

'I'm okay,' replied Rebecca. 'This discussion won't upset me.'

'Okay then,' said Luke. 'Let's ignore the telepathy option, and consider other possibilities. Firstly, that consciousness dies when we die and there's nothing beyond death. Or that consciousness continues to survive, but goes elsewhere – an afterlife. Or that consciousness ends but remains accessible, like a recording we can look into under the right circumstances. Maybe it's this third option that the psychic utilises.'[69]

Luke put his knife and fork down on his plate.

'If I could sit in front of a computer and download the essence of being me - my memories and beliefs and history - you could go back to that computer at a later date, ask it something, and appear to get a response from me. But all you really did was access a record, some sort of echo of me.'

Luke went on: 'It may be that the psychic uses ESP to tap into some universal record of consciousness for whoever's passed away.'

Then he added: 'Whether consciousness actually survives death, I simply don't know.'

Rebecca shifted tack: 'Does that mean you think science will eventually explain everything? Will God be made redundant?'

'Not necessarily,' replied Luke. 'God and science aren't mutually exclusive.'

Rebecca appeared pensive, then looked down at her plate and changed the conversation. 'We've hardly touched our food,' she said. 'It'll be half cold by now. Why don't I put our plates in the microwave?'

Luke was two thirds of the way through his serving, but she stood up and took it anyway.

'Until someone categorically tells me otherwise,' stated Rebecca, 'I'll continue to believe that Arthur's spirit lives on. And that he's still with me.'

CHAPTER 21

Thursday morning.

At ten o'clock the next morning, Luke drove back to the Monroe house to meet with Chloe. For the first time since he arrived, the clear sky and furnace dry heat of the desert had absconded, replaced with menacing grey clouds and a mugginess you could chew on.

Luke backtracked the route Margaret had shown him and found the Monroe's road easily enough. He turned through the metal gates and followed the long twisting driveway to the house. The old dog was in the same position as before and stirred, but did not bark. It just lifted its tired head and sniffed the air before lying back down. At the door, Luke was greeted by the housekeeper Leya, who introduced herself.

'Mrs Monroe has just gone out,' she explained in her Spanish-American lilt. 'She asked me to tell you she would be back shortly. Please come in.'

'And Mr Monroe?' enquired Luke as he crossed the threshold. 'Is he about?'

'He is playing golf,' replied Leya. 'Perhaps, you would like to wait in the drawing room?'

Luke checked his step. 'Sure.'

He wandered down the hall and into the drawing room. The early mutterings of rain began to make their presence felt on the glass of the patio doors and in the distance came the rumble of thunder. It was growing darker so he turned on the main lights before moving to the middle of the room where he slowly span around, surveying everything.

Luke walked to the patio doors and grasped a handle. He pushed down but it was locked and did not give. He crouched low to look for a sign of damage or forced entry. There was none.

On the other side of the room, he noticed a pair of speakers positioned next to a sleek rosewood cabinet. When the drawing room doors were open, they were not easy to see and he must have missed them on his first visit. Luke strolled across and opened the cabinet to reveal an expensive stereo with a chrome face. He pressed eject on the front panel, and the device spat out a compact disc. He pushed it back in, and turned the volume to low, before pressing play.

The room filled with a deep orchestral harmony.

He stopped the music then pulled the stereo unit forwards in the cabinet to reveal the sockets at its rear. There were only three cables coming off the back and he traced them to the wall socket and two speakers. Satisfied that everything seemed quite normal, and at the same time clearly uncertain what he should be looking for, Luke pushed the unit back into place, squaring its front edge with the shelf. There was a magnetic click as he closed the cabinet door.

He began to pace around the room, but little else caught his eye. He took an interest in the air conditioning vents recessed in the ceiling and stood underneath each of them on tiptoes, peering up, looking for anything out of place. Cool air fell onto his face, but behind the grates there was nothing but blackness.

Another clap of thunder sounded, this time much closer.

His eyes came to rest on the vases above the fireplace, and he went across to inspect them. Up close there was rather more to them than Luke had first thought. They were slim, but elegant in shape, with ridges and troughs carefully engraved like contours on a map. Subtle shifts in glaze highlighted their intricacies and craftsmanship.

Luke reached up and carefully lifted one of them off the mantelpiece with both hands. He was surprised by its lightness and he bobbed it up and down, as though sizing up the weight of a vegetable.

Do not drop this.

He put it back where he had found it.

At a loss, Luke left the drawing room and made his way to the kitchen where Leya was sitting at a round breakfast table, polishing a silver plate.

'Could I trouble you for a glass of water?' he asked.

'Certainly. I shall bring it through.'

'That's okay,' replied Luke. 'I'll get it.'

Leya deferred and pointed Luke towards the cabinet of glasses. 'There are bottles of water in the refrigerator,' she said before returning to her work.

Luke helped himself then watched Leya fastidiously work at the silver plate. She was a nervous looking woman in her fifties, with short black hair and grey highlights. She wore dark green sweatpants and a sports top, and had a pair of gold stud earrings in each ear.

The metallic smell of the polish filled the room.

'So, are you a big football fan?' asked Luke pointing at the badge on her sweatshirt.

She looked up: 'Football? Ah yes, very much. You?'

'Absolutely.'

She put the plate down.

'We occasionally get to watch some of the matches from England. Very fast, no? Lots of running around.'

'Keeping warm,' joked Luke.

Leya relaxed a little. 'Gary Lineker,' she said. 'I always liked Gary Lineker.'

'The golden boot from the 1986 World Cup,' replied Luke.

'Held in Mexico,' beamed Leya, and Luke returned her warmth.

Luke took a final gulp from his tumbler then held it up. 'Thanks for the water.'

'Just leave it by the sink, I will wash it later.'

He did as instructed, then walked over to the table and rested his weight across the back of a chair.

'So where's home for you?' he asked.

'I'm originally from Nogales. Just across the border.'

'You still have family there?'

'Some. Most of them are up near Phoenix, although my daughter is in Albuquerque. She's about your age. Very pretty. Very clever too.'

Leya raised her eyebrows provocatively.

'And how long have you worked here?' asked Luke.

'For Mr and Mrs Monroe. About three years.'

'Before them?'

'Another couple, further down the valley.' Leya paused. 'But I had to leave. When the Lady of the house died, her husband… well he decided that I should become his new wife.'

'He what?'

‘He tried to chase me around the kitchen. Thankfully his walking frame tangled with the cat and I managed to escape.’

Luke glanced over his shoulder. In an effort worthy of vaudeville, he chewed on his lip, lowered his voice and asked: ‘What are the Monroes like? Is it good working here?’

Leya stiffened. ‘It is fine,’ she replied.

‘Go on,’ said Luke seductively. ‘I won’t tell.’

She looked at him suspiciously. ‘I am just the housekeeper, Mr Jackson. They are fair employers.’

Leya put her head down and returned to her polishing, so Luke picked up a salt cellar that was yet to be polished and began to play with it, passing it from hand to hand.

‘What sort of hours do you keep?’

Leya concentrated on the plate, ‘I’m usually here around seven. It is best to arrive early, and do the chores before the heat gets too strong. I’ll stay until maybe lunchtime then come back later in the day at three or four. And stay until seven or eight.’

‘You go home for lunch?’

‘Yes, I have a house further south, down the freeway,’ she said proudly.

Luke put the salt cellar down on the table. ‘How would you feel if you lived here?’ he asked. His fingers tapped quietly on the table top. ‘Things seem a bit spooky.’

‘Yes, Mr Jackson. A little strange.’

‘Call me Luke,’ he said invitingly. ‘What do you think is going on?’

Leya did not budge.

‘It’s just between you and me,’ he assured her. ‘You can be as indiscreet as you like.’

Leya spoke: ‘I really am not of much help.’

‘Oh well,’ said Luke. He took his time to peruse the room. ‘Am I right in thinking Mrs Monroe asked you to dispose of the candle from the dining room?’

‘Si,’ said Leya momentarily dropping into Spanish.

‘You felt okay about that? Some people might have felt uncomfortable.’

‘I have God to protect me,’ came the reply. She put down her work and pulled out a gold crucifix around her neck, which she showed to Luke before tucking it away. Then she placed both hands in her lap.

'What do you think about that message on the mirror?' enquired Luke. 'It seems like the Monroe's must have upset someone?'

Leya blinked.

'Have they ever upset you?' The question was delivered casually.

Leya looked uneasy.

'No disagreements with Mr or Mrs Monroe?' he added.

'Nothing bad,' she replied. 'There was a small problem some months back. I asked for some time off to visit my sister. But Mrs Monroe said I should have given her more notice.'

'So you stayed?'

'It is one of those things. I will see my sister later.' She quickly saw the direction the conversation had taken and added urgently, 'I am not involved with the bad things here.'

'I never said you were,' advised Luke. 'I'm just interested in working out how this house operates, whether it's one big happy family.'

'I am the housekeeper. I am not family, Mr Jackson.'

Luke allowed the moment to pass.

'Sometimes weird things can have quite regular explanations,' suggested Luke. 'People do something, then forget they've done it. Or they do things because they need help…'

Leya paused then shook her head.

'Mr Jackson. Luke. You think there is a rational explanation for all this? But what is normal? It is different for each person. I have no problem believing in ghosts or spirits.'

'So you think there's a spirit in this house?' asked Luke.

'It would not surprise me.'

From the hallway came the sound of a door slamming and several moments later Chloe walked into the kitchen holding a pastry box. She looked at the pair of them suspiciously and Leya dutifully rose to her feet.

'I'm sorry I'm a bit late, Luke,' she said. 'I see Leya has made you comfortable.'

'Yes she has. Well, Leya – sorry to drag you away from your work. Thanks for the glass of water.'

Chloe placed the box on a side counter: 'Why don't we go through to the drawing room. Leya can you deal with this?'

'Yes Ma'am.'

Chloe led Luke from the kitchen.

'Funny weather at the moment,' she stated. 'There's heavy rain sweeping in from the west. Have you ever seen a really good desert storm?'

'No.'

'They're short but intense. Rolling thunder, lots of lightning. I can't remember the last time we had rain, but my goodness do we need it.'

'Isn't Jack on the golf course?' enquired Luke. 'Not the best place to be holding a metal rod.'

'You know what golfers are like. They cut things a bit fine. Mind you even if Jack did get struck, it wouldn't do him any harm.'

CHAPTER 22

Thursday morning (2).

'Why don't we go sit down, over there?' said Chloe.

She took Luke by the arm, and manoeuvred him across the drawing room.

'I hope you don't mind,' said Luke, 'but I had a nosey through here whilst you were out.'

'Find anything?'

'Unfortunately not.'

'Well I'm not surprised. Jack had a very careful look around the day after we heard the strange whisper. He couldn't find anything either.'

Luke pointed at the rosewood cabinet behind the doors. 'I was toying with your stereo. Do you often listen to music in here?'

By the sofa, Chloe released her grip, and the two of them sat down, side by side.

'Yes,' she replied. 'Most evenings. It helps us unwind.'

'And I realise this might seem a bit obvious, but is there any chance the noise came from the stereo?'

Chloe looked at Luke as though he was silly. 'I doubt it. If it was Puccini floating up the stairs then perhaps. But the sound was quite unlike any music we possess.'

'There is a radio function. Any chance it was that? Either a station, or interference of some kind.'

'We never use the radio.'

'And no television in here? You haven't got one hidden behind a picture or anything?'

'A television? No. When we must watch something, we do so in the kitchen or Jack's study. We don't watch much TV.'

'Where is Jack's study?'

'At the front of the house. Off the first hallway as you come in the front door.'

'I don't suppose the noise could have come from there?'

Chloe batted away the proposition. 'Definitely not. I'm certain it came from in here. But, to be honest Luke, it's the least of our worries. I'm more concerned about the bathroom mirror.'

Luke could see Chloe tense up at the recollection, so he reached across to touch her hand comfortingly. 'Well, there's been no actual harm to you, or the house, has there? It's not like the tyres were slashed and the vases broken. And I guess candles are designed to burn.'

Chloe brought her free hand over to rest on Luke's.

'But the signs, if that's what they are, seem to be getting more overt,' she said nervously.

'You'll be fine. We'll make sure you come to no harm.'

Chloe breathed out in an exaggerated fashion, and patted Luke's arm.

'You're very kind to be doing this. People have really come through for us: Chet, Margaret, even the children. You've all been wonderful.'

The rains had travelled down the Canyon valley at speed and large droplets now beat at the windows whilst the howl of the wind whistled around the house. Chloe seemed to have regained her poise and the two of them broke their physical contact.

'Are you from a big family, Luke?' she asked.

'No, I'm an only child.'

'Where do your parents live?'

'Well my Mother lives in Kent, just outside London.'

Chloe interrupted: 'I know Kent. Jack and I have made several trips to England, and we once stayed in Canterbury. Where does your Father live?'

'He died some years back.'

Chloe made no further comment but bowed her head in acknowledgement.

'So, what made you become a parapsychologist?' she asked, changing the subject.

'I just kind of fell into it.'

'An unusual profession to fall into. You must enjoy it?'

'Most of the time,' he said, looking at his watch. 'Chloe, don't think me rude, but my Aunt is flying in from Guyana this morning. And I said I'd be back at the house by eleven, to greet her.'

'Of course.'

'Why don't we take a look around the house? And you can fill me in on the bits and pieces as we go along.'

'Okay,' said Chloe rising to her feet. 'Why don't we start in the garage?'

The garage was the width of four cars, with white brick walls and a cement floor. The doors were controlled electronically with the motorised drive units mounted to the ceiling. There was little in the way of tools or equipment on display, simply a pair of grey metal tool chests pushed against the back wall. As Luke and Chloe entered, two cars were parked up.

'A tidy garage,' noted Luke.

'Jack's rather fastidious. We have a storage outbuilding, hidden behind the tennis court for all the junk.'

She pointed at the farthest space. 'Jack always parks on the end there.'

She pointed at her car, which still pinged and popped occasionally, as it cooled down from its earlier outing: 'That's my space. The other car is Leya's. You simply cannot leave a car out in the sun around here.'

They walked around the edge of the garage to Jack's bay.

'And his car was in this space when the tyres went down?' he asked. Chloe nodded.

Luke felt somewhat foolish, standing there in an empty parking space, with literally nothing to look at. But he soldiered on gamely, pacing around the space inspecting it closely.

'There's not a lot to it, is there?' said Chloe.

'Nope,' replied Luke with a half smile.

He scanned the area. 'At night, you keep these garage doors closed?'

'We keep them closed all the time, otherwise the air conditioning wouldn't cope. They're only opened to take a car in or out. They're on remote controls, you know, those zapper things.'

'Who has controllers?'

'Jack, myself, Leya. I think there's a spare in the kitchen.'

'Can you hear the doors opening when you're in the house?'

'No, they're very quiet,' she replied.

Luke pointed at the door that led from the garage back into the house. 'That door,' he said, 'is it normally locked?'

'At night.'

'Where do you keep the key?'

'Umm, it stays in the lock, on the house side.'

Luke stared down at the concrete floor and took his time to think things over. 'And just remind me,' he began, 'on the night the tyres went flat, it was just you and Jack in the house?'

'Let me think,' replied Chloe. 'Jack, myself-'

And...

Chloe thought carefully.

'- and Harris, our eldest son.'

Luke waited for booming thunder to crack outside, in true Hollywood fashion, as the villain was revealed. But there was none.

'Oh that's right,' said Luke. 'I remember now. He mentioned he'd been staying here.'

Chloe looked embarrassed. 'He'd had too many drinks, and has had various run-ins with the law in the past. I told him to slow down, but in the end I thought it more sensible if he stayed the night.'

'Was he amenable to that?'

'He didn't seem to mind.'

'Well, I think I've seen enough in here,' said Luke decisively. 'You don't mind me asking all these questions, do you?'

'Not at all. I'll tell you when you ask something I don't want to answer. Why don't we go look at the dining room?'

They left the garage, with Chloe pulling the door shut behind her.

As they walked across the house, Chloe tried to make small chat. 'You've been to Eagle Canyon before?' she asked.

'I have indeed.'

'And what do you think of our little old town?'

'I very much like it.'

'Good. Both Jack and I think much the same thing.'

The dining room was accessed through double doors with ornate and oversized brass handles. As they entered, Chloe called out an inventory to the room: 'table, chairs, dresser at the far end there,' she began. When she had finished listing items she turned to the ceremony she and Clarice had conducted: 'It was at this end,' she stated, 'but Jack found the burnt candle at the other, on the dresser.'

Twin candelabras sat prominently at the far end, and Chloe motioned Luke towards them.

'The left hand one, end holder on the right,' she said, as they approached.

He picked it up and examined it with care.

It was tall and heavy, with five arms spreading out from a central post. Pristine red candles were in place. Luke placed it back on the sideboard.

'Do you eat in here often?' he asked.

'It gets used now and then, Christmas, Thanksgiving, some bigger Family Events. Jack and I tend to eat out quite a lot, but when we take supper at the house, we tend to eat at the kitchen table.'

Luke acknowledged the information.

'These candles,' he said motioning at the holders, 'they're the same as the ones you had in place when you had your ceremony?'

'The very same. They complement the wallpaper.'

'Where are they kept?'

'At the bottom of the dresser,' replied Chloe. 'Open the door on the left.'

Luke crouched down, opened the door and pulled out a case that listed twenty-four candles on the front label. He removed the lid and quickly counted the remaining candles. There were thirteen left.

'And on that night,' he began, 'the candelabras were on the dresser here, they weren't on the dining table?'

'As you see them,' responded Chloe.

Luke held a candle up. 'Mind if I take one with me?' he asked.

'Be my guest,' said Chloe.

Luke placed it on the table and returned the box of candles to the dresser.

'This little ceremony you had in here, did you think it would work?' he asked.

'I wasn't sure,' said Chloe plaintively. 'I guess, from our discovery the next morning, it didn't.'

Luke stood and surveyed the dining table. The top had recently been polished and the beeswax odour was unmistakable.

He shuffled on his feet for a moment. 'Let's fast forward to the next morning. Jack found the candle, then what?'

'He got me, and Clarice up, and the three of us gathered in here.'

‘What time was that?’

‘Around eight.’

‘Had Leya arrived yet?’

‘No. I think she was running late that day. She joined us in here when she came in. About five past.’

Luke glanced back at the candelabra.

‘And then you asked her to dispose of the candle?’

‘Yes,’ said Chloe. ‘I didn’t want it in this house.’

Luke walked over to the candles once again, and examined them closely.

‘How far down, had the candle burned?’

Chloe took a moment: ‘I’m not sure. Two to three inches, maybe a little more.’

‘And under normal circumstances, that would take how long?’ he asked.

‘Under normal circumstances? I have no idea. This was the first time I’d bought those particular ones.’

Luke continued to examine the candles, and rubbed his fingers across one of them lightly. ‘Do these candles burn up their wax?’ he asked.

‘I don’t understand.’ said Chloe.

‘Does the wax burn up as the candle does? Or do you get a pool of dried wax?’

‘Umm, I don’t know. Did it not say on the box?’

Luke turned and smiled: ‘No, but it’s not a problem,’ he replied. ‘Any matches or lighters nearby?’

Chloe pointed at a drawer, and Luke found a box of matches.

He looked at the strike patch down the side but there were no marks. Slowly he placed the matches back into the dresser and pushed the drawer closed.

‘I think I’m done in here,’ he said. ‘How about the bathroom?’

‘You want to use the bathroom?’

‘No, the bathroom with the message on the mirror,’ explained Luke. ‘Can I see that?’

‘Oh right, of course. Please follow me.’

Chloe led them back into the hall, where Luke briefly diverted to place his newly acquired candle by the front door. ‘So I don’t forget it later,’ he explained.

Then they began to climb the stairs. At the top, Chloe pointed out the master bedroom, the first door off the landing. 'As you can see,' she said, 'we're close to the hallway. It's probably why we could hear the noise so easily. As the sound travelled up.'

On the landing, a large picture window that overlooked the front of the house allowed a clear view of the rain's intensity. As they gazed out, a bolt of lightning trailed across the sky.

'The bathroom is this way,' said Chloe.

They walked down a long corridor and stopped outside the bathroom. She opened the door, turned on the light and ushered Luke inside.

It was just a bathroom.

Shower, bathtub, basin, toilet.

An extractor fan embedded in the wall began to hum.

'Across there. In red.' Chloe pointed. She remained by the door, reluctant to enter.

The mirror had a bevelled edge and took up a large part of the left hand wall. It ran from the top of the basin to the ceiling. All the other wall surfaces were laid with white tiles.

'Leave Now.' confirmed Luke. 'That's what it said?'

Chloe nodded.

'What style of writing was it?'

Chloe shook her head, as though she could not recall.

'Was it clear writing? Big letters? Joined up?' prompted Luke.

'Several inches in height,' she finally replied, before adding: 'It was scrawny. Whatever it was written in, the liquid had run. Each letter had little trails running down the mirror.'

'And what do you think it was written in?'

'I couldn't say, but it reminded me of blood.'

Luke peered very closely at the mirror. There was no sign of anything unusual on it.

'Where exactly was the writing?'

Chloe walked over and touched the mirror. 'It started here and ended here,' she said.

Luke breathed out heavily onto where she pointed; his breath misting the mirror up, but nothing was revealed. 'Have you had the mirror cleaned at all?'

'Yes, I asked Leya to do so.'

Luke leaned back and slowly bent down, resting his weight against the bathtub's edge.

'Out of interest, what made you come in here, that day?' he enquired.

'I heard the extractor fan and saw the light was on. I came in to switch them off.'

Chloe glanced towards the light switch by the door.

'Was anyone using this bathroom?' asked Luke.

'Yes. My Grandson – Davy. His room is directly across the hall.'

'Presumably you asked Davy if he'd seen anything.'

'He said he saw nothing.'

Luke pondered. 'Where was Leya?' he eventually asked.

'She often works a half day on a Saturday. I can't remember if she was at the house, or had left.'

Luke pulled away from the mirror, and faced Chloe.

'I don't want you to take this the wrong way,' he began, 'but I need to know whether you're on any medication.'

Chloe stiffened

'I need to know,' repeated Luke.

'Nothing serious. Just some medicine for arthritis. And I've been on it for several years now.'

Luke could see the discomfort on Chloe's face. The stress of revisiting each scene was beginning to bite.

'Would you say you were tired when this happened?' continued Luke. 'Had you been sleeping properly?'

She looked at him timorously. 'Not so well. It had been stressful being in this house with everything going on.'

She rested against the edge of the doorframe and her eyes began to redden.

'This has just been so difficult,' she said as tears began to form.

Luke pulled some tissue from a holder by the sink, and passed it to her.

'I just want everything back as it was,' she said, dabbing at each eye. 'Maybe it's time to go elsewhere. Maybe Pete was right when he said make it someone else's problem.'

Then she scrunched up the tissue in her hand. She looked weary.

'You wouldn't want to sell up here surely? This is a great house,' stated Luke. 'You don't strike me as the sort of person who would walk away from a little difficulty like this.'

'No,' sighed Chloe. 'But neither Jack nor I are spring chickens. We simply don't need this sort of hassle at our time of life. Jack's even got ideas of how he'd redevelop the site.'

'Really?'

'His last hurrah,' explained Chloe.

She looked down at her watch: 'Luke, did you not say you had to be home by eleven?'

'I did.' he replied.

'It's ten to eleven.'

CHAPTER 23

Thursday late morning.

As the storm seethed overhead, Luke made his way through the torrent that had spilled forth. The windscreen wipers rushed from side to side and the rain pounded the roof and glass angrily. Pools of standing water had formed that straddled sections of tarmac and required careful negotiation. At the road's edge, surface water rushed towards the storm drains.

Luke pulled up to the house and noticed his Grandmother's car parked under the carport. Wet tyre tracks led from the street.

He hurried up the path into the house and through the front door and found his Aunt in the living room. She was sitting on the floor with a stack of notebooks spread out in front of her. She stood up.

'Samantha, hello,' said Luke pleasantly, wiping water from his face. He placed the candle he had taken from Chloe by the sofa.

Samantha replied with a perfunctory: 'Luke.'

He wiped his wet hand on his trouser leg and stepped forward, then gave her a hug and kiss on the cheek. She squeezed his side.

'I'm pleased we were able to reach you, Grandma was a bit concerned we wouldn't get hold of you in time.'

Samantha took a step back. She looked greasy and had the fusty smell of travel about her. 'Indeed,' she replied.

'How long have you been here?'

'About twenty minutes.'

'Oh,' said Luke. 'I thought you were due at eleven. You must have landed early.'

'The pilot wanted to get the plane down before the storm came through,' she replied brusquely. 'It's a shame my Mother had to drive all the way to the airport by herself to collect me. Especially in this weather. Perhaps you could have saved her the trip?'

'I offered,' said Luke.

'She's in no fit state to be gallivanting across the countryside.'

Same old Samantha.

'She said no,' explained Luke.

'You should have insisted.'

Luke shrugged. 'You know what she's like.'

Samantha sharpened her tone. 'Where the hell have you been? Doing this stupid paranormal thing?' she asked.

'I've been to lots of places-'

'-Damn it Luke!' she snapped. 'Don't get cute. You need to think a little bit more about the others in this family. If your ridiculous ghost busting bullshit is more important than your bereaved Grandmother, then I suggest you just pack your bags and save us all a lot of bother.'

Luke felt the needles of anger rise beneath his skin. 'Just take it easy Samantha,' he said gruffly.

'She's bound to say she's fine,' offered Samantha. 'That's how she is.'

Luke's speech became very deliberate. 'Look, you must be tired from travelling and all that, and we're all upset about Grandpa, but whatever frustrations you've got, don't lay them on me.'

'Don't be a smart ass.'

Luke stopped to lower his voice: 'Is she here?' he asked, pointing towards his Grandmother's bedroom.

Samantha shook her head. 'No,' she replied irritably. 'She went next door to see Mrs Tyler.'

Luke returned to his regular volume: 'You know. Sometimes it's better to let people make their own decisions, and do as you're asked, when you're asked. She wanted to pick you up, and said I wasn't needed. If there's one person I can think of who doesn't need mollycoddling, it's Grandma.'

'Oh really?' asked Samantha sarcastically. 'You know her so well, do you?'

Luke recalled Rebecca's instructions to be nice to Samantha. A fight was never going to be productive. He decided to end things there.

He stuck his tongue out, and blew a loud raspberry.

Samantha seemed unsure how to respond. 'What are we,' she spluttered, 'eight years old again?'

He did it once more, even more loudly, then added merrily: 'Anyway enough about me. How's the travel writing business these days?'

Samantha looked lost.

'Umm. Fine,' she replied somewhat flummoxed. She looked down at the notes spread on the floor in front of her. 'It's fine.'

Luke perched himself on the arm of a sofa. 'Revising the Guyana book?'

Samantha gave up trying to reprimand Luke and sat back down on the floor. 'That's right. It was fortunate I was in Georgetown when I heard about Dad. If I'd been out in the sticks, it would have been impossible to get back in time.'

Samantha never seemed to age. To Luke, she was always the same person. A petite firestorm with reading glasses on a chain around her neck and curly dark hair that was always scraped back. Luke's Grandfather referred to her, somewhat obliquely, as The Contrarian.

'How's life with you these days?' she asked ponderously.

'It's good.'

'You seeing anyone?'

Luke nodded.

'Anything serious?'

'I think so.' And as Luke began to expand his answer, the front door flew open, striking the doorstop with a bang. Rebecca walked through holding an umbrella in one hand and a chocolate cake in the other.

Samantha looked at the cake intently. 'What on earth is that?' she asked.

'It's a cake,' replied Rebecca. 'From Bernice. To commemorate Arthur. Does someone want to give me a hand over here?'

Samantha did not move. 'Does Bernice realise Dad has died? She's not under some misconception it's his birthday, is she?'

'Hush Samantha,' chided Rebecca. 'It was a considerate thought.'

Luke got up and closed the door, then followed Rebecca into the kitchen.

'My, it's wet out there,' she remarked. 'But boy did we need some rain. Why don't we have some of this cake now?'

'I'll put the kettle on,' said Luke.

Rebecca looked at him, and with a sly glint in her eye asked: 'How are you two getting on?'

Luke chose his words carefully: 'Great guns.'

'Honestly?'
'Honestly.'

Luke boiled the kettle and made tea. Rebecca cut the cake. They loaded a tray and headed back to the living room, where Samantha remained installed on the floor with her work.

'It's so good to have you both here,' said Rebecca sincerely. 'Circumstances could have been better, but I love you both dearly and being here is of great comfort.'

Rebecca passed out the cups and plates and tried to start up the conversation. 'Sam honey, Luke's been telling me a little about his work.'

Samantha did not look up. 'Oh yes. I'm sure it's been enlightening,' she replied disinterestedly.

Rebecca looked at Luke and rolled her eyes.

From then on, Samantha chose the topics of conversation. She wanted to know more about arrangements for the funeral and her Mother's plans for the future. Every so often talk would switch to reminiscences and childhood histories.

After an hour or so, matters reached a natural break and Rebecca glanced at the window to comment that the rain was stopping. 'It's beginning to get brighter,' she added.

Samantha asked if she might be excused to shower and rest.

'There are fresh towels on the rail, and there should be plenty of hot water,' said Rebecca.

She turned to her Grandson. 'Luke darling, perhaps you wouldn't mind doing some errands for me?'

'Not at all,' he said, eager to be of help. Samantha's barbed comments had sneaked through and he had begun to feel guilty.

Luke spent the afternoon scuttling around the Canyon. He visited the post office, the florists and the dry cleaners. He went to the Madison Hotel where the reception was to be held, and then on to the undertakers to deliver Arthur's burial suit. The undertaker asked if he would like to see the body, but he declined.

It was not until mid afternoon that he got back to the house. Neither Samantha nor Rebecca was about. Luke sat quietly in the kitchen and telephoned his airline to rearrange his ticket. The doorbell rang three times for flower deliveries, including the ones Amy had sent. He texted her to say they had arrived. There were no vases left, so some of the flowers went into a bucket of water, and Amy's went into a china teapot then onto the dining table.

Later, Luke thought he could help out further by making dinner. He popped out to the store to buy ingredients, then spent an hour or so chopping and creating. The others finally appeared, and the three of them spent a quiet and largely uncontroversial evening, eating curry and drinking beer.

CHAPTER 24

Thursday night.

Chloe's sleep patterns had become more and more irregular.

As Jack slumbered next to her, she stared at the ceiling and grew restless. Her relationship with her home had changed and a new awareness had evolved. Familiar noises like the muted whoosh of the air conditioning, that she had heard thousands of times before without apprehension, were logged and analysed. Unexpected noises and shapes were attended to. Shadows were scrutinised closely.

That evening Chloe had a strange feeling. One of expectancy and foreboding.

The linen felt restrictive and Chloe wanted out. She slid out of the bed and made her way to the back of the room, where it overlooked the garden. Quietly, she pulled back the curtains, opened a window and gazed out into the peaceful night. For several minutes she stood there, resting against the window frame taking succour from the tranquillity of the dark. She began to feel calmer and more assured so returned to the bed and climbed back in.

Something was not right.

She glanced back towards the windows. There was a noise coming from garden. She listened closely then turned to Jack.

'Jack,' she whispered.

He remained asleep.

'Jack!' She shook his shoulder.

He awoke with breathlessness: 'What is it?'

'Wake up.'

He rolled towards her with a groan of irritation: 'Why? What do you want?'

'I can hear something in the garden,' said Chloe.

'So?' he said grumpily. 'It's probably an animal.'

'Will you go look?'

Jack's mind was sluggish: 'What?'

'You heard me.'

'Oh for Christ's sake.' He sat up with a growl, and shot his wife a filthy look. 'This is ridiculous,' he muttered, getting out of bed and crossing to the windows.

He pulled back the curtain.

'Can you see what it is?' asked Chloe.

'Yup,' he said bluntly. 'It's an owl. It's sitting on the ground eating something.'

'What did you say?' Now Chloe made her own way across the bedroom to the window. On the ground was a large owl with a mouse in its talons. It tore at the flesh with its beak then momentarily stopped and looked up at the window.

'Just an owl,' repeated Jack.

'It's more than that,' said Chloe. 'It's a long eared owl.'

'Whoopy do.'

'Do you have any idea how unusual it is to see one around here?'

'No,' replied Jack. 'Owls are nocturnal and I'm not.'

'This is quite some coincidence.'

'Not really.'

'In Indian culture, the appearance of animals holds meaning.'

'We're not Indian.'

'That doesn't mean it's not significant. Owls are considered sacred. Owls are considered bad omens.'

'Of course,' said Jack. 'Heaven prevent us actually getting a good omen right now.'

She sounded unequivocal: 'Often, they represent death.'

'Chloe,' said Jack. 'I could have looked out the window and seen anything and you'd have attached some significance to it. A snake, a frog, a coyote.'

'Perhaps,' conceded Chloe. 'But we didn't see a coyote. We saw an owl. And a rare one at that.'

Maybe it was a snagging fear that something was genuinely afoot, maybe it was the time of night, but Jack began to lose his temper: 'Chloe, get it together. You're talking crazy. It's folklore.'

'Jack, the situation in this house is hardly normal,' she replied calmly. 'Maybe we should start paying more attention to the signs around us?'

Jack sounded exasperated: 'Well, what do you want me to do? Pack our bags? Get my gun? Telephone Luke?'

He lifted the receiver of an imaginary telephone: 'Excuse me, Luke,' he said. 'Do you mind coming over right now. There's an owl in our garden, and as Chloe has pointed out, it's a symbol of death.' He raised his voice an octave: 'What? Yes! We have gone stark raving mad!'

But Chloe had stopped listening to him. She turned her face back towards the bed and took on a look of intense concentration.

'Quiet,' she said. 'There's more.'

CHAPTER 25

Friday morning.

The smell of grilled bacon, the sizzle of frying eggs, and the gurgle of the coffee maker greeted Luke.

'Good morning,' said Rebecca, looking up from her newspaper. 'Grab a mug.'

'Morning,' he replied, ambling across the kitchen towards her.

'How did you sleep?' she asked.

'Very well, thank you. Funky dreams though. Probably thanks to our curry,' he replied.

Samantha stood by the hob, angrily poking at a frying pan with a spatula.

'And how did you sleep,' he asked her.

'Fine,' she replied abruptly. 'Would you like a fried egg?'

Have you spat in it?

'If there's one going,' he replied.

'Grab a plate, they're almost ready. The toast has just gone on the table, help yourself to some bacon. It's keeping warm in the tray under the grill.'

Luke pulled a plate from the cupboard and moved across to the grill. He was busy trying to stab a rasher with a fork when the phone rang. A handset was mounted on the wall next to the hob, and Samantha leant across to answer it. She tucked the mouthpiece under her chin and returned to prodding the eggs.

'The Archer residence,' she said tersely.

There was a pause.

'Yes, he's right here. Hold on, I'll just get him for you.'

Samantha held the receiver out for Luke: 'Jack Monroe for you.'

Luke put his plate down and took the phone.

'Hi Jack,' he said. 'How are you?'

'Is this a convenient time?' enquired Jack. There was a quiver of nervous excited energy in his voice.

Formalities over.

'Yeah, no problem.'

'Last night,' said Jack, 'Chloe woke me up to say she heard something rustling in the garden, and I went over to the window to see what it was.'

Luke was clearly in Samantha's way, so he moved away from the hob, towards the breakfast table. The phone cord trailed behind him, bisecting the room.

'A rustling,' repeated Luke.

'Yup. I drew back the curtains-' Jack sounded very excited, '-and there was this owl with big ears, on the ground eating a mouse or a small rabbit or something.'

Wow.

'I don't know how much you know about Indian tradition Luke, but animals are often viewed as signs. Chloe was telling me frogs have something to do with rebirth and coyote's with trickery. Anyway, Chloe seemed sure this owl was a sign; they can be seen as a portent of death you know.'

Where's this going?

'Anyway, Chloe is explaining this to me, when she stops. "There's more" she says. And she's right. In the background, I hear it too.'

Jack paused for dramatic effect.

'Something other than the owl?'

'Damned right! Our noise in the house, our whisper, it's floating up the stairs again.'

'Really?'

'And best of all, I got it!'

Luke's interest rekindled. 'You got the sound on tape?'

'Yup, as you told me, I kept my tape recorder to hand. It was by the bed and I got the sound!'

'Is it clear?' asked Luke.

There was now some hesitancy in Jack's voice. 'It's not bad, but it's not brilliant. I started recording in the bedroom and then crept as quietly as I could down the stairs. I made it into the hallway when it stopped. Obviously the sound got better, the nearer I got.'

'And any idea what the source was?'

‘No. Nothing obvious. I had a really good look through the drawing room afterwards. I couldn’t find a thing.’

‘Have you got the tape player with you now?’

‘I certainly do. You want me to play it for you?’

Samantha pushed the frying pan onto another ring and switched off the hob. She turned, but found herself boxed in by the stretched out phone cable. She made her displeasure known with a loud tut that Luke chose to ignore.

‘Before you do anything, Jack,’ said Luke, ‘I want you to pull the tab out on the cassette, so you can’t record over it.’

‘Good thinking,’ agreed Jack.

Luke could hear a spring-loaded click, and the sound of plastics sliding over each other. Jack came back onto the line.

‘Luke, I’m gonna have to find a pin or something to prise the tab out. My fingernail’s too big. Shall I do it now?

‘Better safe than sorry.’

‘Okay, back in a mo’.’

An unexpected development.

Luke rested against a kitchen cabinet and waited until Jack came back onto the line.

‘Okay. I’ve popped the tab. I can’t record over it now.’

‘Excellent, now can you play it for me?’

Jack slid the tape back into the dictaphone and pressed play. He held the speaker over his end of the phone.

Luke listened intently. For the first few moments, all he could hear was the sound of replayed silence. Suddenly it was overcut with a voice. It was Chloe mumbling, followed by Jack grumbling. ‘Yes, I’m aware how it works,’ he was saying, ‘I bought the damned thing.’

The tape continued to play.

After twenty seconds, Luke came across his first glimpse; short and muffled.

Then it went quiet again.

He waited, and in due course, the sound reappeared.

And then a third time.

But he struggled to make out what was being said.

On the other end of the line, Jack began to provide a commentary: ‘About now, Chloe and I are heading onto the landing.’

Luke closed his eyes and concentrated. The passing of relative quiet, and there it was again – rhythmical and real, but unclear.

‘Walking down the stairs about now,’ added Jack.

Luke pictured Jack tip-toeing down the staircase, holding the tape recorder out in front of him.

'We were in the entrance hall now. By the front door. About to turn and face the drawing room.'

The sound began to uncloak itself.

It was definitely language. But not one Luke was familiar with.

There was a click, as Jack stopped the tape.

'That's it,' he said.

'Nothing more?' asked Luke, hiding his disappointment.

'Nope. It all went quiet as we moved down the hall.'

'I wasn't able to make out what was being said,' stated Luke. 'Were you?'

'Nope,' replied Jack. 'I can't tell either. But Chloe was right. It isn't English.'

Samantha gesticulated at Luke to move the phone cord out of the way.

'Well. There you have it,' said Jack proudly.

Luke sucked briefly on his lower lip. 'Well done. Good job,' he said.

'The tape recorder's speaker hasn't got much clarity,' explained Jack. 'I listened to the tape a few times on a pair of headphones and the quality was a little better. You still can't pinpoint words, but whatever they are, it's beside the point. The tape proves that something is in this house. It shows we have a ghost.'

Luke thought for a moment.

'And you had a good look around, right after the sound stopped?'

'Yup. Couldn't find anything untoward. The doors were locked. The stereo was switched off at the wall.'

Samantha pulled on the phone cable causing Luke to spin around. She gesticulated again, irritably, and Luke walked back to the phone's base. Samantha began to dole out the eggs.

'Right then,' said Luke, 'what we need to do next, is find a way of cleaning up the sound. Boost the definition as best we can. It would be good to find out what we're actually listening to. Whatever's being said is likely to mean something, be some sort of message.'

'But we don't think it's English,' said Jack.

'Then we'll try to get it translated.'

'True. Where could we go to get the sound cleaned up?'

'We'll need to find a sound lab.'

Luke swapped the phone around in his hands.

'The University in Tucson might have one,' proposed Jack.

'Possibly. Or maybe there's a commercial firm. Can you hold on a sec?'

'Sure.'

Luke put the phone down on the floor.

'Is the yellow pages to hand?' he asked Rebecca.

'I tidied it away. You do tend to make a mess, Luke. Hallway cupboard, bottom drawer.'

He retrieved it and returned to the kitchen, then crouched with the directory across his lap and thumbed through the index, He picked up the phone.

'Still there?'

'I'm still here, Luke,' was the assured reply.

'I'm just looking through the phone book right now. Seeing if there's anyone who can help us.'

'And?'

'Well there are a couple of maybes. I'm looking at an advert for a company that works on film transfers.' He read from the directory. "We convert old film and video to DVD". They might be able to help.'

'Breakfast's getting cold,' said Samantha peevishly.

'Jack, I'm just about to eat,' said Luke. 'Let me give them a ring and call you back a little later. What have you got planned for today?'

'Nothing any more,' laughed Jack.

'Well I'll speak to you soon then.'

Luke returned the phone to its home.

'Developments?' asked Rebecca.

'Seems so, I might need to pop out later,' he declared.

Samantha glowered.

He collected his plate. 'But first, breakfast. Samantha, this smells wonderful.'

You've spat in it, haven't you?

CHAPTER 26

Friday morning (2).

The three of them sat around the table eating breakfast, with the quiet broken by the percussion of cutlery on crockery and the shouts of the garbage men doing their round, out front.

'So this thing you're doing,' said Samantha after some time. 'You'll soon be finished?'

'I don't know,' replied Luke, 'things are beginning to move along, so quite possibly.'

'Huh,' she grunted, cutting into some bacon. 'I hope it's all worth it.'

'You're not being very supportive, Sam,' offered Rebecca.

'Well you know what I think about the paranormal,' she replied. She looked at Luke, and a pre-rehearsed spiel began to flow: 'I saw something interesting a few weeks back, in this little village in Guyana. A young couple had a sick little girl, who the doctor had given up on. They were desperate to save her and this man who claimed to be a healer waltzed into town. He said he could cure her and they paid him handsomely to heal the child. That night I watched him perform. With bare hands he appeared to open up the child's abdomen, dip into her stomach, and pull out a tumour.'

'That sounds awful,' said Rebecca.

'Then, when he had finished, he took his money and left the village. There were many more people who needed his help, he said. Two days later the child died.'

'Hold on,' said Rebecca.' He put his hands into the child's stomach and pulled out a tumour? With no scalpel?'

'It's a con,' said Samantha.

'It's sleight of hand,' said Luke. 'It's known as psychic surgery.'

‘How does it work?’ asked Rebecca.

Luke put down his fork ‘The healer appears to cut into the patient with his fingers, then palms a chicken gizzard or something equally unpleasant from up his sleeve. He’ll hold it up for the onlookers then have it whisked away by an assistant before anyone can inspect it too closely. He may even wear a false thumb filled with blood, or have a small vial of blood up his sleeve, which he squirts over the patient when making his incision to show he’s penetrated the skin. At the end, he wipes it away and hey presto - the wound is closed. As an added touch, he might scratch a fingernail over the stomach - for a short while it gives the appearance of a scar. This type of thing is particularly popular in the far east.’

‘And you wonder why I’m sceptical,’ said Samantha.

Luke saw through the insinuation.

‘You can’t seriously suggest psychic surgery is related to parapsychology,’ he stated.

‘Well, the last time I saw you,’ said Samantha, ‘I remember you talking about healing.’

‘I remember the conversation,’ responded Luke. ‘I was talking about DMILS. Direct Mental Interaction with Living Systems. It’s got nothing to do with stage acts like the one you saw.’

‘DMILS?’ asked Rebecca.

‘Looking at whether consciousness can interact with, or influence, biological systems.’[70]

Rebecca put down her knife and fork and gave Luke her full attention.

‘What do you mean by influence?’

‘Well, there’s a host of measures. Can consciousness affect the rate of bacterial growth[71], or tissue regeneration in mice[72], or the re-growing of a salamander’s tail?’[73]

Samantha looked unimpressed.

‘At the other end of the spectrum,’ continued Luke, ‘there have been studies that use people in place of animals.’

‘Ha!’ exclaimed Samantha. ‘Aren’t we getting into alternative therapy nonsense?’

‘That’s not what I’m talking about,’ replied Luke. ‘But on that matter, there’s no doubt many of the claims alternative therapists make need to be taken with a pinch of salt.[74] Then again, though it’s easy to mock “wacky” remedies - we need to be fair. Drop preconceptions and examine therapies impartially and objectively.’

Samantha quietened down.

'Anyway, as I was saying, there have been experiments which have looked at consciousness effects on human beings. Things like the haemolysis rate of blood[75], or the activity of the nervous system.[76] The results suggest that under certain circumstances variables like heart rate, blood pressure and autonomic arousal can be influenced remotely by a third party.'[77] [78]

'Oh come on,' said Samantha. 'How do you reach that conclusion?'

'You take two people and separate them so they're isolated in controlled environments,' began Luke. 'One person, "the receiver", gets hooked up to equipment that measures the activity of their nervous system. The other person, "the sender", sits in front of a computer screen, which instructs him to try to increase or decrease the receiver's arousal. The instructions are fully randomised, so that the receiver has no idea which experimental condition they're in, at any moment.'

'The receiver can't guess and somehow adjust themselves accordingly?' asked Rebecca.

'No,' replied Luke. 'We factor that out. The receiver is not asked, per se, to do anything. They're just requested to just sit there, in as relaxed and quiet a manner as possible.'

'Does that mean I could cause someone in the street to have a heart attack?' asked Samantha sarcastically.

'Is that something that appeals?'

Rebecca looked displeased, so Luke moved on swiftly: 'In the lab, changes in arousal operate within the normal physiological range. It's likely these experiments work because the receivers are amenable to the setup. In the real world, you wouldn't be.'[79]

Luke went back to his food.

'So what about healing people?' said Rebecca. 'Making them better.'

'Healing studies tend to look at whether you can speed up a patient's recovery from illness. Researchers will take two groups of patients, one to be healed through volition, and the other to have no intervention. Obviously for ethical reasons, you don't get trials where people try to slow down or prevent healing – that would be unacceptable. People are willed to get better, but the healer never operates in the presence of the recovering individual, nor meets them. This is to rule out placebo or expectancy effects. In fact, there are studies where the patient is not informed until after the study that they were being willed to recover.'[80]

'And the results?'

'A bit of mixed bag really. There have been positive results, but also null ones, where no effect was visible. When you get positive results, it's difficult to draw out what's happening, in terms of causation. Are senders interacting with receivers and healing them directly, or are they just helping the receiver to self-heal? Recently, we've seen experiments that look at directing healing onto objective physical systems such as Random Event Generators, and so far the results have been pretty positive.'[81]

'You were talking about salamanders and mice just now, is it not true that some animals might hold psychic powers?' asked Rebecca.

'So called Animal Psi or Anpsi,' replied Luke. 'There have been some funky experiments over the years. Cockroaches and baby chicks have been tested for PK. Kittens have been tested for ESP. Lots of other species including gerbils and rats have also been involved.[82] In many ways, Anpsi makes logical sense. If human beings display psi abilities, couldn't other members of the animal kingdom?'

'Well I'm not convinced,' said Samantha.

Luke shrugged. 'There's a long way to go before we get a good handle on the nature of these effects,' he said.

'Anyway,' said Samantha abruptly. 'Anyone for more food? There's still some bacon under the grill.'

CHAPTER 27

Friday morning (3).

From the street came the sound of a car horn.

'That'll be my ride,' announced Luke as he made his way out the front door. 'I shouldn't be more than a couple of hours.'

'Okay,' called Rebecca after him. 'Have fun. No need to rush.'

Samantha skulked in the background.

Outside the house, Luke walked the path towards Jack. The Canyon had returned to its more conventional weather state. There was no sign of the rains that had blown through town the day before. Jack waited in his car with his hand on the passenger's headrest and watched Luke draw near. He reached across the cabin to open the passenger door. Across the road, a sprinkler worked at a small patch of grass with its characteristic *sh-sh-sh.*

'Hop in,' said Jack, buzzing with excitement. 'To Tucson we go!'

Luke had just about closed his door when Jack jabbed at the throttle sharply. The rear tyres protested with a momentary squeal before traction was restored and they charged down the road.

'I can't believe we got it on tape,' said Jack patting the top of the dashboard in excitement.

'I know,' said Luke, rapidly pulling on his seatbelt.

'This guy you got hold of. You really think he can help us?'

'He seemed optimistic enough on the phone. And if he can't, we'll find someone who can.'

Jack contented himself with a thigh slap, which sent the car into a momentary wobble.

'The tape recorder's down there,' he said, pointing at a cubby-hole between the seats.

Luke picked up the metallic black unit and ran his fingers along a plasticized chrome strip. He popped the eject button and slid out the micro-cassette. Someone had written "hidden whisper" across the label, in blue biro.

Luke put the tape back into the machine: 'Did you bring any headphones with you? You said the clarity was a little better.'

Jack shifted his eyes from the road to the cubby hole.

'Are they not down there?' he asked.

'No.'

Jack ran his fingers around the driver's door pocket.

'Oh.' He returned to concentrating on driving. 'I must have left them at home.' Luke returned the tape recorder to its resting place.

'How's Chloe about all this?'

Jack screwed up his face: 'Mixed emotions really. She's pleased we've got something to show that we're not going nuts, but at the same time, it kind of demonstrates we've got bigger problems.'

The badly punned "Reel Deal" was on the outskirts of Tucson, nestled in a small industrial estate. Jack negotiated the busy feeder road with precision, skirting past fractured tarmac, eighteen-wheelers and delivery trucks. From the car, Luke spotted their destination.

'Over there,' he said. 'Middle of the block.'

They pulled into a small parking lot and put the car in a reserved space. Luke slid the tape recorder into his pocket, and the two of them walked together up to the building's entrance. On the frosted glass front door, red vinyl lettering with the company's name and opening hours had begun to peel away. Luke pushed on the door but it did not give, so he rang the buzzer and waited.

A blurry shape finally appeared through the glass. When the door opened, a man in a Van Halen t-shirt and back to front baseball cap greeted them.

'Sorry about that,' he said. 'When no-one's in the front office we lock the door.'

'Are you Terry?' asked Luke.

'Yes Sir.'

'Good. We spoke on the phone earlier – I'm Luke Jackson.'

'Ah yes,' came the reply. 'Come on in.'

He pulled the door wide.

'And this is my friend, Jack,' added Luke.

'Howdy.'

The front office to the Reel Deal was little more than a cramped reception area with three chairs and a desk. A perspex brochure stand filled with pamphlets advertising the company's services stood against the wall, and next to it, three packing cases were stacked high. An elderly computer and printer crowded the desk's top.

Terry shepherded his guests towards another door at the back of the room, which led to a spacious but windowless workspace lit with fluorescent tubes. A long metal workbench in battleship grey was positioned along one wall and upon it, a selection of video cameras, cases, and tripods had been deposited. On a separate bench sat a number of DVDs and a large transparent bag of polystyrene peanuts. On the other side of the room were two closed doors, marked Edit Suites. Above the first door, an old fashioned 'Do Not Disturb' sign was illuminated.

'Organised chaos,' explained Terry. 'Please, pull up a pew.' He pointed at some dilapidated office chairs. Upon his desk was a sign that read: "You don't have to be mad to work here. But it helps."

Taxi.

Terry took a seat behind his cluttered desk and cleared a small working space using his forearms and an elbow. Then he adjusted the angle of a large flat-screen monitor, and repositioned a trolley behind him upon which a large television and a pair of speakers were placed.

'Your phone call,' he said speaking in a fast easily absorbed voice, 'you said you needed to clean up some sound recording. That should be no problem. We've got state of the art gear.'

'I'm afraid it's not very exciting,' replied Luke.

'Well that's okay,' said Terry readjusting the computer monitor.

The edit suite door opened and another man, with large headphones around his neck came out.

'You done, Kev?' asked Terry.

'Nine tenths, baby. I'll finish up this afternoon and ship tonight.'

'Cool.'

'I'm gonna go meet Casey right now. If you need me, you know where I am.'

'Cool.'

They exchanged victory signs before Terry turned back to Luke.

'You were saying?'

Luke smiled diplomatically: 'Shall we get started?'

'Yup, soon as I finish booting up.'

There was nothing more to add, so Jack chipped in. 'What sort of work do you do here, mostly?'

'All sorts. Weddings, local TV ads, digital transfers. We've got a big project right now, making a training video for an engineering company. We have a studio in a warehouse across the road for the professional spots.'

Terry lifted his head and looked at his screen: 'Okay,' he declared, 'this should be fairly simple. You got the recording?'

Luke reached into his pocket and pulled out the tape recorder. He passed it to Terry who looked it over and examined its sockets. Then he spun in his chair and from a drawer behind him, produced a thin cable. He plugged it into the recorder, and then disappeared under his desk with the other end. As he did so, he whistled to himself.

Having reappeared, Terry turned towards his computer. He started working the mouse with clicks and double clicks then held up the Dictaphone, pressed the play button and nodded knowingly.

'Good to go,' he reported.

Suddenly the room filled with an uncomfortably loud hiss and Luke winced.

'Yowzah!' exclaimed Terry. 'I'll turn that down.'

In a flash, he went back to his mouse, and scaled back the volume.

'That's better, huh?'

The three men listened to the contents of the tape, which opened with Jack telling Chloe that he knew how to use the recorder.

'Ignore that bit,' said Jack.

Then came the first muffled sound that Luke heard earlier that morning. It sounded clearer than over the phone, but was still almost impossible to distinguish.

'That's what we want to clean up,' said Jack at the appropriate point on the tape.

The first repetition ended.

'What is it?' asked Terry, somewhat bemused. 'Someone talking?'

'I think so,' said Jack vaguely.

The three of them continued to listen as the cycle began again. Two to three seconds of noise then quietness for fifteen seconds. Several more cycles endured before Jack pointed at the speaker: 'That's all we have. That was the last one,' he said.

'I can stop the tape here?' queried Terry.

Jack nodded, and Terry clicked a button on his mouse and started typing on his keyboard. Then he went back to the tape recorder, pressed stop and removed the cable.

He passed the machine back across the table.

'Don't you still need it?' asked Jack.

'What I've done,' began Terry, 'is digitise the recording.' He picked up a remote control lying on his desk and without looking pointed it towards the television on the trolley. It breathed into life and showed a computer screen desktop.

'The image you've got on the television is what I can see on my screen here,' explained Terry touching his monitor once again.

Luke and Jack looked at the TV. Across the top half of the screen was a graph with a flat line followed by regularly spaced dense squiggles of activity. They grew slightly larger in size as the recording progressed.

'This is the sound wave for the whole recording. The flat parts represent the moments when nothing was picked up – the moments of relative silence.'

'We were very quiet,' whispered Jack to Luke. 'Ghostly quiet.' He had a chuckle to himself.

'The squiggly parts,' continued Terry, 'are the periods of speech you want cleaned up. As you can see, these squiggles get slightly bigger the further into the recording you get. I guess whoever made this tape was getting closer to the source. It was getting louder.'

Jack leaned forward in his chair.

'Am I right in thinking we can concentrate on the squiggles?' asked Terry. 'We're not so interested in the quiet stuff, are we?'

'No,' replied Jack.

'Good, it'll speed things up if I cut them out.'

The mouse moved over the sound wave, and Terry began to highlight the noisier parts. When he had finished, he typed at his keyboard and moments later the relevant sounds were displayed individually, in little boxes, one on top of the other.

'So the first thing I can do is apply some filters and clean up the sound as a whole.'

Jack and Luke watched as the mouse pointer moved across the screen, dropping down various menus and opening boxes. Terry entered numbers on his keyboard and when he had finished, a small hourglass appeared in the centre of the screen. Shortly afterwards, it disappeared.

'Hmmm, that's interesting,' murmured Terry. His eyebrows were knotted in concentration.

'What is?' asked Jack.

'I can compare the characteristics of each sound. Examine the similarity between them.'

Jack continued to look at the TV monitor and Terry went back to tapping at his keyboard. A box appeared on the right hand side of the screen filled with reams of numbers.

'Yup. I thought so,' said Terry. 'It's the same sound.'

'What do you mean?' asked Luke.

'Each sound is the same. Identical. This software can look at structure and factor out any differences in volume or ambient noise. There's no doubt, it's exactly the same sound repeated over and over.'

'I still don't get you. We know it's the same sound,' said Jack.

'Yeah, but you thought it was someone speaking. If that was the case, you'd expect to see small differences across each clip.'

Terry searched for an example: 'If I was to ask you to say a sentence, I don't know…the cat sat on the mat?'

'The cat sat on the mat,' said Jack dutifully.

'Yeah,' replied Terry, 'if you were to say that a bunch of times-'

Jack began to open his mouth.

'-there's no need, right now,' interrupted Terry. 'If you said it a bunch of times, although each one would be very similar, it's unlikely they'd all be identical. You'd find slight differences in the various elements that make up the sound - pitch, sound length, et cetera.'

Terry looked back at his monitor: 'And these noises are identical.'

'And what might cause that?' asked Jack.

Terry leaned back in his chair and thumbed at his ear. 'Umm, I'd guess that whoever made this tape was recording some stuck record or a skipping compact disc. They've caught it through all five repetitions.'

'I see,' said Jack. 'But can we determine what's actually being repeated?'

'I'm sure we can.'

Terry clicked on the final sound box and the others dissolved away in a digital twinkle.

'We'll focus on the final recording. It's got the highest clarity.' He played it. Then he worked at control menus.

Every so often, Terry would try the occasional playback and each time the sound quality got slightly clearer. His head nodded in satisfaction each time.

'Hold on,' he said. 'This should do it.' He hit a key on his keyboard and there it was, coasting through the air.

Clear and sweet.

The three of them listened in silence.

i 'ap 'i hud ki:kam. Gm g hu 'u:pam hi:m.

He played it again.

i 'ap 'i hud ki:kam. Gm g hu 'u:pam hi:m.

The sound danced around the room and they were all transfixed.

i 'ap 'i hud ki:kam. Gm g hu 'u:pam hi:m.

'Well that's it. But I have no idea what it means,' pronounced Terry. 'Sounds like Navajo or something. Once more?'

He began to play it back again, but halfway through the sound cut out and the speakers began to hiss.

Terry looked surprised and squinted at his screen.

'Problem?' enquired Luke.

'That's odd,' replied Terry, more to himself than his guests.

He tapped away at the keyboard, but the sound did not reappear.

'Some ghost in the machine?' suggested Jack.

Terry stood up and looked at a black amplifier with green lights behind him. He went back to the computer and clicked on his mouse before returning to the amp. His hands moved around the back, pushing cables more firmly into slots. A crackle of feedback, then nothing.

'Hmmm,' began Terry, 'must be a dud connection somewhere. I'll have to look at it later.'

He turned towards his clients: 'Do you want to hear it some more or will that do? I can hook up another amp is you want.'

'That'll be fine,' said Luke.

'It's clearly not English,' said Terry. 'If you want to know what it means, you'll have to find someone who can translate it. I only speak American.'

'I doubt we'll bother, we were just wondering what it was really,' said Luke. 'Terry, you've done a great job. Before we go, perhaps you could make us a copy of this cleaned up version?'

'Sure. Any particular format?'

'Err, just burn me an audio file on a CD. Thanks.'

'No problem. Let me just find a blank disc.' Terry stood up and wandered down the bench looking in various boxes and under bubble wrap.

Luke turned to Jack, who simply looked back at him in silence.

'Here we go,' said Terry, walking back to his desk. He picked up the remote control and switched off the television, before placing the blank CD into a burner behind him.

'I'll record two tracks. The whole recording. Then the final clip that we've just been listening to. All cleaned up.'

The equipment began to whirr as Terry spoke: 'About the bill. Do you want me to invoice you now, or send one out?'

'I'll take care of it now,' said Jack reaching into his jacket.

'Okay, that's cool. Our accounts system is next door in the front office. I'll just go print up an invoice for you.'

Terry left the room leaving Jack and Luke alone.

'Well so far so good,' said Luke. 'All we need to do now is find someone to translate for us.'

'Yes, but who? Or where?'

'We could try the phone book again?'

They both sat cogitating.

'I was in the Silver Dollar Casino the other night,' said Luke. 'It's an Indian owned casino, right? I'm sure someone there could help us.'

Jack looked deep in thought.

'No, I've got a better idea,' he said. 'There's an art dealer on the way to the border. A real nice guy called Ben Rose. I've bought a few pictures from him over the years. He's an Indian fella, in fact he once told me he was on the tribal council. I'm sure that he could help us and I'd prefer to use him as I know he'll be diplomatic.'

'How far?'

'Just twenty miles south of the Canyon.'

'Will he be there, now?'

Jack looked at his watch. 'It's coming up for midday. Yes, he should be. I'll phone him once we leave here, and make sure.'

'Right,' acknowledged Luke 'Well, let's stop at my Grandmother's on the way. I'll pick up my laptop so we can play the disc.'

Terry returned, clutching a paper in his left hand. He walked over to his desk and looked at his screen, then nodded: 'All done' he said, removing the CD from its slot. He placed it into a jewel case then passed it across the desk along with the invoice. Jack reached for his wallet.

'Is a credit card okay, or would you prefer a cheque?'

'A cheque will be fine, Sir. A cheque will be fine.'

CHAPTER 28

Friday midday.

As they drove back to Eagle Canyon, Jack seemed self absorbed. He did not talk and drove in silence with his eyes fixed on the road straight-ahead. Luke did not intrude and took his opportunity to make sense of the day's developments.

Eventually Jack decided to speak. 'My mind's racing,' he said.

'I'll bet,' answered Luke.

'Do you mind if we chat? It might relieve some of the tension.'

'Sure,' replied Luke. 'Choose a topic.'

Jack blew out his cheeks and hesitated.

They were a half mile further down the road when he spoke again:

'Okay, you remember when that storm blew through the other day?'

'Yes.'

'I was on the golf course playing a foursome with a buddy of mine and a couple of his out-of-town friends. Anyway, when the thunder started, someone made a joke about meeting our makers, and then one of the others - a guy named Bobby - said he hadn't quite met his maker, but he got halfway there.'

'Sounds intriguing.'

'It was about six or seven years ago. He'd gone into hospital for a little exploratory surgery, nothing major, but something which required a general anaesthetic.'

Jack rubbed his nose.

'Somewhere in the middle of it all, he finds himself floating up and out of his body, into the top corner of the operating theatre. He was up there for a few minutes, just watching and listening. He said he could clearly remember the doctor in his green scrubs wearing a pink surgical hat. He remembered the nurses, the tray of surgical instruments they put out and the heart rate monitor in the background. It continued to beep so he told himself he couldn't be dead.'

Jack glanced at Luke then continued: 'As his experience came to an end, Bobby said he just floated down, and went "pop" back into his body. One of the other golfers – Jeff – said that Bobby was probably hallucinating. What do you think? Do you know anything about Out of Body Experiences? They can't be all that common?'

'Well they're not that uncommon,' replied Luke taking his time. 'Something like 5-10% of the population can expect to have a naturally occurring OBE during their lives.'[83]

'What? You can have an unnatural one?'

'Sure. Certain types of drug use[84] or meditation can precipitate them.[85] You can even try and bring them on in the lab.'[86]

'Are they like dreams?' asked Jack.

'No. They're vivid experiences, more like being awake. Like Bobby, people often feel themselves leaving their body and journeying to a new vantage point. They might enter a secondary body. Sometimes this second body is reported to connect with the actual one via a cord.[87] OBEs tend to be both pleasurable and quite tranquil. But they shouldn't be confused with near death experiences. They're not one and the same.'

'What can prompt OBEs?' asked Jack.

'They've been claimed under lots of different circumstances, although the vast majority seem to take place when people are sleeping and resting. Alternatively, they can happen during quite unlikely moments. You could be driving down the road, on your way to work.'

'Bobby's lasted a couple of minutes, is that normal?'

'Pretty much. Spontaneous experiences tend to be quite short in duration and the return to the body is often gradual. Having said that, other returns have been reported as sudden, with a shock as the person re-enters their body.'[88]

'Sometimes,' continued Luke, 'the person having the OBE might travel to another place and "visit" someone else. This other person sees them as an apparition, and the experience is known as a Reciprocal Out of Body Experience.'

'And what's the explanation for OBEs?'

'There are three main ones. Either it's all an illusion, or it's some form of psychic functioning like clairvoyance, or it shows that we can transcend physical life as we presently understand it.'

Jack looked across: 'A soul, you mean?'

'That's one word for it.'

The road sign for Eagle Canyon appeared on the right, prompting a change in subject.

'You still want me to stop at your Grandmother's?' asked Jack.

'Yes. I need to grab my laptop.'

Jack turned off the freeway and criss-crossed Eagle Canyon towards Hummingbird Lane. At the house, Luke pushed through the doorway to find his Aunt and Grandmother in a locked embrace. He felt the embarrassment of intruding on a private moment. Rebecca noticed his arrival and pulled away from Samantha.

'Luke,' she said with a sniff.

'I forgot something,' explained Luke. 'I'll just grab it from my room.'

Samantha looked up at him under swollen red eyes.

CHAPTER 29

Friday lunchtime.

The Ben Rose Gallery was 25 minutes south of the Canyon and tucked away from the main road in a small pavilion of art and craft showrooms. When Luke had gone into his Grandmother's house, Jack had taken the opportunity to telephone ahead and it was a quizzical looking Ben Rose that came out to greet them.

'Jack. Good to see you,' he said in a deep voice.

'Ben,' replied Jack. 'This is Luke.'

They exchanged pleasantries and Ben led the way into his gallery. There were no other customers, and he hung an "out for lunch" sign across the door, and pulled the blinds. They all went to stand next to Ben's desk where Luke laid down his laptop and began to power it up.

'We won't be disturbed,' said Ben. 'I wasn't quite sure what to make of your phone call.'

'Well it's a bit unusual to be honest,' said Jack.

Ben pointed at a chair: 'Do you want to sit down?' he asked.

'No I'll stand,' replied Jack looking around nervously. 'Ben, you're gonna think this sounds way out, but we started to have some strange events at the house, about six weeks ago…'

Jack recalled the events. He spoke precisely and made sure that no detail was missed.

Ben's gallery was an end of terrace unit. From the outside it looked most unprepossessing, but inside it was light and airy and there was a natural warmth to it. On the walls were broad sweeping canvases of traditional Indian living. Paintings of men on horseback and women in the villages. Behind Ben's desk was a large cabinet lined with black velvet shelves that displayed silver jewellery finished off with turquoise and amethyst.

Luke loaded the CD into his laptop as Jack completed his account of life at home. He watched the two men in conversation. Ben was an older man whose body language gave little away. He was tall with plaited white hair that stretched down his back. He listened to Jack and stood immobile with his eyes focussed on the floor and his arms folded across his body.

'And so here we are,' concluded Jack. 'We thought you would be so kind as to translate it for us.'

'I see,' said Ben. 'Well I must hear this recording you have.'

'Great.'

Jack gestured towards Luke.

Luke picked up a pair of earpieces that were in the computer bag and methodically unwound the coiled cable that led off them. He passed them to Ben, as Jack began to fidget.

'Go on, take a seat,' suggested Luke eager to lessen Jack's restlessness. Jack did so and Ben lifted himself up onto the desk so that his feet dangled slightly above the floor.

Everyone was in place, and when Ben gave the signal Luke pressed play.

He set it to repeat.

Ben closed his eyes and listened. He continued to give nothing away. It was not long before he took out the earpieces, and spoke.

'Well, it's very clear,' he commented. 'The people in Tucson did a good job for you.'

There was a silence.

Ben spoke once more, loudly and with purpose: 'i 'ap 'i hud ki:kam. Gm g hu 'u:pam hi:m.'

Jack chewed his lip.

'The words are instructions, of a sort.'

'Instructions?' asked Jack. A little of the colour drained from his face.

Ben rewound the earpiece's cable then passed it back to Luke.

'Yes, instructions.' He seemed in no rush to expand his explanation. 'It means – You are not from here. Go back home.'

Jack repeated Ben's words without sound.

'And there's no ambiguity in the message?' asked Luke. 'I mean, it doesn't have different possible interpretations?'

'Not really.'

'Oh,' said Jack flatly.

Ben tried to look sympathetic.

'Have you come across anything like this before?' asked Luke.

Ben blinked slowly and sighed: 'I have not come across anything like this before. But the world is big and many things are possible.'

Jack scrunched his face up and thought for a moment. 'Why Chloe and me? Why us, and our house? What does it mean by "home", we've been in that house for a long time.'

Ben dropped his head: 'I'm sorry Jack. I don't know. There may be many possible reasons.'

There was another silence.

'Can we do anything to appease the spirit?' asked Jack.

'It may be possible,' said Ben solemnly.

The remainder of the conversation was odd. They talked for a few minutes, with Jack asking questions and Ben providing answers that were often impenetrable. Eventually, it became clear that little else could be prised out of him. He told Jack that he would try to find out more information. He would consult others and see what could be done.

Luke made the first move: 'Well, thank you for your help,' he said, putting his laptop into its bag. 'Jack, we should be off.'

Two minutes later Jack and Luke were standing in the car park, where Luke began to rummage through his bag. 'I just need to check I didn't leave anything in the gallery,' he said. 'Give me two secs.'

Jack was in his own world and waved Luke away.

Back in the gallery, Ben was at his desk writing out price tags.

Luke picked up a business card from a holder on the desk. 'I'm going to give you a call when I get home, if that's okay?'

Ben nodded: 'That would be a good idea.'

Back in the car, as they made their way home, Jack chimed in first. 'Well, if nothing else, we know what it says. The same as the message on the mirror.'

He gripped the steering wheel tighter, so his knuckles grew white.

Luke shifted the issue: 'What do you want to do?' he asked.

'I don't know, you tell me. Perhaps we can get someone in? Maybe Ben can put me in touch with the relevant parties?' He thought for a moment. 'Right now, I have to go back and tell Chloe what's happened. I don't think she's going to be very happy.'

'You'll be able to put her mind at rest,' stated Luke.

'I'm not sure my mind's at rest,' said Jack categorically. 'What's more, is it safe to stay in the house? Maybe we should do as we're told and leave?' He grimaced a little.

Luke tried to sound reassuring: 'I'm sure you'll be fine. My Grandfather's funeral is tomorrow but after that, I have a day or two in the Canyon. There are a couple of things I've been pondering that might sort you and Chloe out.'

Jack did not respond.

'Will you at least wait a couple of days before making any decisions?' asked Luke.

'Is there any point in waiting? We've identified the problem. Now we need to implement a solution,' said Jack, businesslike.

'Well as I said at the beginning, I have little experience with haunts or poltergeists but I know people who do. What we don't want to do is rush in without taking advice.'

Jack looked out the side window briefly.

'All right,' he finally said. 'A couple of days can't hurt, I suppose.'

'And I think that this tape recording remains on a need to know basis,' said Luke. 'Don't tell anyone else.'

They drove back to Eagle Canyon in silence and when they arrived at Rebecca's, Luke took a moment before exiting the car. 'We'll work this out, Jack,' he said. 'You've just got to hang tight for a couple of days. In the meantime, if you or Chloe want a friendly shoulder to lean on, don't hesitate. Pick up the phone and call me.'

Jack seemed touched: 'Thanks Luke. That's good of you.'

Luke closed the passenger door and headed up to the house. His Grandmother's car was not in its space, and as he unlocked the front door, he called inside.

'Hello? Anyone here?'

There was no reply, so he walked straight into the kitchen and pulled out the business card he had taken from Ben's desk.

Carefully, he dialled the number: 'Hi there, this is Luke Jackson...'

CHAPTER 30

Friday afternoon.

Luke phoned Chet to tell him there had been progress and arranged to meet, as before, in the Sun Café.

It was early afternoon and the place was quieter than during his previous visit. The lunch crowd had dispersed and a sense of calm had descended on the place. The lack of customers extracted all sense of immediacy from the waiting staff.

Luke arrived to find Chet already there, twiddling his thumbs. He stood to welcome Luke then raised two fingers in the air towards one of the waitresses, who was busy chatting with a cook. She acknowledged his signal and fetched a pair of mugs and a stainless steel coffee-pot.

'So where do we stand, Batman?' he asked.

Luke took his seat, and the waitress came over to pour the coffee.

'Well Robin, there have been developments,' he said. There was an emphasis on the final word.

Chet looked him square in the eyes. 'Enlighten me.'

The waitress finished pouring and turned away.

'I got a phone call this morning from Jack,' said Luke. 'It turns out they heard the voice again in the house last night. What's more, Jack managed to record it.'

Chet looked up from stirring sugar into his coffee with a look of surprise across his face.

'You're kidding me,' he said.

'Nope. He got it on tape.'

Chet put the spoon down onto the table with a clang: 'Well I'll be damned. I always thought the voice thing was the weakest part to the story. I was never properly convinced it had actually happened.'

'Unfortunately,' said Luke, 'it was pretty hard to make out what was being said. So this morning we went into Tucson and had the sound cleaned up.'

Chet ran his tongue over his front teeth. 'And?' he asked excitedly.

'It turned out to be a message. In Indian. It said - you are not from here. Go back home.'

'Wow,' exclaimed Chet in a low rush. 'You're sure it means that? Who translated it?'

'A man called Ben Rose. Do you know him? He's got a gallery outside town.'

Chet indicated that he did. 'So where does that leave us? The Monroe's have an Indian spirit that wants them out?'

'There's more,' said Luke. 'This whisper Jack picked up, there's an odd property to it.'

'Which is?'

'Each of the clips, each "You are not from here" is absolutely identical in form. All five renditions.'

'So?' asked Chet.

'Doesn't that strike you as strange? The exact same thing repeated every fifteen seconds?'

'Well I don't know. I hadn't really thought about it. But we're not talking about the world you and I inhabit. We're talking about a spirit source. There's no reason to presuppose it follows some conventional pattern.'

Chet looked at Luke then shook his head: 'You don't agree?'

'Well, we should consider the possibility that there isn't a paranormal source,' said Luke. 'That it really is one sound clip played over and over.'

'Okay,' conceded Chet, 'but, if that's the case, who made the recording and where's it coming from? Jack and Chloe thought it came from the drawing room and you've, presumably, looked through there pretty good?'

Luke looked at him glumly: 'Yes.'

'You didn't find anything?'

Luke cocked his head to one side. 'No.'

Both men raised their coffee mugs and took sips.

'When I got home,' said Luke, 'I gave Ben Rose a call. I wanted to talk in private, without Jack over my shoulder. Let's just say Ben was… sceptical of the situation. In particular, he thought it unlikely that the Monroe house was on any type of sacred land.'

'Well, I've tried chasing Pete for that report,' said Chet looking embarrassed. 'I just keep getting his secretary.' He cleared his throat: 'As we're spitballing here, I've got a theory.'

Luke waited.

'What about the idea that Chloe is our source? She moves the vases and lights the candle, but suppresses the memory. She sees the message on the mirror - or doesn't really, if you know what I mean.'

'And the sound?'

'Maybe she created the sound unconsciously, using psychokinesis?'

'But it's in a language she's unfamiliar with.'

'So?' replied Chet. 'I've read about mediums who've suddenly started speaking in a language they've never known. There's even a name for it.'

'Xenoglossy,' said Luke.

'Xenoglossy, right. Could that not happen with Chloe?'

Luke appeared unconvinced.

'Well, I'm just offering some alternatives,' said Chet slightly hurt, before trying his luck once again. 'Of course, there's one explanation that you might not have considered fully.'

Luke raised his head: 'Which is what?'

'There really is something going on in that house. For whatever reason, the Monroes have a ghost.'

Luke gave no reaction.

Chet expanded his explanation: 'Maybe because you know there are often rational explanations for haunts and poltergeists you've become a little biased? I mean there's a chance that some ghosts might be real, isn't there? You might be able to explain most haunts in terms of misperception or PK phenomena, but maybe this is the real deal?'

Luke was deep in concentration. 'No,' he eventually said, 'I smell something fishy.'

This statement puzzled Chet.

'You smell something fishy?' said Chet, raising his head and sniffing the air.

'Yes. Something dodgy.'

Chet did not hear. 'Nope, I don't smell it,' he replied taking a deep breath through his nose.

'Chet. Stop,' instructed Luke. He rubbed his right eye briefly. 'You remember I told you I thought Harris was behind the flat tyres?'

'Sure.'

'Well, to begin with I thought Harris was simply being opportunistic. But then I went to see Clarice, and her charming child let slip that Harris had picked up a speeding ticket in the last month. Apparently Clarice warned him about driving too fast around "old people" and it got me thinking.'

'Oh yes.'

'What if Harris got busted around the "old people" in Eagle Canyon? If that's the case, it doesn't fit with Harris's story that he'd only been to see his parents three times this year - Christmas, his Mother's birthday, and the night he recently spent at the house. And if that's correct, what was he doing in Eagle Canyon?'

Chet took a moment then made a suggestion: 'There's no guarantee he was in the Canyon.'

'True,' admitted Luke, 'but what about the idea that Harris is behind more than just the tyres? We know from Jack that the vases were moved on the thirteenth, what we need to do is find out where Harris was on the thirteenth. It would be quite a coincidence if his ticket was on that day, in Eagle Canyon.'

Chet dropped his voice: 'I know a man,' he said confidentially, 'at the Sheriff's department. I helped him out with a…delicate matter, and he owes me a favour. He can find out when that ticket was issued, and even who issued it.'

'Can you call that favour in?'

'For sure. But remember, even if it turns out Harris got a ticket on the thirteenth. It's not proof that he's responsible.'

'No, but it would give us a clearer picture and possibly some leverage.'

Again, they both took sips of coffee and contemplated matters. Chet looked at his watch.

'Let me go give him a call right now,' he said.

'While you're at it, perhaps you could run a license plate for me.'

'Run a plate?'

'Yup. The guys from the casino the other night.'

'I told you. They were probably just punks.'

'What's the harm?'

'Okay,' sighed Chet. 'What's the number?'

'It was a white Dodge Polara from the sixties or seventies on Arizona plates,' recalled Luke. 'The first three letters were LKA.'

Chet wrote the information on a napkin. 'I'll go call from the car,' he said. 'I don't want anyone over-hearing.' He disappeared out the front door.

Luke waited for Chet's return by perusing the menu. When that was done, he read the small print on the back of the ketchup and mustard bottles. Then he thought some more about the Monroe conundrum and swilled what little coffee remained in the bottom of his mug clockwise and anti-clockwise.

The waitress came over. 'You want a refill, sweetie?' she asked. 'Or are you happy playing?'

'I'm good thanks.'

'Well you let me know,' she said with a click of her tongue.

Finally, Chet returned and slid back into his seat.

'What's the story?' asked Luke.

'Sorry that took so long. They were having computer problems. Firstly, you're in luck. There's only one car that matched the plate you gave me. It belongs to a guy from Tucson called William Jones, but he doesn't have a record so if you want to find out anything more about him, it'll take some time.'

'Don't bother. I must be getting paranoid.'

'More interestingly, Harris Monroe had a bad couple of weeks. He picked up two speeding tickets. The first was here in Eagle Canyon.'

Luke perked up.

'Don't get too excited. It was on the tenth. That's three days before the vases were moved.'

'Oh,' replied Luke unhappily. 'Of course the question still remains as to why he didn't mention his trip to Eagle Canyon that month.'

'Maybe he was visiting someone else. Or maybe he forgot. From what I hear, the kid is half wacko. Anyway, he got a second ticket on the night of the 4th this month.'

'The night of the candle,' said Luke sharply.

'Indeed. But that ticket was written up in Phoenix, at four in the morning. That's a good 130 miles from here. I think it unlikely he's our man,' said Chet. 'And for argument's sake, assuming he moved the vases, how did he know his parents were going out that night? How did he get in?'

'A key?' suggested Luke. 'He's probably had one at some stage. And maybe his sister told him they were all having dinner?'

'Maybe the sister was in on it?' joked Chet.

Luke put his head in his hands and stared down at the table. All of a sudden, he looked up and smiled.

'What did you just say?'

'Maybe the sister was in on it,' repeated Chet.

Luke's smile grew broader and he leaned back in his seat. 'Now, funny you should say that.'

'I'm kidding,' said Chet. 'Clarice is a sweet kid.'

'Hear me out for a moment,' replied Luke. 'I've been concentrating on the idea that there's a rational explanation for everything at the Monroe's house and that a person, not some sort of spirit, is responsible. But what if it's more than one person? What if there's a group behind all this?'

Chet looked at Luke with bemusement. 'That sounds pretty leftfield to me.'

'Throughout this, it's struck me that lots of small things don't fit. First up - the land report. Where is it?'

Chet shrugged.

'And what's more - do you remember when we went to meet Pete? We were about to knock on his office door when one of his employees came out with Pete shouting at him.'

'Yes.'

'Pete looked pretty angry, pretty het up. Then just as we sit down he gets a phone call from his secretary telling him there's a problem on his building site and he has to leave straightaway.'

'I remember.'

'Don't you think it strange how calmly he took it? He'd just been raging at that other man. If I was really angry and got more bad news, I suspect I'd be pretty cheesed off and I'd say something pretty fruity. And why didn't his site manager call him in person? You wouldn't leave a message like that with a secretary would you? You'd tell the boss man directly.'

'You think he wanted us out of there?'

'I reckon so. I'll bet he told his secretary to ring him back a couple of minutes later and give him an excuse to get out of there. I remember her saying "I understand" as we stood by her desk - curious words to use if she was simply told to send us to his office. Pete didn't want to talk to us. So, what are the chances there's no actual report?'

Both men thought the scenario through.

'Okay, you've got me interested. For argument's sake let's hear the rest of this conspiracy theory,' said Chet.

'We know that for three of the four episodes, one of the kids was on the premises. Harris for the tyres, Clarice for the candle, and Pete for the message on the mirror.'

'Which leaves the vases, and the voice in the drawing room?' added Chet. 'How did they create the whisper?'

'Hmmm. I'm still a little stumped on that one,' conceded Luke.

Chet removed his thick glasses and laid them on the table. He took both hands and began to massage his eyes. 'Why would the kids do it?' he asked. 'What possible reason is there?'

'That's the million dollar question,' replied Luke. 'One thing got my attention when I saw Chloe yesterday. She said: "People have really come through for us... even the children". Even the children? What does that mean?'

There was a delay, but then Chet's eyes widened. 'Hold on,' he said. 'About a year ago there was a big family dispute. Nobody wanted to talk about it and Jack would clam up straightaway if you tried to bring it up. But one night Chloe had a few too many glasses of wine and when I asked what the problem was, she replied "money, what else?"'

'Any specifics?'

'No. But around the same time our local arts council asked Jack and Chloe if they'd consider bequeathing their house and art to the public when they passed on, as some sort of museum. Although it's quite a big town, we don't have anything like that at present. With the Monroes being patrons of the arts as they are, they really liked the idea.'

'Everything seems hunky dory with the children now,' commented Luke.

'Well I guess they sorted out their differences,' said Chet. 'Why do you think the kids are doing this?'

'Well, they want the parents out of the house that's for sure,' replied Luke. 'The Monroe property must be worth millions, and if Jack and Chloe upped and left now, do you think Jack could resist one final redevelopment? Who would stand to benefit? Monroe Land Development presumably - now owned by Pete, Clarice and Harris. If the children did stand to lose their inheritance, they'd get it by the back door.'

'It's possible,' admitted Chet. 'But we'd need the motive corroborated.'

'Look,' continued Luke, 'I'm not really sure what motivation sits behind all this, but it seems clear to me that the poltergeist isn't real.'

Chet picked up his glasses and returned them to his face. 'So Jack and Chloe have disturbances at home and the family circles the wagons, before easing Mom and Pop out? But Jack's a sceptical guy. How did the kids know their parents would buy into this?'

'Lots of people are sceptical. Until things happen to them. Do you believe in voodoo or witch doctors?'

'No.'

'So you wouldn't mind me getting someone to place a voodoo curse on you?'

'Touché,' conceded Chet. 'Well you might be right, but it's a very elaborate ruse.'

'That's why it's effective. By making it complex, there's less chance of anyone connecting the dots.'

Both men leaned back in their seats.

'It's just an idea,' said Luke. 'Do you have a better one?'

'But would the kids want to go after their parents like that?' asked Chet. 'Chloe could have had a breakdown or something.'

'They would if they thought they were going to lose a lot of money, a large chunk of their inheritance. Maybe they thought it was a victimless crime? No-one got hurt. Everything was kept in the family. The parents would move out, they'd keep their inheritance and earn some payback for being left out in the first place.'

Chet licked his lips.

'Luke, what you're saying has some value, don't get me wrong. But it's basically guesswork. We've got no evidence and you sure as hell can't go telling the Monroes their kids are behind this without some proof.'

'I agree.'

'The only real evidence we have is the recording. If the children created it, there must be a trail. Especially since they would never have thought outside people would get involved. Can we analyse the tape further? Maybe there's some sound in the background that gives them away?'

'It's a bit of a long shot.'

'Could we find out who recorded it? Get them to squeal.'

'I wouldn't know who to ask,' said Luke. 'And what if it was Pete or Harris who recorded it? They're not going to tell us.'

'We could do some voice analysis. Like in the movies.'

'No, I think we're gonna have to keep this simple. The whisper seems to emanate from the living room.'

'Uh-huh,' said Chet.

'Then the source must be in there.'

'I don't want to keep harking back to this. But nothing's been found. Maybe the source is in another room or even outside the house?'

'But Jack and Chloe seem certain.'

'Then we need to go in and tear the place apart. You can explain things. Excuse me Chloe, we think this whole poltergeist thing is a plan by your once estranged kids to prevent you bequeathing the house to the people of Eagle Canyon. We think that the voice comes from this room and want to rip it apart to find out where.'

'Yeah it might be tricky,' admitted Luke.

'Then again, maybe I could get them out of the house for a few hours,' suggested Chet, 'and you go in with some sort of detecting equipment? We'd probably have to get Leya onside.'

'We can't put her in that position,' said Luke. 'She'd lose her job if the Monroes found out.'

'Well they needn't find out,' said Chet.

'They would if we found something. We'd have to admit we'd gone in without their knowledge. And what if we found nothing and they discovered I'd been in the house? You'd have to talk them out of pressing charges. It would be trespass.'

'I'm sure you could handle yourself in the county slammer,' said Chet with a grin. 'Everyone's real friendly in there.'

They both laughed.

'But seriously,' added Chet, 'there must be something playing the voice into the house. How would the children get it in? It's all a bit risky?'

'Well I'm sure they would have had occasion to do it. Jack and Chloe go away on holidays I presume. As long as they were patient, they would have had loads of opportunities to plant the device. Maybe Leya's involved in some way? She gets a cut. As for being risky, Pete and Clarice have been close to what's going on. If Jack got too suspicious, they could just get everything removed.'

'True.'

'Anyway, if there is something hidden, I don't have any equipment to find it. And I don't know how to sweep a place for bugs. We'd have to find a professional and as this is pretty much illegal they'd probably want a fair bit of money.'

They both looked away.

'How about you try to flush one of the kids out?' asked Chet.

'What? Tell them we're on to them?'

'Yes. Maybe they'll get scared and show their hand?'

'I doubt that would work. They know I leave Arizona in a couple of days. They'll just deny everything and wait until I'm out of here.'

Luke clasped his hands together, interlocking his fingers. He looked pensive. 'What about bringing Jack in?' he finally asked. 'Explain what we think is going on? If things were bad with his children previously, maybe he's still a little suspicious of them?'

Chet thought the suggestion over. 'I don't think that would work. He'll want evidence. And let's just take a step back here. What if you're wrong? What if this explanation of yours isn't on the money?'

'Well that's possible,' admitted Luke. He sat up in his seat. 'All right, this is what I think we should do. I'll go see Harris and tell him I know he let down Jack's tyres.'

'But he virtually told you that himself.'

'Then I'll tell him I have my suspicions that the whole poltergeist thing is fake. And that I reckon he's responsible.'

'He'll probably deny it, like you said.'

'Let him. I'll also say that I reckon Clarice was involved, and Pete too.'

'You're gonna blow your whole wad?'

'Yup.'

'And what about when he asks for your proof?'

'I'll tell him I've got it.'

'And then?'

'I'll ask him whether he thinks I should tell his Father? Whether telling his parents is in the best interests, of "everyone". If the price is right, I'll say, then maybe I'll be quiet. Let's see if he bites.'

'Luke I don't think blackmail is going to work.'

'I'll make clear that for a small payoff I'll be happy to disappear from the scene without a word said.'

'He might be a little weasel but he's not stupid. He'll just stare you down. And of course there's still the chance you're wrong.'

Luke stopped to think this through, but Chet broke in: 'But what the hell, if we're wrong we're wrong; we'll just say sorry, tuck our tails between our legs and slink away. When are you going to do this?'

'The funeral's tomorrow,' replied Luke. 'How about the day after? That gives us one day to get it together.'

'Well you let me know what I can do,' said Chet. 'Sleep on it tonight and make sure you're certain this is what you want. If it doesn't work out, you could end up with egg on your face. We both could. Jack would probably forgive me because of our friendship and because I'd make clear I'm old, goofy and led astray easily.' Chet gave a trademark wink. 'But he probably wouldn't forgive you and he could make life difficult, especially as you're in academia where reputation is so important. You understand what I'm saying don't you? Your career could be under threat.'

'Hmmm. Who wants to work, anyway?' offered Luke.

CHAPTER 31

Saturday morning.

The day of the funeral had arrived and at Rebecca's everyone awoke early. The atmosphere in the house was claustrophobic and unrelenting, and melancholy seemed to pervade every room. Rebecca, Samantha and Luke all moved through the house like figurines on a cuckoo clock – on the same plane but never quite interacting with each other.

Conversation was only exchanged when necessary.

Rebecca seemed most dejected, and passed on breakfast, satisfying herself with a cup of tea. Samantha encouraged her to have some food but did not press her case.

At nine o'clock, Luke went to collect his suit from the dry cleaners and by ten the three of them were ready – an hour ahead of schedule. There was very little to do except wait as the undertakers had taken care of all the arrangements. They were well practised in a retirement town where the average age exceeded seventy.

Rebecca sat at the dining table, penning last minute changes to the short speech she planned to give and Samantha stayed in the kitchen reading a book. For the first time Luke could remember, Samantha had her hair down.

The waiting began to eat at Luke and he wanted to get out of the house. So he drove to the nearby pharmacy and spent thirty slow minutes choosing toothpaste. Three different members of staff stopped to see if he needed help. When he got back, he spent the rest of the wait doing the crossword on a four-day-old newspaper.

I hate crosswords.

The black limousine arrived to collect the Jackson household at 11.15 and transported them the short distance to Rolling Pastures

Crematorium. The only other service scheduled for that day was in the late afternoon, so they waited in the main reception area for their guests to arrive. Rebecca had wanted to stand outside, but Eagle Canyon was back to its hottest and black clothes only exacerbated matters.

The crematorium started to fill at a quarter to twelve with most guests drawn from the local area. Nonetheless, Luke met a couple who had journeyed from California to be there, and another who had come from Florida.

Chet and Margaret sat together and for the first time Chet looked smart. He wore a dark suit and a navy blue tie and his shirt cuffs were held together with elegant silver cufflinks. Margaret wore a big hat, and kept a handkerchief permanently to hand.

The service was conducted by Reverend Small, who steered clear of mentioning the Church and God as best he could. Instead, he talked of the personal nature of faith and how Arthur had certainty in what he believed.

After that, a number of people stood to give short eulogies. A man's seventy year life, distilled into a few hundred words.

Arthur Jackson, the marine biologist.

Arthur Jackson, the friend.

Then it was Rebecca's turn and she moved to the lectern to speak.

Her tone was firm, her voice was clear: 'I thought long and hard what to say here today,' she began, 'for Arthur and I had been married almost fifty years. Like all couples, we went through good times and tough times and when I sat down to write this speech I made a list of the things I could include. I thought of the stories from our travels around the world, of Arthur's work, and of our life together.

I began to write about his loyalty and decency and kindness, and made light of his sometimes curmudgeonly nature.

I listed his work in marine conservation, and the awards he received, and the changes he helped bring about.

And as I was doing all this I remembered an incident in The Bahamas some years back. It just popped into my mind.

We were walking down the beach at sunset and Arthur stopped to scoop up a handful of sand. He turned to me, and with it running through his fingers, said:

"On the ground, each grain of sand is the centre of its world.

On the ground, it will never see the beach".'

Rebecca looked up briefly from her notes: 'So if you'll indulge me dear friends, this speech won't be about the things I mentioned, for the past is the past. Instead, I would like to talk about what he meant on that beach in The Bahamas, for it was something that exercised him greatly.'

She looked down again and spoke carefully, hitting every word with clarity and precision.

'We live in an age where man has never been more fragmented or disenfranchised or disconnected.

In an age of great technological advancement and knowledge, we have never been lonelier, or more capable of inflicting damage on ourselves and our planet.

And seeing this state of affairs, Arthur had an idea as to how we got here.

It is because the individual has replaced society. Self interest has seeped into every facet of modern living. We have learned to treat our brothers as competitors, and to define ourselves not through our successes, but through the relative failures of others.

Our self-importance has bred isolation and fostered arrogance. It is a way of life that brings out selfishness, intolerance and prejudice, and leads to divisions against those who do not share our philosophies, skin colour or religious belief.

We covet our views at all cost and believe them to be unerringly right. There is little grace or humility when we fail.

Some might say that's nature for you - evolution in action, the biological imperative. Maybe it is, maybe it isn't – but our future requires us to work together for a common good. For mankind to succeed we need to reconnect with each other, and with nature, and realise that the generations to come will not forgive us for our selfish attitudes and short term viewpoints.

This is not a new message I appreciate, and one that is often made by people more eloquent than I. But it is a message we have grown accustomed to, like some sort of background noise.

Arthur fretted over such matters. He used to say that the seas could look after themselves as long as man learned to respect them.'

Rebecca paused and looked up: 'Goodness, I make him sound like a bit of a hippie; which we know he certainly was not.'

A ripple of laughter ran through the audience.

She carried on: 'Just three months ago, we had a conversation at the dining table when Arthur said: "Rebecca, I am an optimist. Man has an unbounded capacity for hope, vision and survival. We just need to wake up every so often, and realise so."

As you leave here, and with reference to that beach in The Bahamas, remember that we are not the centre of our universes, and that we need to consider our world from outside, as well as in. Arthur understood that. We need more men like him. He will be missed terribly.'

Rebecca bowed her head and stood down, and Reverend Small continued with the service. The congregation was invited to join in the final prayers and as they finished, the Reverend gave his final blessing and pressed the red button on his control panel. At the front of the room, curtains opened and Arthur Jackson slid silently out of sight. As his coffin cleared the curtains, they closed and it was over.

Only then did Rebecca cry. A solitary tear down her cheek.

Samantha held a single yellow rose.

After the service, the guests decamped to the Madison Hotel for the reception. In line with Arthur's wishes, it was a simple affair, and around fifty people stayed for the buffet and drinks, which was held in one of the function rooms. Rebecca was stoic and walked the room endeavouring to speak with each of her guests. In turn, she was the last to leave.

The limousine returned the Jackson family to the house just after four and Luke poured a large glass of wine for himself and collapsed onto the sofa. Rebecca went to lie down. She seemed sluggish.

Samantha joined Luke for a drink then went to her room.

That evening they re-gathered but no-one was in the mood for eating.

By ten-thirty, they were all in bed.

CHAPTER 32

Sunday morning.

D-day.

Luke sat on his bed. As Chet had suggested, he had slept on matters, then made his decision. On the bedside table, the candle he had taken from the Monroe's dining room stood in a holder he had found in the kitchen. It had a charred wick. He listened once more to the recording Jack had captured.

'i 'ap 'i hud ki:kam. Gm g hu 'u:pam hi:m.'

He switched off the player.

Sod it.

Luke left the house early and took breakfast at a small diner on the edge of town. He rehearsed the conversation he planned for Harris. He tried to come up with the excuses and escape angles Harris might play, and how he could counter them. He might have to get personal and hope the fog of anger overcame Harris's self control.

Luke parked directly outside Harris's home and checked his watch. It was nine thirty in the morning and he had not forewarned Harris of his visit. There was no guarantee Harris would be either present or awake.

Luke knocked on the front door loudly, and as the seconds ticked by without response, he began to grow disheartened. He pinned his ear against the door to listen but there was no sound inside. He pulled out his mobile and rang the house. He could hear the phone ringing from the doorstep but there was no answer. After half a minute, he gave up.

Crap.

Luke turned and sat on the step. He reached into his pocket, and pulled out the list of phone numbers Jack had given him. At the bottom was a number that Jack had marked as "Harris Cell".

Luke took out his mobile and dialled it.

From inside the house he heard a jazzy ringtone start to play.

Crap.

He hung up.

Luke sat on the step, put his phone back in his pocket and tried to think of an alternative plan. As he did so, Harris walked up the pathway carrying a brown grocery bag. Luke noticed him first.

'What are you doing here?' said Harris slightly taken aback

'Just in the neighbourhood,' replied Luke quickly getting to his feet. 'I thought of a couple more things I needed to ask.'

'I'm kind of busy at the moment, my friend,' replied Harris nonchalantly. He placed the bag on the ground and began to look for his keys.

'Oh right. That's a shame. I'd only be a couple of minutes. I thought I'd cracked the poltergeist. Thought you'd be interested to know what I uncovered.'

Luke stood there motionless as Harris's interest grew. 'Cracked it huh?' he said. Then a look of intrigue spread across his face. 'Well I'd love to hear this. I suppose I can give you a few minutes. Come in.'

He opened the door.

'Would you like a coffee? And a bagel? I'm just making some for myself.'

'Just the coffee thanks.'

'Go through,' instructed Harris pointing down the corridor.

Luke did as he was told. He went into the living room and sat down on the sofa. The room was tidier than when he was last present. There were no discarded shirts or shoes cluttering up the place. The mannequin art piece had been moved from Harris's studio into the corner of the room, and it stood there dominating the space.

Several minutes later Harris appeared, bearing mugs and a bagel on a plate. Luke took a sip and complemented Harris on the coffee, keen to establish some rapport. If he was going to get Harris to spill the beans he might as well start by being friendly.

'So you've cracked it,' said Harris. 'I'm all ears, my man.'

'Well, maybe cracked is too strong a word.'

Luke glanced away briefly then began. 'First up, I'm convinced there's nothing paranormal at the house.'

'Oh yeah?'

'Yup. I think we can look at a more conventional explanation.'

He let the sentence hang in the air.

Finally, Harris asked: 'So, what is it?'

'Why don't you tell me?' replied Luke.

Harris's face twisted in confusion and Luke stayed quiet.

'What do you mean?' queried Harris.

'You tell me.'

There was a momentary delay.

'Are you feeling all right?' asked Harris slowly. 'I have no idea what's going on. I thought you came here to educate me.'

This doesn't look good.

'Harris,' said Luke with a crafty smile on his face, 'look I don't give a monkey's for whatever reason you're doing it. If you want to screw with your parents so be it…'

A deadpan Harris looked back. He was totally expressionless.

'Go on. Spill the beans,' said Luke invitingly.

Harris's eyes narrowed: 'I really don't know what you're talking about, and frankly I'm insulted that you think I would do such a thing.'

The indignation was strong and Luke got a bad feeling in the pit of his stomach. At least that was until he saw the slight twitch at the edge of Harris's mouth.

'In fact,' said Harris, 'screw you Luke. You come into my house and give me shit. I should throw you out on your ass, right now.'

Change tack.

'C'mon Harris. Level with me. When I was here last time and you were telling me about the tyres. I could see you were almost gloating.'

Harris hesitated. 'You're talking about the flat tyres?'

'Yup.'

'And the other stuff?'

'Oh that? I don't know what's happening there.'

Harris relaxed visibly.

'The tyres huh?' he repeated. 'Gloating?'

Both men sat in silence whilst Harris weighed up his position. Luke got to his feet and walked across the room towards the mannequin.

There was a bang on the front door.

'Expecting someone?' asked Luke.

Harris pursed his lips before getting up and going over to the door. He looked through the peep hole then over his shoulder at Luke who had turned to face him.

'Excuse me for a moment,' he said coldly. 'Some business I need to attend to.'

Then he opened the door a few inches and spoke through it.

Whoever was on the other side sounded agitated. It was a male voice but Luke could not hear what was being said. Harris raised his left hand to placate the visitor before glancing back over his shoulder once more.

'Gimme five,' he said to Luke before moving through the doorway, making sure that the gap remained small and Luke could not see the visitor.

Harris's words had seemed strained.

Something's happening here.

Luke put down his mug and quickly moved from the living room to the kitchen. He pushed up against the window that overlooked the street, eager to check out whom Harris was talking with.

He peered out but neither Harris nor the caller was to be seen. Luke checked left and right, up and down the street, but he had disappeared. There was now a dark blue Mercedes convertible parked in front of Luke's car. Its roof was up and he could not see the driver.

His bad feeling came back.

Rapidly he pulled out his phone and tried to call Jack.

Leya answered. 'Monroe residence.'

'Morning Leya, it's Luke Jackson.'

'Oh, good morning,' she replied courteously.

'Is Jack about? I need a quick word with him.'

'Certainly. Please hold.'

Luke watched the street. No movement from the Mercedes.

Maybe he owes more money? Maybe it's just a friend?

Jack came onto the line.

'Luke,' he said.

'Hi Jack. Thought I'd call and see how you were today.'

'Yeah doing okay, thanks.'

'And everything's quiet at the house?'

'Nothing new to report from here.'

'Listen, I've been doing a bit of research and was wondering if you were going to be in later this morning. As this is my last full day in Arizona, we need to get on with things.'

'Umm, yes, I had no real plans for this morning. I was just going through some paperwork. Come round whenever.'

'Excellent. Have you told Chloe what the Indian message translated as?'

'Yes. She took it like a trooper.'

'I thought she might. You haven't told anyone else yet, have you? You remember we thought it wise to keep things quiet.'

'Oh yes,' there was a faltering in Jack's voice. 'Well Pete called. I didn't see the harm in telling him. That was only about fifteen minutes ago in actual fact.'

'What did Pete say?'

'He sounded a bit alarmed. Maybe all this time he thought that we were imagining things. He said he was going to swing by.'

'For any particular reason?'

'I don't think so. Probably just to make us feel better.'

'Maybe I should come over, when he's there. I've thought of one more thing I need to ask him. What time's he due?'

'He said he'd come right on over. He was at his office, so he'll probably be here in thirty or forty minutes.'

'Okay, well I'll try to be there in thirty also. I'm in Tucson myself.' Luke coughed before adding jovially: 'If I see him, I'll make sure I give him a wave. What car does he drive?'

'Umm, I'm not sure,' replied Jack. 'He keeps changing them. Some sporty Mercedes, one of those two-seater jobs.'

'I'll keep my eyes peeled. What colour is it?'

'Blue.'

Luke continued to look out the window.

'See you soon, Jack,' said Luke. He hung up abruptly.

At the other end of the line, Jack looked at his handset irritably.

Chloe walked in. 'Who was that?' she asked.

'Luke,' replied Jack. 'And he just cut me off.'

Luke rapidly scrolled through the call history in his phone, and dialled Chet's house.

It rang and rang.

He gave up and tried Chet's cell phone.

It rang eight times before Chet answered.

'Hello?'

'Chet, it's Luke. Where are you?'

'I'm at home,' said Chet straightforwardly. 'Where are you?'

‘I’m at Harris Monroe’s house. I just tried you at home.’

‘Oh I thought I heard it ring. So, has Harris confessed yet?’

‘Not really, but things have taken a sudden turn. Just as we were getting down to business, a visitor pitched up. I can’t be sure but I think it could be Pete Monroe. He’s outside in his car right this instant.’

‘Did he not come in and say hello? Huh. Terrible manners.’

‘Jack just told Pete about the tape, less than fifteen minutes ago. Chet, I’ve got a funky feeling about this. I think our horse is about to bolt.’

Luke continued to watch through the window, looking for any sign of action. He gave Chet some instructions. ‘Phone Jack. Tell him I asked you to help me this morning. Then go over to his house and wait for me there. Jack said Pete was on his way over and he’s going to have a head start on me. If they think they’ve been rumbled, they might panic.’

‘So we’re going with the conspiracy idea?’ confirmed Chet.

‘That’s right. If there’s something in that house, they might want to get rid of it, and we can’t let that happen. Get over there and don’t let anyone remove anything.’

‘And how am I meant to do that?’ enquired Chet.

‘Think of something. Be creative. But for God’s sake don’t accuse anyone of wrongdoing at this stage. We might need some wiggle room.’

‘I can’t keep my eye on every room Luke.’

‘No, that’s fine. Just stick with Pete. He’ll want to go wherever the evidence is. And, as we reckon, that’ll be the drawing room.’

‘You got it, boss,’ said Chet excitably.

Luke’s mind raced. From the window, he watched Harris exit the Mercedes. He slapped the roof as it pulled away with speed.

Luke continued: ‘And we might need to buy a little bit of time when I arrive. I’ll scoot round to my Grandmother’s and collect my laptop. We can pretend we need it for some sort of analysis.’

‘Analysis?’

‘Just go.’

‘Yes boss,’ said Chet emphatically.

Luke watched Harris stop at the bottom of the path and take a deep breath.

‘Pete will be with you in twenty to twenty five minutes,’ said Luke. ‘He’s just taken off like a bat out of hell.’

'On my way.'

'And have you got a tool kit?'

'Sure.'

'Take it with you.'

Luke snapped his phone shut at the exact moment Harris re-entered the house.

He looked surprised to see Luke staring out the kitchen window, but it quickly seeped away. 'Luke,' he said warmly, 'sorry about that. A friend of mine.'

Harris stared at the phone in Luke's hand.

'Just got a call,' explained Luke. 'The signal's better here, by the window. Hey I think I'm gonna have to head off now. Family problems I need to sort out.'

He held up the handset to emphasise the importance of the call and minor panic crossed Harris's face.

'Err, umm,' stammered Harris, 'before you go, I think I should tell you about the tyres. Why don't we sit down and I'll explain everything? Clear things up a bit.'

Harris pointed towards the living room and the mannequin in the corner. Luke looked across but remained where he was.

Harris tried again: 'I'm gonna be honest with you Luke. You were right. But I can't just admit it and let you leave without some sort of explanation. You'll think really badly of me. I'm actually a pretty nice guy.'

Luke's gaze returned to Harris. He spoke. 'Like I said, there's a problem at home that I need to attend to sharpish. Why don't we run through things on the phone later?'

Harris ignored him. 'It might help me to get all this off my chest. Y'know, catharsis? It was bit low what I did, but I saw an opportunity to get some money off my parents. We haven't always had an easy relationship you know? Come let's sit down.'

He pointed once again and now it was Luke's turn to ignore him.

'I think it's commendable you telling me this,' said Luke. 'And I'm more than happy to discuss it later.'

The urgency in Harris's voice increased: 'You want to help me and my parents get back on an even keel, don't you? You can't stir everything up then walk away.'

Luke looked casually back at the mannequin.

Then his mouth curled into a sneaking smile.

Harris became unnerved. 'Luke? You okay? Is something funny?'

He waved his hands across Luke's line of sight.

Luke's smile stayed in place. 'Sorry Harris, nothing funny. Look, I really need to go.'

All of a sudden Harris rapidly closed the gap between the two of them. He grabbed Luke by his shoulders.

He had a look of pure violence in his eyes and his face was contorted.

'I don't think you understand me Luke,' he said threateningly as spit launched from his lips. 'I really need to talk these things through.' He continued to speak through gritted teeth: 'I need to get matters off my chest. I'm not a bad guy, just a bit misunderstood. It's important that you understand where I'm coming from. That I'm not a terrible person. Now let's go sit down and talk.'

'Okay. Relax,' said Luke calmly. 'You're right. Let's go chat.'

The evil look on Harris's face began to subside and he relaxed his grip on Luke's shoulders. As this happened, Luke made his move.

He dropped his left shoulder and brought his hands up between Harris's outstretched arms. Then he fired his fists into the elbow joints, breaking the lock.

Harris looked startled.

In a split second, Luke's right arm was drawn back and he struck a fist hard into Harris's stomach. Harris stumbled backwards in small steps. He doubled over struggling for air, then dropped onto a knee to support himself. Luke said nothing and began to head for the front door. Suddenly, Harris rose back onto both feet and tried to lunge at Luke, but Luke stepped to one side before taking careful aim and striking Harris with his elbow, on the side of the head.

Harris slumped back onto the floor and Luke was gone.

CHAPTER 33

Sunday mid-morning.

Luke sped down the freeway back to Eagle Canyon, gunning the car and without concern for the Highway Patrol. He drew up outside his Grandmother's house and dashed inside. As usual, his aunt was sprawled on the floor working from her notebooks, but Luke simply rushed past without comment and grabbed his laptop from his room. He stuffed it into his bag and ran back towards the front door.

'In a hurry?' asked Samantha.

'Yes.'

He slammed the door behind him.

Back in his car, Luke worked his way across town to the Monroe's house. He found himself hampered by a group of cars travelling at a leisurely rate. Impatiently Luke used his horn and when it became clear that made no difference, he simply went around them. The drivers took umbrage and loud honks followed him.

Luke pulled up at the Monroe house. In the driveway, he recognised Chet's car from the parking lot outside the Sunflower Café and the blue Mercedes he had seen at Harris's. A third vehicle was also familiar.

Luke got out of his car and went to the front door. It was open so he walked in and found a commotion in place. Jack and Chloe stood to one side of the hall looking bewildered. Chet and Pete were on the other.

Pete looked angry and was remonstrating with Chet who looked stressed. His eyes widened when he saw Luke.

'Ah! Dr. Jackson,' sneered Pete. 'Maybe you'd like to explain what the hell is happening here?! Why Mr Baker has decided to tell my family what they can and can't do in their own house.' His inflection was harsh, his volume loud.

'Oh hi, Pete,' said Luke affably. 'How are you today?'

'Cut it out, wise-ass!' replied Pete.

Clarice walked into the hallway from the direction of the kitchen.

'Clarice,' said Luke. 'I thought that was your car, outside.'

She looked at him cautiously.

'Just popping by?' he continued.

'I was in the area and decided to come see my parents,' she said. 'If that's all right with you of course?'

'Of course. It's nice to see you close to your parents.'

Jack looked bemused: 'Luke, I'm not quite sure what's going on here. But this is all a little bit much. We were having a quiet day at home, when Chet bounds in-'

Chloe cut across him: '-Then Clarice, then Pete, now you. What is going on?'

'I'm not sure,' replied Luke. 'I can't speak for the others but I did ask Chet to join me here. Look, I've brought a bit of kit that might help us out.'

He held up his laptop case.

Jack looked at him suspiciously.

'How's that going to help us?'

'I can take some readings.'

'You never mentioned this previously.'

'I only thought of it this morning,' explained Luke. 'It's a program I use for other work. I thought of a way to adapt it.'

'Right,' replied Jack, 'and what specifically are you going to measure?'

Luke ignored him.

'So Pete,' said Luke, 'I was round at Harris's this morning. I saw your car outside. You should have come in and said hello.'

Pete went on the offensive.

He spoke to his Father: 'Dad, this is bullshit. You and Mom are going through the mill and this idiot's just making matters worse. He's a fruit loop.'

Then he shifted his attention to Luke: 'This is one grade-A waste of time. You've taken a lot of liberties, and upset my family. Clarice says you were rude and abusive when you went to see her.'

'You what?' asked Luke.

Clarice appeared dazed but regained her composure: 'Erm yes. Rude. And Abusive.'

She appealed to her Mother. 'Surely you can't let him act like this?'

Chloe's face creased with anger and she glowered at Luke.

Luke changed tack: 'Jack, Chloe. Things are getting a little out of hand here, but I reckon I can solve your poltergeist problem.'

Pete cut across him: 'Dad, he's a charlatan. He doesn't know what the hell he's doing. He's wasting your time and mine.'

Jack held his hand up with his fingers spread wide: 'I don't think he's a charlatan, Pete. And Clarice, I'd be surprised if he was intentionally rude or abusive. Perhaps you simply took something the wrong way.' Jack nodded at Luke then said: 'Go ahead and do your thing.'

'Oh for Christ's sake!' began Pete.

'Be quiet, Peter,' instructed Jack.

Swiftly, Luke began to walk down the hallway towards the drawing room, and Chet had to catch him up.

'Well I want to see what you're doing in there,' said Pete beginning to follow.

Luke stopped and span around.

'Sorry Pete, in taking these readings, the calibration is really sensitive. If too many people are in the room, it'll give false negatives. It's two people, max.'

'Well that makes no sense, if you and Chet are both in there-'

'-Erm, with due respect Pete, I do know what I'm doing,' interrupted Luke, 'and if you just leave us alone, we'll be quicker.'

Pete appealed to his Father once again.

'Dad?'

'I told you,' replied Jack, 'be quiet.'

'Yes Sir,' replied Pete stone-faced.

'Why don't you wait in the kitchen?' suggested Luke. 'We'll come get you when the results are in.'

'That sounds a good idea,' said Jack categorically. 'Everyone follow me.'

As they left for the kitchen, Luke whispered to Chet: 'Well here we go. It's all or nothing.'

'I hope you're right Luke.'

'Me too.'

They made it to the drawing room doors.

'Did you bring your toolkit?' asked Luke.

'Oh rats! No! I forgot it. In the excitement to get over here it slipped my mind.'

'Right then, would you go see if Jack has one?'

Chet about-turned and headed for the kitchen and Luke made his own way into the room. He dumped his laptop onto a sofa and surveyed the scene. The pictures, the vases, the sculpture. Everything was as he had last seen it.

Chet came in holding a plumber's toolbox.

'How's it in the kitchen?' enquired Luke.

'Tense. Pete's going ape. Why do we need a toolkit?'

'Because we might need some tools,' replied Luke matter-of-factly. He started to open the toolbox. 'Tell me what happened when you got here.'

'I only arrived a moment or two after Pete.'

'What? You live ten minutes down the road, he had to come in from Tucson. How could he have beaten you?'

'Erm, I might have chosen a poor route.'

'In your own town, going to an old friend's house?'

'Well there was traffic and I was flustered. Anyway, time-out kid, bring me up to speed. What are we looking for?'

Luke finished rummaging through the toolbox.

'I kept thinking there must be a secret transmitter of some sort in here,' said Luke. 'Something in a ceiling grate or the fireplace. But it occurred to me this morning that Pete and the others probably didn't expect this to go so far, so maybe things aren't quite as sophisticated as I imagined. There must be something more overt in here.'

'Well that makes sense, but where?'

'You know Harris is an artist.'

'Yes.'

'He's just completed this big ugly electronic mannequin and is now working on some monstrous spider that raises its legs and hisses when someone wanders in front of it.'

'Sounds god-awful.'

'I really can't believe I've been so slow to catch on. What's the one thing in this room that's a recent addition?'

'I'm not sure,' said Chet.

‘Something that Jack and Chloe never bought for themselves? Something they feel compelled to display. And something the giver insisted be positioned in a particular place.’

Luke swept his shoulder round and pointed.

‘Chet Baker. I give you Harris’s clock.’

‘The clock?’

‘It’s got to be.’

Chet looked nervous. ‘You’re sure?’

‘Well in my mind it seems perfectly logical.’

‘Is Harris smart enough to do that?’

‘Yeah, I think everyone underestimates him. Which worked to his advantage in this case. He could sneak in under the radar. All we’ve got to do now is open it up and confirm the hypothesis.’ He paused. ‘Or open it up and run for the hills.’

They both walked over to the clock and Luke lifted it off the sideboard onto the floor. He turned it over.

‘It’s heavy,’ he said.

Chet bit his lip.

‘Don’t worry,’ laughed Luke. ‘I’ve been in worse scrapes. Here pass me a medium Phillips head screwdriver.’

‘A what?’

‘A cross head screwdriver.’

‘Oh right.’ Chet began to rummage through the toolbox. After 10 or so seconds he spoke. ‘I can’t find one.’

‘At all?’

‘Nope?’

‘All right, what about a medium flathead?’

‘Yup got one of those. Here.’

He passed Luke a screwdriver with a yellow and black plastic handle and Luke began to unscrew the base. He had just finished the second screw of four when he heard the sound of the front door slamming shut.

‘Rats abandoning ship,’ he commented confidently.

He undid the third screw.

There were raised voices in the corridor, then the pounding of feet that got louder and closer.

Luke was halfway through undoing the fourth screw when Jack burst into the room, closely followed by Harris. Some dried blood had congealed around his ear.

Jack seemed furious.

'Luke!' he bellowed. 'Harris says you attacked him! Have you gone stark raving crazy!?'

'Ah Harris,' replied Luke calmly, 'I wondered how long it would take you to pitch up.'

'Did you strike him, God damn it!?' demanded Jack.

'I was just defending myself,' replied Luke.

'I owe you a beating!' shouted Harris angrily.

Pete brought up the rear and looked ready for a fight.

Luke lifted the screwdriver menacingly in his hand. 'Sit Down!' he demanded with a ferocity that surprised them all.

Chet took a rapid sideways step, away from the Englishman.

For a stunned moment nobody said anything, then Jack spoke: 'If you think you can speak to me like that in my own house…'

Luke reduced his volume and spoke in a reasonable manner: 'Jack.'

Jack steadied and Luke continued: 'I tell you what. In about 5 seconds from now, everything will be made clear. Just let me finish, all right?'

'God help you, if you are wrong about this,' said Jack. 'I'll…'

The threat remained empty.

'Look, you asked for my help,' replied Luke. 'And that's what I'm trying to do.'

Chet watched Harris whose eyes were fixed on the clock.

'Undo the final screw, kid,' he instructed Luke.

Luke turned back and began to undo the final screw. Harris toppled onto the chair beside him.

With the heat taken out of the moment, Jack recovered his sangfroid and asked politely what Luke was doing. Luke did not reply.

The final screw slid out and the case was free from the base. Luke lifted it clear.

For a second or two nobody moved.

There was total silence.

Luke looked down then finally spoke.

'Everyone makes mistakes now and then,' he said in a subdued voice. 'But I guess this isn't one of mine.'

Chloe and Clarice entered the room and Clarice's hand went up to her face as Luke stepped aside to reveal the clock and its innards.

'Jack. Chloe. I just couldn't believe the voice was genuine. I give you… your Indian ghost.'

With the screwdriver, Luke began to point at the various components. He started with the back of the clock face.

'The clock mechanism is this bit,' he said. 'It's absolutely bog standard and can be purchased at any electronics store. It takes a regular double-A battery.'

Then Luke twisted the base to reveal more of the innards.

'And if that's the only bit responsible for timekeeping,' he began, 'it begs the question, what the hell are these bits for?'

Luke's right hand dropped and directed his audience's attention towards an array of electronics. There was a large battery, cables, circuit boards, and most visibly a speaker.

'Jack. Chloe. You've got a trojan clock on your hands,' he stated.

CHAPTER 34

Sunday mid-morning (2).

'Harris, perhaps you'd like to explain this?' invited Luke.

There was a delay in the room, as everyone absorbed Luke's revelation. Eventually Harris began to mutter a response.

'Ermm,' was all he could muster, squirming in his seat, searching for a plausible explanation.

The seconds passed and Harris tried to buy time by scratching at the congealed blood on his ear. Then he spoke. 'Ermm, originally when I built the clock, I was going to have it play music every hour, but in the end I couldn't get it to work properly, and I-'

Luke made a noise, as though a contestant on a game show had made a wrong answer. 'Wah-waaaah.'

Harris tried to continue: 'Like I said, originally-'

'C'mon Harris. That's bollocks.'

He could see Harris floundering. He had no contingency.

'I hope you don't mind Jack but as I was driving in from Tucson I took the liberty of phoning an electronics expert. It's always a good idea to get things corroborated, don't you think?'

Theatrically, Luke looked at his watch. 'He should be here in about forty-five minutes. Although I know a fair bit about these things, he should be able to give you the complete low-down on this device. Impartially.'

Jack looked at his eldest son, who looked at Pete.

Luke quietly moved over to Chet, who had maintained his distance since Luke had brandished the screwdriver. He whispered very quietly to his partner: 'We've got forty-five minutes to get a confession out of this lot, or make the machine work.'

'What? There's no expert?'

‘Of course not. Where would I have found one at such short notice? Plus, I didn’t think it would pan out like this.’

‘Can’t you make it work?’ responded Chet.

‘I have no idea.’

‘You said you knew about electronics.’

‘Well, that wasn’t exactly the truth. If our forty-five minutes run out without a confession, we’ll have to get the clock out of here and then find someone who knows what they’re looking at. You distract the Monroe lynching party, I’ll grab the clock.’

Chet held his hand up to his forehead. ‘Heavens above,’ he muttered.

‘Who is this expert?’ asked Jack from across the room.

‘Clive Sinclair. A researcher at the University of Arizona,’ replied Luke quickly. ‘When I spoke with him he seemed a bit perplexed to be honest, but I promised him a couple of hundred bucks, if he could make it here a.s.a.p.’

‘Well, I guess we’ll have to wait,’ concluded Jack, before turning to speak with Harris. ‘But, if Luke is right, you’d better come clean right now. I don’t want the embarrassment of some outsider knowing my own damned son did this to me.’

Harris remained defiant. There was a teenager’s petulance about him.

‘What are we going to do until then?’ asked Chloe. ‘Sit around here in silence.’

Luke took the opportunity.

‘Well since there is a certain reluctance to be honest here, perhaps I should take the time to explain the broader picture?’

‘Yes, that’d be good,’ said Jack. ‘Please go ahead.’

Pete moved across the room and whispered something in Harris’s ear.

‘I don’t think there is anything paranormal going on in this house. Whatsoever,’ said Luke.

Harris looked up at Pete and glared at him.

‘Let’s start at the beginning with the vases that moved all by themselves.’

Luke turned towards the vases on the wall and pointed at them with his left hand. Harris interrupted: ‘Okay Luke. No need to go on. You can quit your grandstanding.’

‘Grandstanding?’ Luke turned to Chet. ‘Moi?’

'Luke's right,' continued Harris. 'The clock is your sound source. And what's more, I was also behind everything else.'

Both Jack and Chloe looked appalled, and Pete shot Luke a daggered smile.

'Harris, it was you?' confirmed Jack.

'Yup, the whole thing.'

It couldn't have been.

Harris continued: 'I needed the money. I knew you wouldn't give it to me, if I simply asked for it. Not after my chequered history.'

'But we paid up,' said Chloe.

'A little more never goes astray.'

Harris looked at his Mother. 'I heard you were having dinner with Clarice last month, so I came down to the house and moved the vases. I let down the tyres when I was here. I snuck in and lit the candle the night Clarice was here.'

Jack seemed genuinely shocked and took a seat. But Chloe walked across the room and slapped Harris hard across the back of his head.

'You did all this?' confirmed Jack.

'Yup?'

'For the sake of eight thousand dollars?'

Harris stumbled across his words: 'Well yeah. And a little bit of payback maybe, for all the crap you put me through over the years.'

'How'd you get in?' asked Jack.

'I had a key cut ages ago. I never knew when it might come in handy.'

Chloe interjected: 'And the message in the mirror?'

'I was hiding upstairs,' said Harris. 'I just cleaned the mirror off, after you went in there.'

'And was this clock going to haunt us forever?' complained Jack.

'No. I was gonna come and collect it. Take it away for repairs or something. Everything would then have stopped.'

'The clock,' said Jack. 'Make it work. Now.'

Harris reluctantly got to his feet and his Mother had another swing. This time she missed.

He trudged over to the case and slid a finger underneath one of the circuit boards. There was a click and then the room filled with the same haunting noise that had earlier invited such consternation:

i 'ap 'i hud ki:kam. Gm g hu 'u:pam hi:m.

'Son of a bitch,' said Jack, with a smile on his face. He almost seemed proud, but his expression soon gave way to one of confusion. 'But this thing never got going when we were in the room. If it did, we'd have realised it was the source pretty quickly. And for that matter, it only came on at night – how'd you get that to happen?'

Harris explained: 'It was programmed to activate after ten o'clock at night, and when the room was empty. I disguised some infra-red sensors in the case; if it picked up anyone nearby, it wouldn't activate. That's why I put it right here, on this table. It could sense anyone coming down the hallway if the drawing room doors were open. And if they were closed, opening the doors would also shut it down. I didn't want people getting too close when it was operating.'

'So, was it set to run every night?'

'No, that would have been too much. I only activated the system when I moved the vases, and there's a minimum length of time between any two events happening. It's really quite sophisticated you know.'

'I can't believe this,' said Chloe. 'You did this to your own family. Do you have any idea how sick with stress this whole thing made us feel? Do you?'

All Harris could say was: 'I'm sorry.'

'I'm really quite impressed you could make such a thing,' said Jack. 'I didn't think you were capable of doing something this ingenious.'

'Jack!' remonstrated Chloe.

Jack shrugged his shoulders.

'Harris?' said Luke.

'What.'

'Why don't you give us the real story?'

Jack went back to his look of bemusement. 'That isn't it?'

'You don't have to take all the blame,' said Luke.

Harris looked coy. 'I don't know what you're talking about.'

Now Chet joined in: 'Harris can't be acting alone,' he said. 'He's taking one for the team.'

'It's true,' added Luke. 'Pete and Clarice are also in on it. Ask yourself, how come they both arrived here minutes after Jack spoke to Pete? What was that song and dance Pete was making in the corridor all about? Talk about reluctant to let me in here. He didn't want me getting to the clock.'

'I came over to be supportive,' said Pete. 'I didn't want you coming in and upsetting everyone. At the time, I thought you were out of line. Now, I see you were just doing your job. I want to apologise for getting you so wrong.'

Clarice stayed quiet.

'You think they're all involved?' asked Jack.

'Yes,' replied Chet.

'You know that for a fact?'

Luke walked over to a chair and sat down: 'Start at the beginning. The clock is delivered for your birthday. Harris takes a lot of care and attention to put it in the right place. But you don't really like it much.' He looked at Chloe. 'I'll bet you mentioned how little you liked it to Pete or Clarice.'

'I may have.'

'Did they urge you to leave it there, so as not to hurt Harris's feelings? Did they say - leave it out a few weeks then quietly get rid of it?'

'Umm. I don't remember. Quite possibly,' said Chloe.

'Luke, tell Jack and Chloe the whole story,' urged Chet.

'Okay, the vases. Quite an obvious one really. The night of the 13th. And you were out for dinner with Clarice and her husband. Harris comes around and shifts them. And as he just said, he activated the clock.'

'Why the vases?' asked Chloe.

'Because they're so important to you. He knew you'd notice and that they'd have an immediate effect.'

Clarice interjected: 'You think that proves I'm involved. Because I told Harris we were all having dinner? He could have found out Mom and Dad were away that evening from anyone. Leya might have told him. He could have swung by the house and found it empty.'

'Hold your horses Clarice,' said Luke. 'We'll come back to you. Then there's the tyre episode. Harris comes around to tell you about the problems he's having, has "too many" beers, and you make him stay. He comes down in the night and depresses the valves.'

'Is that what you did, Harris?' asked Chet.

Harris nodded meekly.

'Clarice, you ask how you were involved, well what about the candle episode?' continued Luke. 'We know Pete was out of town on business, so it couldn't have been him. And I know for a fact Harris couldn't have done it. So that only leaves you.'

'Oh you know for a fact I was involved, do you? But he just admitted he did it,' said Clarice.

'Well that would have been rather difficult. You see he was in Phoenix that night.'

'You can prove that can you?' challenged Clarice.

Harris's hand went up to his face.

'Err yes,' said Chet. 'He got a speeding ticket on the Interstate north of Phoenix, at four o'clock in the morning. He can't be in two places at once.'

'Oh,' replied Clarice.

Luke spoke to them all. 'I took one of the candles the last time I was here and lit it at my Grandmother's house. The candles release wax as they burn. So you'd have expected to see a puddle of dried wax on the dresser the next morning. According to Chloe, there wasn't one, so I guess Clarice took a fresh candle from the box when she went to bed that night - when the little ceremony in the dining room had been concluded.' Then he turned his attention onto the Monroe's daughter. 'You lit the candle in your room and swapped it for one in the candelabra in the middle of the night, didn't you?'

'Conjecture,' she replied flatly.

'And the message in the mirror?' said Chloe. 'It was really there, on the glass?'

'Of course. And that would have to be Pete's doing. He must have written it. Then being the first up to the bathroom, he wiped it off before anyone else saw it.'

'Garbage,' said Pete. 'Columbo here has got everything all mixed up.'

'And whilst we're talking about Pete – I never got to see that land report which said this house was on sacred land,' continued Luke. 'Are you sure you faxed it to the right number?'

There was no response.

Luke faced Jack: 'I spoke with Ben Rose yesterday afternoon, after we'd seen him at his gallery, and asked him whether he thought this land was in any way sacred. He said it was exceptionally unlikely.'

Jack looked confused: 'And the story from Harris? About the Indian he owed money to?'

'I don't know. Ask him. Either he did it to add plausibility. Or, he saw an opportunity to get a bit of pocket money out of the deal, on top of getting you out of the house.'

Harris stayed quiet.

'Is that why they did it? To get us out of the house?' asked Chloe.

'That's what you'll have to find out. I'm a little shaky on motive. You need to work out how they would benefit, if you left here. Whatever their reason, they each had to work together. Each doing their little bit.'

Pete tried a rearguard manoeuvre: 'Dad, Harris has just admitted it was him and him alone. I had nothing to do with this. And nor did Clarice as far as I know. Seriously, swear to God.'

'Harris?' asked Jack. 'Are you going to take the heat for everyone?'

Harris sat there stony-faced.

'Chet,' said Luke. 'Why don't we go outside? I think the Monroes will want some time to work this out.'

'Call your electronics man,' said Jack. 'Save him the trip. Tell him I'll pay him for his time anyway.'

'Oh yeah. Sure thing.'

Chet nodded and the two of them exited the room. Luke pulled the drawing room doors behind him then caught up with Chet and put his arm around him.

'A good job, eh?' he said. 'How are you feeling?'

'Not great,' replied Chet. 'My heart's racing, and you mustn't forget I'm actually quite old – excitement like that could kill me. What's more, I feel like we've put an atomic bomb under this family.'

'Well, it wasn't very healthy anyway. Maybe this will be the start of something better?'

'We'll have to wait and see.'

They reached the front door and went outside.

'It was a bit of a close run thing though,' said Luke.

'It certainly was. And what the hell happened at Harris's? Jack looked like he was ready to murder you.'

'Things got a bit frisky, that's all.'

The dog that lay under the portico came over to say hello and Luke patted it on the head. Both men sat down on a wall that marked out the start of the garden, and took deep sighs.

'So it's all over,' concluded Chet. 'And tomorrow you go home.'

'That's right,' responded Luke.

'Have you got anything planned for when you get back?'

'No. Same old stuff.'

‘So, it’s not normally like this?’ Chet laughed. ‘This isn’t your average day in parapsychology?’

‘No. This has been quite unique.’

They both looked at the dog, which was busy staring at Chet.

‘I still can’t quite believe those kids would do that to their parents,’ said Chet.

Luke agreed. ‘But then again, open any newspaper and you’ll see worse,’ he added.

‘That’s true. Tell you what, let’s go get a beer. To celebrate. And calm my nerves.’

‘You just read my mind.’

CHAPTER 35

Monday morning.

The next morning, it was time for Luke to leave Eagle Canyon. It was cooler in town, almost balmy, and as Rebecca stood out front examining her mailbox, Chet drew up in his old car.

'Morning Rebecca,' he said getting out.

'Chet Baker,' she replied curtly. 'I have a bone to pick with you.'

'Ma'am?'

'What did you do to my Grandson? When he made it back here yesterday after your little celebratory outing, he was a wreck. What on earth were you two drinking?'

Chet tried to look ashamed: 'We got going on tequila slammers.'

'Well at least he's a happy drunk,' said Rebecca with a smile on her face. 'Sam and I had a lovely evening watching him fall around the place, talking nonsense.'

Chet shuffled on the spot.

'So, you're taking him to the airport?' he asked.

'Yes, Samantha and I both will.' She looked at her watch. 'Goodness is that the time? We need to be leaving before too long. Let me go see if I can find your partner in crime.'

At that moment, the front door opened and Luke popped his head out.

'I thought I heard voices,' he said. 'Howdy.'

'Ah. The man of the moment,' exclaimed Chet. 'Rebecca, your Grandson here did a great job with that problem we had.'

'I knew he would,' said Rebecca proudly. 'Why don't I leave you both to it for a moment? Luke, we'll depart for the airport in five minutes.'

'Okay, I'm all packed.'

She disappeared indoors.

Luke stood back and surveyed the old man suspiciously: 'Are you sure that tequila was legal? I'm still sweating booze and I feel like a mule has kicked me in the head. How come you look all right?'

'Strong constitution,' said Chet slapping his stomach. 'I just wanted to come by and say, au revoir. It's been a very interesting few days with you here.'

'For me too. Spoken to Jack?

'I rang Jack last night to check things were okay.'

'And what's the fallout?'

'The tequila buzz may have clouded the conversation but from what I remember, the kids were still there. I'd have thought there was a lot of "talking" going on.'

'Had they owned up?'

'Apparently so, it took a while, but Harris finally snapped and told Pete he wasn't going to take the fall all by himself.'

'And where's it going to go from here?'

'I'm not sure. It was a lousy thing to do. But Jack can be magnanimous. Surprisingly so. He might forgive them.'

'And Chloe?'

'Ooh, Chloe's a different kettle of fish.'

Both men laughed out loud.

'Where's your rental car?' asked Chet. 'You didn't come back last night and take it out for a spin did you? It's not in some ditch, is it?'

'Nope, they kindly collected it this morning.'

The kitchen window opened and Samantha called from it.

'Luke,' she said. 'I think Mom's ready. Why don't you come grab your bags.'

Then she noticed Chet. 'Oh hi there. How are you today?'

'Fine. Top of the world, thanks.'

Not fair.

'Hold on two minutes,' said Luke. 'I'll get my bags and then say goodbye properly.'

Back in the house, Luke collected his luggage and checked over his room one final time. When he returned outside, Margaret had also pitched up. She rushed over to hug him.

'Oh Luke, I heard about yesterday at Jack and Chloe's. Our very own super sleuth.'

Once again, Luke found his arms pinned to his side. He struggled to breathe.

She released him.

'You have a safe journey back now, you hear?' she continued. 'And who knows, maybe we'll see you back here before too long?'

'Yeah, I look forward to it.'

'I'm sure we can find another ghoul for you.'

Samantha and Rebecca came out to join the trio.

'Right then,' said Rebecca. 'Luke, put your luggage in the trunk and we'll be on our way. I think I'll drive, I don't trust your hangover.'

He did as instructed then turned and hugged Margaret and Chet one last time.

'See you next time,' he said before walking around the back of the car and getting in. Rebecca reversed out of the car port and aimed the car down Hummingbird Lane.

And as she did that, Luke and Samantha looked out of the side window at Chet in his shorts and bright t-shirt, and Margaret in her colourful printed dress.

Luke waved.

And then, for no apparent reason, Chet started to tap dance.

It was no half hearted measure. He gave it all he had.

His arms reached up and down. His legs shimmied in a blur.

Chet had a manic grin in place.

It caught them all by surprise.

'What is that crazy man doing?' asked Samantha sternly.

'I don't know,' replied Luke with a broad smile across his face. 'But he sure seems happy.'

ENDNOTES.

[1] **Extra Sensory Perception (ESP).**
The term 'Extra Sensory Perception', although already in existence, gained widespread recognition following the 1934 publication of J.B. Rhine's book (wait for it…) "Extrasensory Perception". Rhine (1895-1980) is credited, in much of the popular media at least, as being the father of modern scientific parapsychology and founded an eponymous Research Laboratory in North Carolina, in the United States.

Extra Sensory Perception often gets abbreviated to ESP, and whilst this phrase remains in common use, many researchers now prefer to use the term psi (from the Greek letter Ψ; pronounced "sigh"; see Thouless, 1942), originally employed to refer to the unknown factor in psychic functioning, but also appropriated widely to refer to 'psychic functioning' itself . Psi thus includes both ESP and Psychokinesis (the idea that you can use your mind to bring about change in the environment), as there is some thinking that both phenomena are, in actual fact, different aspects to the same mechanism. A mechanism of information transfer.

There are three facets to Extra Sensory Perception.

i. Telepathy, which is basically mind-to-mind transfer.
ii. Precognition, when you predict an event that is yet to take place. This event is unforeseeable through the use of inference or deduction from information held at the time.

iii. Clairvoyance, the contemporaneous information gathering of unseen and unknown places and objects, without the use of regular perceptual channels. A commonly misapplied term - it is not 'predicting the future'.

[2] Whom to test?

One question of interest is whether everyone has psychic abilities, or only a certain few. Although many of today's experiments work with regular people who don't present themselves as psychically gifted (undergraduate students being a popular participant group in University settings), other studies have utilised specialist groups, including creative types (Dalton, 1997) and practitioners of meditation (Schmidt & Schlitz, 1989; Matas & Pantas, 1972).

The idea that twins might hold heightened telepathic abilities has also intrigued many. Indeed the very first volume of the Journal of Parapsychology detailed an experiment by Kubis & Rouke (1937) that worked with one identical set and five non-identical sets of twins. Under the research protocol, an experimenter would work through a set of ESP cards, viewing each card one-by-one, and at the same time, the twins would simultaneously call what card they thought was being viewed. The researchers were interested to see whether the twins made the same calls, but no significant overall effect emerged.

[3] Centres of Parapsychological Research.

Some of the bigger centres include (in no particular order): The Koestler Parapsychology Unit, University of Edinburgh, UK; Institut für Grenzgebiete der Psychologie und Psychohygiene (IGPP), Freiburg, Germany; Rhine Research Laboratory, North Carolina, USA; The Mind-Science Foundation, San Antonio, USA; Centre for the Study of Anomalous Psychological Processes, University of Northampton;

There are also societies around the world which maintain an interest in parapsychology, and even fund research. Some of the more historically prominent include The Parapsychological Association; The Society for Psychical Research in London, UK; and The American Society for Psychical Research, based out of New York, USA. Both societies also publish parapsychological journals: The

Journal of the Society for Psychical Research and The Journal of the American Society for Psychical Research.

Other parapsychological journals include (in no particular order): The Journal of Parapsychology; The European Journal of Parapsychology; The International Journal of Parapsychology and The Journal of Scientific Exploration.

As touched upon in Chapter 5, modern parapsychology is predominantly concerned with laboratory based investigations into psi. Whilst there is justifiable concern that the artificiality of such conditions may have little crossover with real world activity and may even inhibit certain types of psychic functioning, it is the best way to cut out unwanted and worrisome factors such as fraud and self-deception. This is not to say, that alternative approaches are not undertaken. Investigators have invoked qualitative approaches (trying to unravel experiences through phenomenology) and survey data (working out how many people experience a particular event) as well as field-based enquiry.

Research is predominantly empirical in nature meaning that scientific discovery is generated through observation and measurement, not theorising. Many experiments conform to the hypothetico-deductive model where a hypothesis is stated (e.g. people who are good at art will outperform less able artists on ESP tasks), and either confirmed or rejected under experimental conditions, by manipulating the relevant variables. E.g. test two sets of participants on the same ESP task – those with very high artistic ability and those with a very low one, whilst controlling for other factors that might have an influence over the experimental outcome.

As there is a certain amount of natural variation in any dataset, statistics are used to compare results between groups and against mathematical probability. The statistics enable the researcher to calculate whether differences are meaningful or whether they are caused by predictable chance fluctuations. When an experimental outcome exceeds a certain level (known as the alpha level) where it is unlikely that chance could account for the outcome, it is known as 'significant'. This level of significance corresponds to a probability, or 'p value', which represents how likely the experimental outcome was to have been caused by chance; $p = .01$ means that there was a one-in-one hundred probability, $p = .001$ means it was one-in-one thousand. The smaller the p value, the less likely that chance can account for the results, and the greater confidence the researcher can hold that a genuine effect is at work.

[4] **Sometimes people won't believe, no matter how good the evidence presented to them is.**
It seems odd that people who represent themselves as scientists can take a strong anti-science position, and unequivocally declare that positive evidence for psi will never convince them of its validity. In one example, (taken from Harvey Irwin's book: An Introduction to Parapsychology; 2004), noted British psychologist Donald Hebb declared way back in the 1950s: "why do we not accept ESP as psychological fact? Rhine has offered us enough evidence to have convinced us on almost any other issue…I cannot see what other basis my colleagues have for rejecting it…My own rejection of [Rhine's views] is - in the literal sense – prejudice." Hebb (1951, p45), cited by Irwin (2004, p253).

[5] **Brickbats aimed at parapsychology.**
Through the years, sceptics (or counter-advocates – as some have chosen to term them) have employed a variety of means and methods to discredit parapsychology. The phrase counter-advocate is in many ways preferable, as all parapsychologists need to be sceptical, cautious and questioning when examining paranormal phenomena.

Rhetoric.
If you say something often enough, whether true or not, people will start to believe it. For many years, sceptics have employed rhetorical argument in place of empirical evidence or proof to bolster their positions. These 'armchair criticisms' range from representing their opinion as accepted fact (e.g. "most scientists do not believe in psi" - the insinuation being that those-in-the-know think it's all nonsense), through to more insidious accusations that fraud is rampant. Mainstream media outlets often make the mistake of accepting these views without suitable scrutiny, thus perpetuating them.

Often the rhetoric has no basis in reality. For example, in 1983 the sceptic Martin Gardner wrote: "Positive evidence [for psi] keeps coming from a tiny group of enthusiasts, while negative evidence keeps coming from a much larger group of skeptics." Gardner (1983, p60). Later, the researcher Charles Honorton took Gardner to task, in a paper that examined the state of scepticism. In it, he wrote: "Gardner does not attempt to document this assertion, nor could he. It is pure fiction. Look for the skeptics' experiments and see what you find." Honorton (1993, p 194). There is a certain irony in fighting rhetoric with rhetoric.

Whilst there have been experiments in recent years by sceptical researchers such as Susan Blackmore and Richard Wiseman, Honorton's overall point remains valid. Sceptical scientists who are actually prepared to go out and conduct quality research over a number of experiments are rare creatures. In many ways, this comes as little of a surprise. If an experimenter does not believe that psychic functioning is valid, they are unlikely to give over much time establishing evidence to support such a view. Why go to lots of time and trouble trying to disprove something that cannot exist?

Give misleading details of events, methodologies, or just getting it flat wrong.

By misreporting (wilfully or through clumsiness) how experiments are conducted, sceptics try to make researchers look amateur or incompetent. Protocols detailing fraud control and experimental safeguards mysteriously disappear in commentaries, which in turn leads to the allusion that positive results probably have conventional explanations, or that experimental data should be considered untrustworthy.

In an ongoing example of such behaviour, the counter-advocate Mark Hansel has continued with a fraud theory way past the point of reasonableness. Commenting on a sequence of experiments (The Pearce-Pratt Series; see endnote 23), Hansel suggested that the results must be due to the subject cheating in some way. During the trials, the experimenter (Pratt) and participant (Pearce) were isolated in separate rooms, in separate buildings, and Pearce asked to determine psychically the order of cards that Pratt observed in his room. Hansel suggested that one way of accounting for positive results was if Pearce left his room, and traversed to the building to where Pratt was working (turning over the cards and recording them), observed the order

through a window above the door, then returned to his own room and wrote down the recently witnessed order. Unfortunately, this explanation turns out to be less than likely. Aside from the fact that Pearce was never seen behaving in such a way during any of the test sessions, Hansel's suggestion that Pearce could have peered into Pratt's room and witnessed the card order from atop a chair in the hallway was based on scrutinizing an incorrect building plan (see Stevenson 1967). The cards could not have been seen from outside the room. Hansel has also provided alternative fraud hypotheses, including collusion between Pratt and Pearce – but unfortunately makes no effort to provide the reader with any evidence.
In the first edition of his book, Hansel pointed out that Pearce had failed to give a declaration that he (Pearce) had not cheated during the ESP trials. Subsequently Stevenson sought and received just such an assurance from Pearce, but Hansel has continued in both of the later editions of his book to maintain that no such pledge has been made. See: Hansel (1966, 1980, 1989).

The problem of 'how experiments get represented' was examined (albeit some time ago) by Irving Child, who was the Chairman of Psychology at Yale University. Child (1985) reviewed various books that detailed the dream telepathy experiments conducted at Maimonides Hospital in New York State (see endnote 15) and found that each of the books misrepresented the methodology in such a way as to create the impression that the experiments were flawed, and therefore invalid. Child concluded that "Some of those books engage in nearly incredible falsification of the facts about the experiments; others simply neglect them." Child (1985, p1228).

In 1991, a separate group of psychologists looked at a large selection of psychological text books to see how they reported parapsychology. Examining 64 such publications, the authors found that the majority were recycling the same-old tired erroneous information, writing: "most of the coverage was cursory…[there was an] over reliance on secondary sources… most textbooks that cover the topic present an outdated and often grossly misleading view of parapsychology." Roig, Icochea & Cuzzucoli (1991, p157-160).

In a more up-to-date analysis, McClenon, Roig, Smith & Ferrier (2003) examined 57 textbooks that were available at the time. They concluded that descriptions of parapsychology were on the whole 'inadequate' stating that many books were sceptical and critical of parapsychology, and that much contemporary research was completely overlooked.

Claiming a lack of replicability.

'Replicability' is the clunky term that refers to whether experimental results can be reproduced by other researchers, in other laboratories, using the same methodology. It is rightly considered a basic requirement of science. A lack of replicability suggests that there may be a problem with the original procedure and that positive results may be due to artefact. One should bear in mind however, that failures in replication are sometimes due to unforeseen experimental variables, and not necessarily flaws in the overall approach. In fact, there may be many reasons why a particular experiment could fail: maybe the procedure employed was taken from a write-up that was incomplete? Maybe other factors were not considered in the earlier experiment that later had a profound effect, such as psychological or environmental differences? Or perhaps the new experiment is not actually a replication? If some new experimental element (however apparently small) was being tried and positive results were not obtained, should this experiment be considered a replication failure?

Sceptics will often claim that whilst some parapsychological experiments generate positive effects, these effects are not replicable. Unfortunately, this line of attack is bogus. Various research fields in parapsychology have demonstrated replicability, including the ganzfeld (see endnote 27) and micro-PK research (see endnote 60). In 1995, Jessica Utts, Professor of Statistics at the University of California was asked by the Central Intelligence Agency to evaluate the state of parapsychological research. She reported that: "Using the standards applied to any other area of science, it is concluded that psychic functioning has been well established. The statistical results of the studies examined are far beyond what is expected by chance. Arguments that these results could be due to methodological flaws in the experiments are soundly refuted. Effects of a magnitude similar to those found in government-sponsored research at SRI and SAIC have been replicated at a number of laboratories around the world. Such consistency cannot be readily explained by claims of flaws or fraud." Utts (1995, p289).

Wrongly attacking the statistics.

Statistics are used throughout the sciences. In medical trials, before any new drug is released, extensive testing is conducted to determine whether the drug does what it is supposed to, and whether there are any side effects. In order to accomplish this, the new drug and alternatives (often including a placebo), will be administered and their effects measured. Then, mathematical comparisons are made between the groups to examine the efficacy of the drug and whether it produces a significant outcome.

In psi research, statistics are also commonly used and the statistical calibre of the analysis is generally very high. But by attacking the statistics, you attack the integrity of the results. In 1983, Ray Hyman, a sceptical researcher, took Charles Honorton's review of the ganzfeld database to task for being incorrectly calculated. This raised a lot of interest in the sceptic camp, which suggested that it was an example of parapsychology failing to do their sums properly. Charles Honorton responded, suggesting that Hyman had not done his sums properly, and the two of them parried back and forth for a while (Hyman 1983, 1985; Honorton 1983, 1985), with both men producing their own formal meta-analyses (a way of combining lots of experiments into one big study). In the end, third parties were called in, to find out who was right, and Robert Rosenthal of Harvard, (one of the top meta-analysts in the world) in collaboration with Monica Harris, recalculated the ganzfeld data. They found that the positive results stood, and could not be attributed to flaws in the methodology as Hyman had suggested (see Harris & Rosenthal, 1988; Harris & Rosenthal, 1988a).

In 1986, Hyman and Honorton came together and issued a 'joint communiqué' detailing guidelines for future ganzfeld research that they hoped would lead to an accepted methodology for such research. Some years later, Honorton, Berger, Varvoglis, Quant, Derr, Schechter & Ferrari (1990) published experimental data that had been conducted in line with the agreed protocols. The results were statistically significant, and thus purported to show that ESP effects were genuine. However, controversy continues in this research area, see endnote 27.

Claiming the results are there – but are due to something else, or that they are trivial.

Having shown that anomalous effects appear to exist, the battleground has recently shifted into one of interpretation. Anomalous effects do seem to exist, informed sceptics grudgingly concede. But then in a bizarre turnaround, they go on to claim that these effects are not due to paranormal functioning, but due to some unknown variable(s). What this unknown variable or error is, they cannot explain, but it is definitely not paranormal.

One of the problems with our current state of knowledge and experimentation is that most paranormal effects are fundamentally statistical in nature. You cannot guarantee any effect will be produced at any given moment. All you can do is highlight how it occurs more often than it should over a series of trials - and that these occurrences cannot be attributed to chance. Often this deviation is small, e.g. micro-Psychokinesis with REGs (chapter 15), and might only involve a 0.5% shift from chance expectancy. Some sceptics argue that because these deviations are so slight, they cannot matter. However, effects that consistently deviate from mathematical expectancy, and which do not appear in control trials, demand explanation. When positive effects coincide with people trying to generate paranormal functioning, and cannot realistically be explained away by invoking chance, fluke or methodological error – there follows (logically) that a paranormal mechanism may be in operation. It may be that sceptics simply don't like this option, and therefore prefer to dismiss the results.

Sometimes, small effect sizes are held up as incredibly important. In the 1980s, a large-scale study was conducted in the United States examining whether low doses of aspirin could reduce the risk of heart attacks. Over 22,000 asymptomatic male physicians were involved, and as the results came in the experimenters saw that the results were overwhelmingly in favour of the hypothesis. The study was ended prematurely in January 1988, because of the strength of the effect (see The Steering Committee of The Physicians Health Research Group, 1988), and advice put out to take an aspirin once a day, to reduce the chances of a heart attack. And yet the effect size from the aspirin study is smaller than that for ESP experiments (as per Honorton's 1985 meta analysis). The question then is how irrelevant can laboratory ESP data really be?

The untrustworthiness of the human condition.
In considering anecdotal psi episodes, the following line of reasoning is sometimes proposed. It is an argument redolent of David Hume's: "On the Nature of Miracles", and advocates that:
i. Paranormal episodes are hugely uncommon, hugely improbable and outside the realm of 'accepted' science.
ii. Human beings regularly misperceive events and/or lie about them.
iii. We should therefore consider paranormal phenomena to be misperceptions or untruths.

Whilst human beings do misperceive events and lie, they also get things right from time to time. Since there is good evidence for psi in the lab, the assumption that it occurs in the real world must surely seem valid? The idea that we can dismiss all anecdotal evidence because psi is not an everyday occurrence and the human condition is apparently 'flawed' seems somewhat misconstrued.

Fraud.
Whilst there is undoubtedly large scale fraud when it comes to commercial psychic operations (whether fairground mediums, phone line psychics, magic amulets or dubious new age practices) one should not make the mistake of tarring everything with the same brush. With that in mind, it is important to note that fraud has been an issue (albeit an infrequent one) in parapsychology, and has taken two forms, either the subject wilfully cheating in a test, or an experimenter fiddling the data.

Two cases where experimenters were believed to have cheated, or been caught cheating were the work of S.G. Soal who is thought to have falsified some of his data; and experiments by Walter Levy, who whilst working at the Institute for Parapsychology in 1974 was caught tampering with measuring equipment. Such occasions do a great deal of harm to the image of parapsychology, and the field responds robustly, by discounting all work by such a researcher.

In the other form of fraud, James Randi's 'Project Alpha' from 1983 illustrates how it may be the subjects who cheat. Randi sent two magician colleagues to volunteer for macro-psychokinetic testing (see endnote 39 for definition), who then employed techniques from the world of magic to dupe researchers. Whilst they were unable to cheat under formal experimental conditions, some introductory (and less controlled) trials excited the experimenters enough to foolishly, but informally, report these results to colleagues. Randi took this as an example that parapsychologists did not knowing what they were doing. Episodes such as Project Alpha are useful, as they show the way forward in strengthening methodologies and preventing repeat occurrences. Modern parapsychology uses tightly controlled experiments that are often designed with the assistance of professionals such as magicians (e.g. Bem & Honorton, 1994) to examine possible threats to the integrity of the research. In turn, there are certain measures of psi (such as influencing radioactive decay) where no-one can explain how magic, conjuring, or sleight of hand can be used by participants to generate positive results (see chapter 15).

Unfortunately fraud occurs in all scientific disciplines, but it may be that parapsychology actually sees less because the 'eyes of the world are upon it'. To suggest that fraud is endemic and can account for the large number of positive results is nonsense, for it suggests a vast global conspiracy by experimenters (which there is no real way of refuting). Secondly, it discounts the validity of well considered, properly conducted research. In recent years, there have been no known episodes of fraud in the field, and yet positive results continue to be produced. Furthermore, experimenters go to serious lengths to minimise opportunities for cheating, and often take on the recommendations of counter advocates. Many experiments now use CCTV to monitor participants, produce multiple copies of raw data so that they cannot be altered, and use 'blind' procedural methods, so that no individual is in a position to tamper with experimental data to alter a study's outcome.

With regard to the idea of subjects cheating, one commonly advocated theme is that parapsychologists spend their time with spoon benders and other 'conjurers', who are out to dupe them into believing they are psychic, over a sequence of trials. This in itself is untrue, as most studies use one subject for one single trial. Even if a cheater gets into the subject pool and manages to cheat, by somehow circumventing the controls, their impact on the experiment as a whole is minimal. In a neat twist to illustrate how positive effects can be obtained with people who would not want to cheat, Schmidt, Morris & Rudolph (1986) recruited sceptics to act as their participants in a psychokinesis experiment. Despite an apparently 'less than amenable' participant pool, a significant PK effect emerged ($p = 0.0032$).

There is no good theory to explain paranormal functioning.
If psi exists, what mechanism is at work? Without theory, argue some, parapsychology will remain a pseudo-science. Whilst there are many theories in parapsychology that purport to explain the phenomena, none can really lay claim to providing "the" answer. As such, parapsychology is predominantly considered a bottom-up approach (i.e. data is collected and theories subsequently formulated) rather than a top down approach (where a theory is made and experiments conducted to test the theory). Some critics suggest that because parapsychology is currently lacking in definitive explanations for how phenomena might operate, it is somehow irrelevant. Ultimately, such a view is difficult to defend. If lots of experiments show something to exist, but the theory lags behind, you cannot simply choose to ignore the data.

Prejudice?
In 1984, the US army asked the National Academy of Sciences to report on various elements of human performance. Its research arm the National Research Council thus formed a panel to look into these elements, which included parapsychology. There were no parapsychologists on the panel (the people you would expect to be most familiar with the research) but there were two strongly sceptical members (Ray Hyman and James Alcock, both executive council members of the sceptical organisation CSICOP). Predictably, the final report (Druckman & Swets, 1988) said that there was no "scientific justification from research conducted over a period of 130 years for the existence of parapsychological phenomena." (p22). Although bizarrely even this does not make sense, the panel only looked at research conducted in the preceding 20 years.

Members of the Parapsychological Association (Palmer, Honorton & Utts, 1989) challenged the findings of the NRC report. In a strongly worded article, they wrote: 'After a careful review of the NRC report, we found that although it is written in scientific language, it does not represent an unbiased scientific assessment of parapsychology and that the conclusion of the report is unwarranted.' (p31). Furthermore: "We have documented numerous instances where, in lieu of plausible alternatives, the Committee's attempts to portray parapsychology as "bad science" have been based upon erroneous or incomplete descriptions of the research in question, rhetorical enumeration of alleged "flaws" that by its own admission frequently have no demonstrable empirical consequences, selective reporting of evidence favourable to its case, and the selective omission of evidence not favourable to its case." (p44).

It also turned out that the panel chairman had telephoned one of the authors of a background paper (Robert Rosenthal of Harvard, mentioned previously) and asked him to withdraw his positive conclusions concerning paranormal research. There seems little doubt that the panel chosen to review parapsychology had made up their minds before writing their report.

[6] **Types of spontaneous ESP experience.**
Louisa Rhine (1953) classified a basic taxonomy of four types of spontaneous ESP experience. Realistic Dreams, Unrealistic Dreams, Hallucinations and Intuitive Impressions. Intuitive impressions can be considered akin to 'hunches'.

[7] **Intuitive impressions account for around a quarter of spontaneous ESP episodes.**
See: Rhine (1962); Sannwald (1963).

[8] **How many people experience spontaneous ESP?**
John Palmer's (1979) US based research suggested that between 50 and 55% of respondents had experienced waking or dream based spontaneous ESP during their lifetimes. In another American based study, Greeley (1987) found the number of people who claimed to have had a spontaneous ESP episode to be around the two-thirds mark.

Haraldsson & Houtkooper (1991) reported research incorporating over 18,000 respondents from the USA and various European countries. They found that over half of respondents in the USA, Italy and Iceland believed they had experienced a psychic episode, and the average across Europe was 46%. Norway and Denmark came lowest in the survey at 24% and 25% respectively, whilst Great Britain weighed in at 44%.

A survey from New Zealand (Clarke, 1995) questioned 385 participants, and found that 46% of respondents believed they had experienced a telepathic episode, and 23% a clairvoyant one. Telepathy is the most prevalent form of spontaneous ESP in both Europe and the United States (Haraldsson & Houtkooper, 1991). PK experiences seem much lower; Clarke (1995) for example reported that only 3% of respondents believed they had experienced PK.

[9] **Themes people experience during spontaneous ESP episodes.** They often involve death, accidents, marriages and illnesses. See: Rhine (1956); Schouten (1981); Virtanen (1990).

[10] **Distance does not seem to prevent spontaneous episodes.** Many examples of ESP at a distance exist within the literature. One example - detailed by Louisa Rhine in her book "Hidden Channels of the Mind" - concerned a woman named Marion who was contemplating suicide in New Jersey in 1947. As Marion's thoughts turned to ending her life, she heard the voice of a friend instructing her not to do so. It was as though the friend stood in the room with her. Marion did not commit suicide and the next day, an airmail arrived from the friend (who lived more than a thousand miles away). In the letter, the friend recalled that she was awakened from her sleep because she thought Marion needed her help right away. Marion reported that: "It was one of the most beautiful and mysterious experiences I have ever had." Rhine (1961, p17).

In the laboratory, distance between individuals also seems to have no bearing. Indeed, way back in 1962, Rhine & Pratt wrote: "When, after some decades of introductory enquiries, better controlled and more systematic investigations were undertaken, the distances that were introduced, often incidentally, did not seem to affect the results in any regular way. In some experiments there were higher rates of success at the shorter and in others at the longer distances." (p67). Distance has continued to show itself to be of little importance. In light of this, some have argued that if ESP operated through conventional energy transmissions (i.e. electromagnetic waves), one would see a diminishing in the strength of any signal, the further one went from the source (the inverse square law). In other words, signals generated by human beings would quickly be no stronger than background level 'noise' where, it is argued, you wouldn't be able to make out the original signal. Whilst the logic of this argument seems plausible, it would be a mistake to dismiss signal based theories too quickly. One does not necessarily need a strong signal to convey a message, one simply needs a detector that is sensitive enough to find the signal within the morass of other signals and noise. Where such a detector might reside in the human body is another matter.

[11] **Low order activity.**
Spontaneous experiences tend to occur when the percipient is alone, and when physical activity is low. Irwin (2004) cites an Australian study he conducted which showed: "Ninety percent of the sample reported being engaged in minimal activity such as sleeping, sitting or standing. The activity level was moderate (as in walking or playing a piano) in 7 percent and substantial in only 3 percent." (p39).

[12] **Breakdown of ESP experiences.**
Rhine (1962) reported that 44% of ESP experiences took the form of Realistic Dreams. In turn, Unrealistic Dreams constituted 21%, Intuitive Impressions 26%, and Hallucinations 9%. It may be that certain experiences (such as dreams) are more likely to be reported as case material than, say, hallucinations, which some respondents may associate with mental illness, and thus be reluctant to mention.

[13] **Around ¾ of precognitive experiences occur in dreams.**
See: Orme (1974); Steinkamp (2000).

[14] **Half of precognitive experiences come to fruition within 48 hours, and 80% occur within a month.**
See: Green (1960); Orme (1974).

[15] **The Maimonides Dream Studies.**
Through the years, various experiments have been conducted to determine whether dream states are conducive to ESP phenomena. Dream Telepathy studies proved particularly popular during the late 1960s and 1970s, due in no small measure, to research carried out at the Maimonides Medical Centre in New York. For a lengthier

explanation and examination into such work, the reader is directed to the book “Dream Telepathy” (Ullman, Krippner & Vaughan, 1986).

In a typical experiment, a participant would enter the sleep lab (where they were due to spend the night), and be introduced to the experimenters, including one who was to act as Sender (the person who tries to “send” a target image telepathically). Then they would be hooked up to an EEG (which measures the brain’s electrical activity), and put to bed. The sender meanwhile would leave the test area, and be given a sealed envelope, within which one of twelve possible photographs had been randomly selected.

Sleep is characterised by distinct stages that repeat throughout the night in roughly 90 minute cycles. As the individual falls asleep and becomes drowsy (stage 1) there is a reduction in what’s known as alpha rhythm (conscious and alert) from 10Hz to around 8Hz alongside an overall reduction of amplitude. As the stages continue, drowsiness gives way to light and then deep sleep. Brain wave frequency and amplitude both continue to slow towards theta waves (4-7Hz) and get interspersed by short active moments known as ‘sleep spindles’ of higher frequency (13-15Hz) that last for a couple of seconds. REM sleep (or Random Eye Movement where the eyeballs move around chaotically) is associated with dreaming, and sees the brain in a highly active state (greater than when the person is awake). It is the fifth stage of the cycle and usually lasts for around 15 minutes, although this period can increase in length throughout the night, and the final REM cycle may last up to an hour.

Back in the laboratory, as the participant slept, an experimenter watched the EEG to determine when REM sleep started and stopped. When REM began, they would operate a buzzer in the room where the sender waited, who then tried to transmit (telepathically) the photograph contained in the envelope. When REM sleep finished, the sleeper was woken and asked to describe the dream they just experienced, which an experimenter then wrote down verbatim. Afterwards, the sleeper went back to sleep, and the procedure was repeated. Every time REM began, the buzzer was buzzed, and the sender tried to send the picture telepathically, then the sleeper was subsequently woken and asked to describe the dream. This would happen throughout the night. Then the transcripts for each described dream were given over to judges who had copies of the 12 possible target photographs. They would then mark each photo based on how close it was to the transcript (basically trying to rank the similarity between each picture and each transcript). The most similar was ranked at number 1, the least at 12. They then passed their judgements to another researcher who compared the ranked list with the target picture. The judges did not know which photograph was the target one. If the real target photo was in the top half of the rankings, 6 or higher, then the trial was marked as a hit, a success. If it came in the bottom half, it was considered a miss, a failure. If there was no effect at play, we would expect an even distribution of hits and misses. 50/50. When the Maimonides data is put together (25 studies combined into one big study), it reveals a positive effect where almost 80% of the studies saw the target photos ranked in the top half. The chances of that - millions to one. Krippner, Honorton & Ullman (1972) also suggested that instead of using the same target over multiple trials, employing different targets for different sleep episodes could facilitate better telepathic scoring.

Dream experiments have also been conducted away from Maimonides. One recent example was by Dalton, Steinkamp & Sherwood (1999), where the trio of experimenters acted as their own subjects in a 32 trial dream-ESP experiment. The sleep and dream periods for each experimenter took place within their home residences, and during the night (usually around 3am) a dynamic video clip was randomly selected by a computer system within the University laboratory where they worked. This clip was then played a predetermined number of times, but no output was made to either a television or speakers; (i.e. the selected clip was read by the video player but not displayed). The next morning the researchers sat down and watched four clips: one target and three decoys. Following this, they ranked the clips according to how closely they matched the dreams from the previous night. Once this had been completed, the researchers formed a consensus vote based on their scores. If the target clip was correctly identified (1/4 chance) then this was marked as a hit, if it was not (3/4 chance) this was marked as a miss. The results showed a 47% hit rate, versus 25% expected by chance, equivalent to a p value of 0.006.

Aside from successes, there have also been failures. Keith Hearne (1981) used emotionally close pairs to examine whether an electric shock applied to one, would be detected and reflected by a change in the heart rate of the other. Various conditions were looked at, one of which was REM sleep, but Hearne failed to find an effect. In a similarly conceived experiment, Hearne & Worsley (1977) investigated emotionally close pairs with a common phobia. The phobic stimulus was presented to the conscious member of the pair, and both heart rate and eye motility were then measured in the dreaming subject. Once again, no significant results were found. Sherwood, Roe, Simmonds & Biles (2002) tested three subjects and asked them to use a majority vote technique in ranking target pictures against dream mentation. The results were non-significant. In a slightly later study, Roe, Sherwood, Luke & Farrell (2002) based out of the same laboratory, used a similar majority vote/consensus judging protocol with dynamic targets, to test clairvoyance. Once again, non-significant results were found.

[16] **Linking events.**
Say you're driving your car and approach a corner where – whoa(!) – you get a bad feeling. You decide to slow down, and as you go around the corner, you find your lane blocked and a ten ton lorry coming the other way. Since you are travelling slowly, you have time to brake to a standstill, but if you had been travelling at your previous speed, there would have been nowhere to go, except straight into an accident. That bad feeling could have saved your life.

Whilst some might view this episode as ESP in action (and it's inevitable ESP exists in the real world, not just the laboratory) there are other options to consider. If the road had not been blocked, would the strange feeling still be considered prophetic? Did the corner look dangerous in a conventional sense, such that your unease was predictable and would have caused you to slow anyway? Was the bad feeling and subsequent driving experience little more than coincidence?

On a mundane level...people often say 'I knew that song was about to come onto the radio'.
Chance and coincidence mean people will correctly anticipate a radio song from time to time, as a matter of course (especially if you listen to certain radio stations with limited playlists). There may also be cueing effects at work that people fail to consciously absorb at the

time. Maybe the DJ mentioned tracks he was due to play, or a particular artist's name earlier in their show? Maybe the song was just an immensely popular one at the time, and its broadcast inevitable?

Picking up the phone knowing who's on the other end.
We tend to be creatures of habit, and are inclined to phone at particular times. Sometimes we think of someone, and five minutes later that person is on the other end of the phone line. The question is whether we were expecting that phone call somewhere in the back of our minds because of some predictable pattern? What about the umpteen times we think of someone who doesn't telephone five minutes later? What about an hour later? What if they don't ring at all?

Waking up moments before their alarm clock goes off.
With the alarm clock phenomena, does the experience happen on a weekday when the alarm clock is set to ring and wake us for work? If so, we must consider our own internal body clock anticipating wake up time. Alternatively, many alarm clocks click ever so quietly just before they go off, as the alarm mechanism moves into place. Perhaps you attend to the click in your partially conscious state, and wake up just before the bell?

Of course, it does not mean that some of these events might not have psi origins, it simply shows the problems in disseminating real world events and fathoming what mechanisms are at play.

[17] Conviction rates for spontaneous ESP - (when people are *convinced* they have had an ESP episode).
People hold a greater confidence in the authenticity of spontaneous psi (e.g. in the real world), than when they are asked to produce psi on demand in the laboratory. Conviction rates vary across different types of spontaneous ESP: 84% for intuitive impressions, 23% realistic dreams, 19% unrealistic dreams.
See: Rhine (1962); Green (1960); Schouten (1981, 1982).

[18] Is the receiver picking up information, or is the sender targeting them?
Some models (e.g. The Psi Mediated Instrumental Response model; see Stanford and Thompson, 1974), have proposed that individuals actively use psychic functioning to scan the environment for

personally relevant information. In other words, information is not put 'out there' by a sender, it's picked up by the receiver. One might argue that such a model would lead to an overload of information, but one can look to conventional perception for comparison, where our progress through the world is governed by constantly monitoring the environment. Whilst some of this is conscious, much of it is subconscious and we only become aware of it when a threshold is breached (e.g. we come across something unexpected or personally meaningful). Cognition is then prompted to adjust one's behaviour in response to the stimulus. Psychology textbooks often illustrate this effect by asking you to imagine yourself at a cocktail party. Even though it's busy and you're having a one-on-one chat with a friend, you can suddenly find yourself tuning in to the conversation held across the room because your name has been mentioned.

[19] **Spontaneous ESP tends to take place between emotionally close people.**
See: Rhine (1956); Sannwald (1963); Schouten (1981).

[20] **Zener Cards.**
Zener Cards were the eponymous ESP targets created by psychologist Karl Zener in response to JB Rhine's efforts to make ESP experiments easier to judge. They were comprised of five distinctive symbols: circle, square, wavy lines, cross and star. Before Zener cards, studies tended to use regular playing cards, which apart from having a low likelihood of being guessed correctly (1/52 on a closed deck) and having inherent biases (people preferring face cards over numbers), have two types of information on them: number and suit. If the Seven-of-Spades was the target card and you guessed Seven-of-Clubs (which was the wrong card, but with the right number and also a 'black' symbol), were you half right? In having a single characteristic, Zener cards simplified matters into simple hits and misses. The use of Zener cards is what is known as a forced-choice protocol, where participants know they can only choose from five possible symbols.

[21] **ESP cards and some of the early experimental approaches.**
Various protocols were developed through the years when using physical cards. Some of the main ones:

i. Cards were placed on a table in front of the experimenter and subject, and the subject was allowed to stare onto the back of the card before calling it.

ii. Cards were first looked at by the experimenter who subsequently placed them face down on the table, before the subject guessed.

There were two obvious problems with protocols i. and ii. Firstly, it was suggested that the experimenter might unconsciously cue the subject and influence their responses. Secondly, it became clear that there were slight differences in the patterns on the backs of early ESP cards (they were hand made), which could enable an individual to 'learn' which card corresponded to which symbol. Once this problem was identified, the immediate solution was to seal each card within its own envelope. Another solution was to remove the cards from the subject's vicinity altogether.

iii. With the ESP cards removed from the test area, a second experimenter in a separate room was responsible for looking at each card and acting as a sender. The second experimenter would work through the stack of cards according to a pre-arranged time schedule (e.g. 20 seconds per card), whilst the first experimenter who sat with the test subject would record whatever calls they made.

iv. The same basic set-up as iii, except the second experimenter (outside the test area) did not look at the cards in his/her care. This experimenter would take a card off the top of the stack (without looking at it), at pre-arranged intervals and place it onto a different pile. The experimenter sitting with the test participant would write down the calls made and once the test run was complete, would compare the guesses with the actual order.

The key thing for these ESP tests was to conduct lots of trials. Although one would expect (on average) to get around five correct calls (out of twenty-five) in a test run, mathematical chance dictates that we would expect to see a variety of other outcomes (whether twelve, or zero, or eight) due to chance, and as a matter of course. So researchers repeated their experiments lots of times to minimise the likelihood of flukes biasing the overall results. The more trials a researcher conducts, the more likely it becomes that statistical bumps get ironed out. In other words, lots of trials should conform to chance expectancy if there was no ESP effect at play. The flip side to this is that when an apparent effect is found, statistical tests can be applied to determine how improbable the results are - if chance alone should be held responsible.

[22] **Clairvoyance vs Telepathy vs Precognition.**
It is important to remember, when examining clairvoyance or telepathy, that one can never rule out precognition as the ESP process at work. It may be that the receiver is simply looking into the future, to a point when the correct information (such as the ESP card order) was revealed to them, and employing that information during the test phase.

[23] **The Pearce-Pratt series.**
The Pearce-Pratt series was a famous group of experiments conducted in the 1950s. A young theology student named Hubert Pearce underwent a series of ESP trials under the supervision of experimenter Gaither Pratt comprising 74 complete runs over four sets of trials. Each run used a full pack of 25 cards, and mean chance expectancy predicted that Pearce would get around 370 correct (from the 1850 guesses he attempted) if no effect was at work. In fact, Pearce chose the correct target card 558 times. The corresponding p value was $p < 10^{-22}$, which if put another way, corresponds to odds that are greater than 1-in-100,000,000,000,000,000,000,000.
See: Rhine & Pratt (1954).

[24] **The Decline effect.**
One effect uncovered from tests with Pearce, and one that can be found throughout many repetitive parapsychological tests, is what's known as the "decline effect". Put simply, the decline effect is where people tend to score more hits during the earlier part of experiments. This phenomenon exists for both ESP (e.g. Rhine, 1969) and PK studies (in 1944, Rhine & Humphrey had noticed the effect during their experiments using dice to test PK). The decline effect has been attributed to boredom taking hold. One can imagine how difficult it is to maintain a high level of interest in guessing hundreds of Zener cards, with little in the way of feedback. Proponents of the Observation Theory of psi (see endnote 59), speculate that the decline effect may be part and parcel of the way psi operates.

[25] **ESP Card data from 1882-1939.**
In his book, the Conscious Universe, Dean Radin examined ESP card data from 1882-1939, incorporating studies from 186 separate publications. A purported ESP effect was uncovered (i.e. the hit rate was above chance, and was attributed to ESP information transfer) that corresponded to odds in the stratosphere.

Radin also looked into what is known as the file drawer effect, which is a theoretical measure that calculates how many null studies (i.e. those where no ESP effect was witnessed and which may thus lurk in someone's file drawer somewhere) would be required to cancel out the positive ones. Radin wrote: "...we find that the file drawer would need to contain more than 626,000 reports. That's more than 3,300 unpublished, unsuccessful reports for each published report. This again demonstrates that chance results and selective reporting cannot reasonably explain these results." Radin (1997, p97).

Side note: Radin's book was reviewed in the science journal Nature in October 1997, by I.J. Good, who suggested that Radin had got his maths wrong, and that the file drawer figure was actually much lower. The tone of the review was therefore critical and negative to both Radin and (by association) parapsychology. Unfortunately, it transpired that Good was the one who had got his sums wrong (Radin had simplified the calculated odds to a level more comprehensible by a general readership, which Good took as the actual figure). Radin wrote to the journal asking them to correct such a clear mistake, and various other letters were also sent (including one from Nobel Laureate Brian Josephson) asking them to amend such factual inaccuracy. In an extraordinary editorial decision, Nature chose to ignore the chorus of dissent, and in the end it took almost nine months from the initial review until Nature published its correction. The reader is directed to Brian Josephson's website for a more detailed explanation. (See Josephson in references).

In an analysis that looked at more recent research, Honorton & Ferrari (1989) examined 309 precognition studies conducted between 1935 and 1987 that incorporated close to two million experimental trials. Once again, strong support for the existence of ESP emerged. The study showed that participants scored hits slightly more often than they should, equating to a p value of 6.3×10^{-25}.

Do the stats add up?
With studies showing positive ESP results, there was a suggestion in the 1930s that assumptions of randomness may be wrong. For example, a study using a Zener pack (closed deck, five cards for each of the five symbols) equates to one-in-five odds of calling a card correctly by chance. The 'maybe there's something wrong with randomness' line of attack was refuted in two ways:

i. Mathematically by the President of the Institute of Mathematical Statistics. See: Camp (1937).

ii. And by empirical means. In 24 separate experiments, card calls from one trial were compared with the actual order from the following trial. As subjects were not trying to guess correctly the cards for the following trial, one would expect hits to correspond to chance expectancy, which they did. In other words, ESP effects stemmed from specific hits on specific cards, and not from random successes. See: Pratt, Rhine, Smith, Stuart & Greenwood (1966).

Problems with the methodology.

Cueing.
As mentioned above, it was suggested that face-to-face protocols where the experimenter and receiver sat across from each other, might lead to unconscious cueing by the experimenter in the form of body language nuances or facial tics. The simple solution to this valid criticism was to separate experimenter and participant. Other potential pitfalls included:

Recording errors.
Where hits (or for that matter misses) were incorrectly marked on the experimenters' recording sheets. The solution was to implement independently collated records, and employ double checking protocols.

Inadequate shuffling.
Where a previously used ESP pack was not shuffled correctly, leading to the possible problem that part of the card order stayed the same. The solution was to introduce better and more thorough shuffling practices.

Optional stopping.
The idea that researchers would choose to call a halt to experiments whilst they were statistically significant. The solution – to predetermine exactly how many trials were to be conducted, and how many subjects were to be employed, before the experiment was started.

[26] **The autoganzfeld.**
The autoganzfeld stemmed from efforts to produce a universal procedure for testing ESP that could be done in any laboratory with any experimenter. It is fundamentally a computerised version of the original ganzfeld methodology, which uses sensory calming (detailed below) to aid participant scoring. It shows how parapsychology has responded to criticism in order to produce better and better protocols, and it's fair to say that the autoganzfeld is a methodology that has satisfied many critics of ESP research.

With the autoganzfeld, a participant (the receiver) enters an isolated sound-attenuated room and is seated in a big comfy chair where halved ping pong balls are taped over each eye, and a red light shone onto the face. Soothing white noise is then relayed via headphones. Fundamentally, the receiver is placed into pleasurable auditory and visual states - for there is the idea that such a state of consciousness (where the participant is highly relaxed and enjoying diminished sensory stimulation) helps facilitate inwardly derived perceptions. There is the further suggestion that ESP is fundamentally a weak signal, in a sea of noise, and that by cutting down on extraneous and diverting information, that signal can be accessed more readily.

In a separate isolated room, the 'sender' is seated in front of a computer screen, and the computer system randomly selects a video clip from a databank. This video clip (known as the target) is shown to the sender who tries to transmit it telepathically to the receiver. The target is shown over and over, for up to half an hour. The experimenter is unaware which target clip has been selected, and remains so until the cessation of the trial.

Back in the receiver's room, the receiver is letting their mind wander, and vocalising their stream of consciousness - they say what they are seeing and hearing and feeling in their world. This stream of consciousness is relayed to the control room, where the experimenter produces a transcript of the verbalisations, and where a hard copy recording (e.g. audiotape/CD) is made.

When the transmission phase of the experiment is complete, the headphones and ping pong balls are removed from the receiver, and the experimenter reads out the transcript. Then, on a computer screen in the receiver's room, four video clips are shown. The real target and three decoys. The receiver has to choose which clip most closely matched the experience they had.

Each ganzfeld experiment is comprised of many trials, and often each participant will only be tested once (e.g. complete one trial). As with the ESP card experiments, the more times the experiment is run, the greater the chances of minimising the likelihood of flukes biasing the overall results. According to chance expectancy, one would expect to see an average hit rate of around one-in-four or 25% across trials if no psi effect was evident.

If people are scoring above chance, it provides a degree of evidence that some sort of information transfer is in effect. Scoring less than chance expectancy is known as 'psi missing', and is a highly infrequent phenomenon.

Cheating.
In an autoganzfeld study, opportunities for cheating are countered by the experimental setup. The two parties – sender and receiver – are physically separated by quite some distance, and there are often closed-circuit cameras or alarms in place, to make sure they don't leave their rooms and collude or spy on each other.

It's important to remember that since the target is not selected until the experiment starts, there is no way any party can find out in advance what said target is. Furthermore, target images are always presented in randomly derived orders, with every stage of the experiment being recorded so that no accusations of data tampering can be made afterwards. As mentioned above, the experimenter is unaware of the selected target during testing, and considered 'blind' to the target until after the judging phase has been completed. This prevents them exerting undue influence (e.g. cueing) on the selection made by the receiver.

Improvements in technology improve experiments.
As technology has progressed, methodologies have benefited. Ganzfeld clips used to be kept on video tape. It was argued that since the target clip was played to the sender many times, there may have been a degradation in picture quality (in comparison to the decoys). An astute receiver could then pick up on this, and work out that since a clip had degraded, it must have been played more often, and that it was the target. To get around this, researchers began to use two video players, one for the sender which could be watched many times and one for the receiver. Nowadays, clips are digitally stored, and the issue of clip quality has gone away.

[27] **Meta analyses for ESP ganzfeld data.**
In 1994, Bem & Honorton produced a meta analysis of the ganzfeld database that included 28 ganzfeld Studies from between 1974 and 1981, and 10 autoganzfeld studies from 1983 through 1989. Of these, the 28 conventional experiments produced an overall hit rate of 35% (corresponding to a p value of 2.1×10^{-11}), whilst the automated experiments equated to a combined hit rate of 32% ($p = 0.0008$). In both sets of data, the expected hit rate, according to chance, was 25%.

Curiously, a 1999 meta-analysis by Milton & Wiseman failed to find the overwhelming results that Bem & Honorton calculated. The authors incorporated thirty additional studies (between 1987 and 1997) that had not been included in the original meta analysis and found no statistically significant effect overall. This prompted a right hoo-ha, with many critics pointing out that the authors had included studies that deviated quite substantially from traditional ganzfeld protocols (i.e. they were elaborations and variations upon the ganzfeld theme), and thus should have been excluded from analysis because they were not faithful replications. This criticism is important as one needs to decide how far an experimental protocol can deviate from accepted practice before it becomes a substantively different procedure and not a replication. By including some of the more 'untried' procedures, the Milton & Wiseman meta-analysis found non-significant results. There was also criticism, as to the 'cut off point' for the included studies. In 2001, Bem, Palmer & Broughton included 10 new studies that were published after Milton & Wiseman's cut off date. With these additional studies included, significantly positive results from the ganzfeld experiments were once again found (overall hit rate: 30.1%; effect size: 0.051; $p = .0048$). Addressing the issue of what to include in meta analyses, the authors advised that future analyses should properly distinguish orthodox replications from less standard or modified ones.

One thing to remember with the ganzfeld is that even with the most successful studies, the results are statistical in nature. One cannot guarantee that any particular trial with any particular participant will produce a positive effect. All that can be said is that over a series of trials, positive results do occur massively more often than they should by chance.

[28] **Creative types in the ganzfeld.**
In 1997, Researcher Kathy Dalton presented the results of a ganzfeld study that worked with actors, musicians, creative writers and artists. 32 participants from each category took part, and Dalton found an overall hit rate of 47% (60 hits from the total 128 trials, z score = 5.2) when 25% should have been expected by chance. This equated to odds of around 10 million-to-one. Musicians proved the most successful group with a 56% hit rate $p = 0.0001$, then artists (50%, $p = 0.002$). Both the actors and creative writers also scored above chance (both at 41%, $p = 0.037$)
See: Dalton (1997).

[29] **Factors at work.**
Long term self-belief.
The importance of 'belief' (confidence in whether paranormal phenomena are real and attainable) has long been considered. In 1943, Gertrude Schmeidler labelled believers as 'sheep', and sceptics (or disbelievers) 'goats'. The importance of belief was highlighted in a 1993 meta-analysis by Tony Lawrence that examined ESP studies where participants had declared themselves sheep or goats. Lawrence

looked at 73 forced choice studies conducted over a 45 year period, involving more than 4,500 participants. The meta analysis showed how goats tended to score at chance levels (not below), whereas sheep scored above chance. Once again, the results were hugely significant $p = 1.33 \times 10^{-16}$ (effect size of 0.029). Lawrence's research tallied with previous work by Palmer (1971).

Other studies have looked at belief and psychokinesis. Gissurarson & Morris (1991), for example, found a positive correlation between PK scores and the sheep/goat measure, whilst both Rubin & Honorton (1972) and Debra Weiner (1982) found likewise.

Short-term belief.

Other researchers have focussed on the importance of belief at the moment when people are asked to produce a psi event. Like many tasks in everyday life, there are moments when we feel more or less able to carry out a chosen task effectively. In terms of psychokinetic functioning (although the sentiment is widely applicable), Batcheldor (1984) has suggested: "What seems to matter is the balance of belief over doubt at the very instant when a PK event is about to occur, rather than the long-term attitude of belief or doubt that exists before the sitting commences." (p108).

ESP, extrovert data.

There has been the suggestion that extroverts are more likely to score above chance on ESP tests than non-extroverts or neurotics, and a multitude of studies have examined this through the years (e.g. Humphrey, 1951; Green, 1966; Shrager, 1978; Thalbourne & Jungkuntz, 1983). A meta-analysis from 1998 (Honorton, Ferrari & Bem), incorporated some 60 independent studies equating to almost 3,000 subjects. They found a very small weighted correlation ($r = 0.09$) corresponding to a p value of 0.000004, but drew attention to the fact that the dataset was non-homogenous (i.e. results were all over the place). Thus, the idea that extroverts do better on ESP tasks is a theory supported by very limited evidence.

Experimenter effects.

One important factor that may influence a study's outcome is the experimenter's belief in psi (see Delanoy, 1997; Wiseman & Schlitz, 1997, 1999; Watt & Ramakers, 2003). If the researcher does not think psi is valid, or does not expect positive results to be obtainable – it is probable that the study will only produce chance results. It may be that something deep rooted is taking place where the experimenter either blocks or facilitates paranormal effects (through his or her own psi functioning), and moulds the study outcome to conform to his or her expectations. The reader is directed to Smith (2003) for a recent discussion of experimenter effects.

[30] **Poltergeist.**
The word 'poltergeist' is German in origin, and translates roughly as 'noisy spirit'. People used to attribute poltergeist events to non-living, discarnate entities.

[31] **Object movement.**
Although object movement has been known to occur in both poltergeist and haunt situations, it is much less common with haunts.

[32] **The fraud hypothesis to explain everything away?**
The fraud/deception hypothesis is a commonly invoked explanation for poltergeist events. As fraud has been uncovered previously, some commentators simply assume that it must be behind all incidents. Fraud might simply be 'inventing a story', or (at the other end of the spectrum) entail sophisticated trickery with elaborately staged events. Even relatively unskilled individuals can make things seem paranormal, and as any magician will attest, distraction is usually the key. A fraudster can bide his or her time, and move or throw a target object when third parties are looking the other way, or not paying attention.

[33] **What percentage of poltergeist cases can be attributed to fraud?**
This figure varies. William Roll (1977) has put the figure at 14%, whilst Gauld & Cornell (1979) put the figure at 12%. In 1989, Huesmann & Schriever reported a fraud rate of 26%, in the 54 cases they had investigated.

[34] **Telepathic hallucination.**
Telepathic hallucination can be considered a comparatively rare form of ESP, where psychically derived information is conveyed to an individual in the form of a strong and realistic perceptual experience, in the absence of conventional external stimuli.

Hallucinations are internally derived perceptual experiences (i.e. they exist in the mind alone) and are very similar to conventional perceptual experiences. Unsurprisingly, this is because they are both underpinned by the same basic neurological architectures and processes. In terms of functioning (and to keep things straightforward), think of perception as a sequence of electrochemical neuronal firings that occur moment-to-moment, within the brain. These firings differ according to the originating stimulus and the processing subsequently employed. Depending on the type of stimulus, a variety of specialised brain structures are employed, and there are qualitative differences in which neurons get fired, their rate of firing, and the pattern of spreading activation across the brain.

Neuronal firing can also be induced artificially. Neurosurgeons, for example, can apply localised electromagnetic fields to patients' brains to study areas responsible for motor activity. Perceptual episodes such as visual hallucinations can be brought on by stimulating the prefrontal cortex (Blanke, Landis & Seeck, 2000), whilst emotions such as fear and happiness can be generated by stimulating parts of the temporal lobe (e.g. Meletti, S., Tassi, L., Mai, R., Fini, N., Tassinari, C.A., & Russo, G.L., 2006). A recent study even managed unexpectedly to evoke the sensation of déjà vu (see Hamani, McAndrews, Cohn, Oh, Zumsteg, Shapiro, Wennberg, & Lozano, 2008).

In turn, one might ask whether ESP (and by inference - telepathic hallucination) is brought about in much the same way that a neurosurgeon can trigger perceptions and feelings. Is there some sort of interaction between consciousness and the receiver's brain that triggers neuronal activation and facilitates a particular experience (even if it is oblique)? Of course, how psi interacts with the actual neuron and tips it over its firing threshold is a separate matter, although speculation has been put forward that there might be some kind of quantum interaction at work (e.g. Josephson & Pallikari-Viras, 1991). If psi is teleological (goal seeking) as some suggest (e.g. Schmidt, 1984), no specific knowledge of brain physiology would be needed by an agent - simply the desire to bring about a particular goal state. Psi would fill in the mechanistic blanks.

Aside from people influencing people, it may be that certain places have characteristics that can trigger brain activation. If someone sees a figure in a supposedly haunted building, one possible explanation is that neurons in the occipital lobe (responsible for vision) become anomalously triggered, and a subsequent 'vision' generated. Peoples' reports of non-descript ghosts (i.e. spectral outlines and shapes) would fit in with the idea that the occipital lobe is activated in a fairly unfocused manner.

One point to consider here is that when people have 'conventional' hallucinations, they often realise that what they are seeing or hearing is not real. People make cognitive evaluations of the experience and search for underlying causes (e.g. tiredness, drugs, over-stimulation, pathology, etc) to help explain the effect. It may be that with certain experiences people struggle to find rational explanations, and thus look to the paranormal for meaning. Clearly, personal beliefs and expectations have a major role to play here.

[35] **Mood affects perception and cognition.**
Although a bit of a cliché, consider the following… it is late at night and you are walking home by yourself. You decide to take a shortcut through the local graveyard. The moon is out, there is a chill in the air and you feel very much alone.

In the scenario above, it stands to reason that you will have heightened apprehension and anxiety (perhaps for good reason). This state freely impacts upon how you perceive events around you. You attend more readily to unexpected or unusual stimuli, such as the wind in the trees or strange shadows, things that might not bother you if you were walking around your garden at midday. In attending to these events, your mind seeks to provide explanations ("it's okay, it's just the way the light hits the gravestone"); but explanations are limited by your knowledge base and understanding of the environment. If something unusual is perceived, and there is no clear explanation as to the cause, the mind may seek to create one. Certain venues, which may have paranormal associations can prompt paranormal explanations far more instinctively. Even something as mundane as a creaking door that sometimes slams shut, may be attributed to something spooky, when in actual fact it is the draught pattern from the corridor outside – a draught pattern that would be very hard to discern without suitable investigation.

[36] Apparitions/Ghosts.

One of the traditional views of apparitions, as characterised in various films, is of an ambiguous swirling mist. In fact, if one were describe a prototypical apparition (taken from people's recalled experiences), apparitions tend to be of quite substantive form, capable of blocking out what's behind them, and visible in mirrors. Having made an appearance, more often than not the apparition will vanish or fade away or leave a room by walking through an actual doorway (walking through walls seems rare). They leave no trace. Apparitions are also reported to be capable of making noises (e.g. rustling clothes, clicking heels) that are appropriate to whatever activity they are doing. Reports seem to suggest that when people encounter perceived ghosts, the apparition itself cannot be touched.

Often the apparition will have no business with the experient, and will simply get on with its own affairs. In rarer cases, the apparition might speak and convey specific information. Apparition episodes occur most often around crisis moments. Apparitions don't have to be dead people, although something like 2/3 of apparitions are of people known to be deceased (see Haraldsson, 1985) At other times, the apparition may correspond to a person who is still alive – it 'pops by' to convey some kind of message. Often apparitions are believed to be people who met their deaths violently (see Haraldsson, 1994).

[37] Sensed Presence.

A sensed presence is the feeling that you are not alone, when in objective terms you are. It seems to be a relatively common phenomenon amongst recently bereaved widows (Simon-Buller, Christopherson & Jones, 1988). In turn, there is crossover with some 'religious experiences' where people believe that God or some divine spirit is with them. It is a phenomenon that has been investigated in particular by Michael Persinger at Laurentian University in Canada. Realising that people with temporal lobe epilepsy were more likely to have 'religious experiences', Persinger sought to induce such states in non-epileptics by subjecting them to weak electromagnetic fields. He created a helmet that did just that, and results appeared to show that by

stimulating specific regions in the brain, the phenomenon could be artificially induced.
See: Persinger & Healey (2002); Persinger (2003).

Subsequently, Granqvist, Fredrikson, Unge, Hagenfeldt, Valind, Larhammar & Larsson (2005) produced their own body of research into sensed presence and temporal lobe activation that failed to find the effect. They suggested that Persinger's work was not properly double-blinded, and that subjects who were prone to religious experiences had 'sensed presence' experiences regardless of whether they were subjected to magnetic fields or not. Persinger responded by pointing out that the Granqvist *et al.* research was not a replication. They had failed to generate "a biologically effective signal" each and every time (i.e. they didn't make sure their equipment was working effectively with each participant they tested), and failed to subject their participants to adequate periods of stimulation. With regard to criticisms of his work, he added that his experiments were correctly double-blinded, and that other research has shown if you co-vary for suggestibility you still get a sensed presence effect.

[38] **Is there something special with the environment in haunt sites?**
Often with haunted buildings, one particular room might get a reputation for being especially 'active'. This has led to research examining whether there's something tangibly different about that room compared to others, and one line of consideration has been to ask whether there are particularly unusual/strong electromagnetic or geomagnetic fields present.

It has been found that many older building have stonework with high iron content in the walls, and if the iron becomes magnetised, it can lead to a pretty decent localised electromagnetic field effect. In much the same vein as the explanation given in endnote 34, it has been suggested that when a person stands within certain electromagnetic fields, there may be some sort of 'influence' over neuronal firing that causes visions.

Two venues that have been investigated for such electromagnetic effects were Dragsholm Castle, Denmark and Engso Castle, Sweden (Nichols & Roll, 1999). By focusing on areas in each building where staff and visitors had reported anomalous experiences previously, some support was found for the electromagnetic field explanation. Interestingly, at Dragsholm Castle, Nichols was standing in an area associated with ghost sightings when *he* reported seeing a figure pass by.

It may be that anomalous electromagnetic fields do not need to interact solely with visual systems to create paranormal experiences. Stevens (2001), has shown in the laboratory how exposure to such fields (at levels similar to those found in allegedly haunted venues) can prompt physiological and psychological changes. It may be that 'a sense of unease' is generated by these fields, which is then attributed to some sort of paranormal source in certain places, or under certain circumstances.

One study conducted in April 2001 (see Wiseman, Watt, Stevens, Greening & O'Keeffe, 2003) tried to examine whether environmental factors such as localised electromagnetic fields or air temperature correlated with areas where people reported 'haunt' (i.e. paranormal) experiences. The researchers asked over 200 participants to spend time alone in various rooms of Edinburgh's underground vaults (subterranean rooms with limited artificial lighting), and note whether they had any unusual experiences (e.g. the feeling of being watched, seeing strange phenomena, etc) in particular spaces.

Edinburgh's vaults are a tourist attraction, and the tour company responsible for guiding visitors has kept historical records of the times and places when tourists have encountered unusual experiences. The experimenters were thus able to rank the rooms in order of how haunted they were perceived to be. (Participants who knew which rooms were regarded as haunted were not included in the data analysis).

The researchers found a significant correlation between the historical records of haunted-ness, and the number of mean experiences the experimental participants had. In other words, there was consistency across time that certain areas within the vaults saw higher numbers of experiences than others. However, analysis of the environmental factors failed to confirm that the venue's electromagnetic fields, air temperature, or air flows were correlated with unusual experiences. Instead the best predictors as to whether any particular room would prompt an experience were: the existence of a dimly lit doorway off the room, a high ceiling and a large floor space. It may be that an individual's sense of vulnerability is heightened by these 'exaggerated' environmental factors.

The Case of Vic Tandy.
It doesn't have to be electromagnetic fields that prompt anomaly. Vic Tandy was an electrical engineer, working alone in his laboratory one time, when he looked up and briefly saw what appeared to be a person (an experience that that his laboratory cleaner had also reported). Tandy had a think and tried to work out if there was a conventional explanation for these supposedly paranormal events. He took some measurements and worked out that a ventilation fan at one end of the lab was part responsible for creating what's known as a standing wave (a fixed-point vibrational pattern). The standing wave was operating at 19Hz, which is a frequency that can have direct effects on the eyeball. In effect, the fan was inducing the visions he and his cleaner had experienced.
See: Tandy & Lawrence (1998).

[39] **Macro and micro Psychokinesis (PK).**
A macro PK event is where the mind is able to affect an object in the environment (e.g. making a chair levitate) and you don't need statistics to see the effect. It's obvious what has happened. Micro-PK, on the other hand requires statistical analysis. If you roll lots of dice and try to make sixes show up more often than not, you need to maintain a record of each throw and then analyse whether sixes actually appeared more frequently than they should have. Micro PK has become the method of choice when investigating such 'mind-matter' events as it seems easier to generate in the laboratory, the safeguards are much stronger, data collection can be fully automated and there is a stronger tie-in with some theoretical explanations as to what might be taking place (e.g. Observation Theories). Modern micro-PK measures use quantum processes (like white noise in circuitry) and the suggestion is that consciousness interacts at a quantum level (see endnote 59).

The experimental literature suggests certain variables can boost PK functioning. It may be that people skilled in meditation are more capable (Matas & Pantas, 1972; Braud & Hartgrove, 1976; Honorton,

1977), and that trial feedback is useful (Braud, 1978). Other factors that can aid performance include false feedback (Isaacs, 1981), competition (Debes & Morris, 1982), hypnosis, and good old fashioned Pavlovian reinforcement. See Gissurarson (1992) for a review.

[40] **Recurrent Spontaneous Psychokinesis (RSPK).**
A phrase coined in 1958 by Pratt & Roll, with regard to the Seaford Disturbances (see endnote 41).

[41] **Michael Lessing.**
Michael Lessing was a twelve year old boy who lived in Seaford, Rhode Island. Michael was believed to be the source of poltergeist activity, which included the unexplained movement of household objects.
See: Pratt & Roll (1958) – The Seaford Disturbances.

[42] **Arnold Brooks.**
Another poltergeist case revolved around Arnold Brooks, a thirteen year old who lived in Newark, and whose home was at the centre of a poltergeist outbreak. Arnold lived with his grandmother with whom he did not get on, and psychiatric evaluations at the time found highly inflated levels of aggression towards her. It is suggested that the poltergeist activity was Arnold's subconscious response to the environment, created to provoke his exit from the home.
See: Roll (1969) – The Newark disturbances.

[43] **Julio Vasquez case.**
See: Roll & Pratt (1971) – The Miami Disturbances.

[44] **Sex bias.**
For some time, it was believed that girls were more likely to be the source of a poltergeist incident than boys, but it seems this may have had more to do with socio-historical propensities than actuality. More recent findings have shown little in the way of a differential. William Roll (1977), in providing a review of poltergeist cases wrote: "[the] favoring of women, however, was due to two early periods. During 1612-1849 there were ten females versus four males, and during 1850-1899, 16 versus three. The proportions then evened out for 1900-1949

to 16 versus 14, and for 1950-1974 to 14 versus 15. Apparently sex was generally not important when determining agency." (p386).

[45] **Problems with RSPK as an explanation.**
Critics have highlighted various potential pitfalls with the RSPK hypothesis.

Firstly, critics (e.g. Martinez-Taboas, 1984) point out that diagnosing psychiatrists were often not blind to the subject's potential role in any poltergeist outbreak, and were therefore (possibly) more open to the idea that psychopathology was present. Conversely, one might argue that the suggestion of bias operating solely in favour of an RSPK hypothesis is flawed; it may well be that once aware of the relevant circumstances, clinicians' prejudices and biases may well have operated in the opposite direction. It should be pointed out that once Martinez-Taboas's line of reasoning is taken to its logical conclusion, the integrity and legitimacy of all non-blind psychiatric evaluations, no matter how mundane should be queried.

Secondly, people argue there's a lack of control data. As Irwin asks: "Are poltergeist agents really in the grip of psychological conflict? Survey data to this effect actually are inconclusive because control subjects have not been surveyed; thus one might well find similar levels of conflict reported by people (especially adolescents) who are not poltergeist agents." Irwin (2004, p159). Some counterpoints to this position can be considered. It may well be that other people hold similar levels of conflict and are not poltergeist agents, but this accordingly does not rule out the legitimacy of the diagnosis. Other individual differences may need to combine to produce an effect. Additionally, although there is no control data, the diagnostic process obviously relies upon the psychiatrist's comparison of any given patient against others with whom they are familiar, including the 'normal' population – a process that, for regular psychiatric diagnoses, is considered legitimate.

Finally, laboratory tests with suspected RSPK agents have proved unconvincing. Roll (1977) reported that 'only' 3 out of 6 studies with such agents produced significant PK performances. One might say it is unfair to criticise the RSPK hypothesis on the basis of this, as poltergeist anomaly is considered (in part) a manifestation of blocked release towards authority figures within the RSPK environment. It seems fair to suggest that testing under incongruent conditions might fail to recreate the psychological conditions required to produce an effect.

Repressed anger and resentment diagnoses were often highly specific to subjects in poltergeist cases, and there has been a lack of similar findings for people in haunting cases. Overall, it may well be that diagnostic bias had some contributory effect when investigating RSPK agents, but this is unlikely to account for the results as a whole. What these cases seem to show is that an inability to release pent-up emotion is in some way fundamental to RSPK, and that RSPK activity provides relief for the individual. Effects tend to be localised because the individual typically seeks to escape from 'problems' associated with that specific environment.

[46] **Psi can operate across time.**
Experiments seem to suggest that psi can operate across time. Some successful PK experiments, for example, have asked participants to influence events that have already taken place (e.g. Schmidt, 1976). Under these protocols, probabilistic events (derived from Random Event Generators; see endnote 59) are recorded by an automated system but remain unobserved (at the time) by consciousness. At some point afterwards, participants try to influence the events by attempting to interact with the REG at the time the events were generated. Various ESP protocols examining precognition have also proved successful (see Honorton & Ferrari, 1989). Support from these experiments suggests that a conventional 'arrow of time' explanation (i.e. time only moves forwards and we cannot jump to different points in it, whether backwards or further forwards) may be incorrect.

[47] **The lingering effect.**
The lingering effect refers to how psi might continue to exert an effect some time after the original interaction was made. In one of the first published examples of the lingering effect, Watkins, Watkins & Wells (1973) carried out an experiment where subjects tried to speed up the resuscitation of anaesthetised mice. It was found that mice recovered significantly faster if placed in a container that had previously been attended to by PK agents - the suggestion being that special properties

were given over to that point of space, affecting systems within that area for a period afterwards.

[48] **The Tohono O'odham.**
Pronounced: "Toh-na Oh-tahm".

[49] **Electronic Voice Phenomena & Psychic photography.**
Electronic Voice Phenomena refer to audio recordings where, upon playback, voices and noises are heard that were not apparent at the time of recording. These voices are often attributed to deceased individuals. Unsurprisingly, the causes of the sounds are incredible hard to authenticate, with explanations being attributed to all sorts of conventional possibilities including electrostatic noise, radio interference and even something as obvious as people making noise in the background during a recording. In turn, the idea that certain noise phenomena are coherent or meaningful may be due to personal interpretation and individual expectancy. EVPs are rare phenomena.

Psychic/Paranormal Photography.
Psychic or paranormal photography developed from the hugely dubious field of spirit photography where images of the deceased were magically materialised onto film (thus promoting the idea that we survived death). Fraud was endemic, but the idea of asking subjects to affect blank film found favour later on, and for a while became a method of 'testing' psychic claimants. Once again, fraudulent methodologies were easy to invoke and many of the results warrant little consideration.
For Kirlian photography, see endnote 63.

[50] **Pre-stimulus Research.**
As the name suggests, pre-stimulus research works by gauging whether people respond to a stimulus before it is presented. The stimulus may take the form of an electric shock, or possibly a 'startle' of some sort (e.g. a blast of unpleasant noise). If the stimulus is designed to provoke an emotional response (i.e. by using emotionally arousing material), then studies are often referred to as pre-sentiment research.

[51] **Pre-sentiment research methodology.**
Under a pre-sentiment methodology, the participant is seated in front of a computer display and hooked up to a device that measures skin conductance. This is a measure of electrical conductivity, and conductivity varies with the level of arousal a person experiences in relation to a stimulus.

Once the participant is ready to begin, they press a button, and several seconds later the computer randomly selects a photo from a database. The participant simply sits and looks at it. Then they press the button again and the process is repeated. For the vast majority of the experiment, the selected images are emotionally neutral, and provoke little in the way of a subsequent physiological response. However, due to the randomised nature of the setup, photos of a strongly arousing nature are sometimes displayed. The physiological response is not only stronger for these (occasional) images but also starts to take place slightly before they are shown. There is no conventional mechanism through which the participant could guess when the provocative material was to be presented. No cueing or pattern effects. The explanation, therefore, is that ESP is utilised to prepare the participant for the provocative material.

Similar sorts of effects can be produced when using auditory stimuli. Relaxing white noise is played to the participant in place of visual stimuli. Randomly, what is known as a 'startle noise' is played and as with the pictures, people begin to respond before the startle is actually offered to them.

[52] **Pre-stimulus and pre-sentiment study outcomes.**
Early research into pre-stimulus effects were conducted by Zoltan Vassy (1978) who found that skin conductance would shift in anticipation of randomly applied electric shocks. Later Radin (1997a) demonstrated substantially different response patterns for emotional and neutral photographs (using measures of electro-dermal response, heart rate and blood pressure volume). Once again, anticipatory effects correlated with the emotive material. In the same year, Bierman & Radin (1997) reported the results from 5 pre-stimulus experiments, concluding that: "...different patterns of material like erotic versus violent, elicit different anticipatory response patterns, i.e., for erotic material peaking is just before the exposure starts while the EDA

[electro dermal activity] preceding violent material peaks 3 sec[onds] earlier." (p689).

[53] **Measuring psychokinesis using dice.**
Dice were seen by researchers as random systems that might be open to psychic influence and enjoyed prominent use in the 1940s and 1950s. Under most protocols, there would be two conditions. i) an intention condition – where participants would try to bring about dice faces according to a pre-selected and randomised protocol (e.g. for each trial the experimenter would tell the participant what to aim for - "Generate Threes"). ii) A non-intention condition where no target number was given out and no deliberate influence attempted. As the statistical likelihood of each face is close to 1/6 (see problems of bias, endnote 57), overall deviations from this figure would help show whether an effect was at work.

With this form of psychokinesis, we are at the micro level, meaning that statistics are required to see what is going on. You carry out thousands of dice rolls, calculate the 'hit rate' (occasions when the target number and rolled dice numbers match) and then determine whether the hit rate falls within chance expectancy.

Examples of dice research through the decades
See: Rhine (1943); Rhine & Humphrey (1944); Mangan (1954); Ratte (1960); Steilberg (1975); Nash (1981).

[54] **Overall, what do dice results indicate?**
A meta analysis into dice research was carried out in 1991 by Radin & Ferrari. It incorporated a mass of data from over 50 years involving 148 studies and 52 separate investigators. They compared conditions where people actively tried to influence the dice (which equated to 2.59 million dice rolls), against those where people did not apply intention (i.e. control studies, c.153,000 dice rolls). Results showed that when people 'willed' a certain face to come up, it did so, ever so slightly more often than it should have (around 1.2% more often). A small difference perhaps, but one that was so unlikely that the chances of it happening by chance were absolutely enormous ($p < 10^{-70}$). A filedrawer analysis (see endnote 25) indicated that nearly 18,000 additional non-significant studies would be required to nullify the observed results, and thus selective reporting was not a reasonable

explanation for the effect. The control studies showed no anomaly, and were within chance expectancy.
See: Radin & Ferrari (1991).

[55] **Different ways to measures PK.**
Through the years, different methods have been employed to test for PK. Individuals have been asked to influence compasses, scales, the physiological systems of other people (so called bio-PK), and the tumbling of polystyrene balls into sorting bins. They have also been asked to bend metal, fog film, and influence magnetometers.

[56] **Casinos make their money, by working the average.**
Casinos stay profitable by playing the average. Whilst the next spin of the roulette wheel is unpredictable, the overall behaviour of the system is predictable (see endnote 59; stochastic systems), and this predictability enables the casino to set odds where they always 'win' over the long term.

The small effect sizes obtained from PK experiments in the laboratory cast doubt on whether it would be possible for an individual to go to a casino and influence a roulette wheel or dice at the craps table to their advantage. The effect size from the dice meta analysis suggests that over hundreds of rolls, your desired face might show up a 'few' times more often than it should (i.e. a percentage shift from chance expectancy of around 1.2%), but the house advantage in a casino for craps is around 2% (as an average across the different wager types). In other words, you should still expect to lose money. Additionally, it's not necessarily the case that laboratory effects can translate into casino effects. In the laboratory, there is none of the psychological stress of playing with your own money, or the presence of other gamblers who might desire different rolled outcomes.

[57] **Problems with dice research.**
Several issues have been raised with dice experiments.

Weight bias.
Consider the six face on a die where the values are marked by 'scooping out' spots. It has six scoops taken out of it. Thus, there is a slightly greater likelihood of throwing a six than a one because a six is

marginally lighter, and heavier faces are more likely to end up face down. For dice with painted faces, the opposite is true.

Throwing the dice.
A practised individual can learn to throw dice in a way that makes desired faces more likely, through (for example) a flat release from the hand. Researchers tried to overcome this by having minimum standards of throwing which included: groups of dice being rolled at once, throwing them over a long distance, and bouncing the rolled dice off multiple surfaces. In addition, automated throwers were sometimes used.

Recording errors.
Another problem was that since dice research was typically conducted before the advent of automated recording devices, the experimenter might have made recording errors when writing down the dice outcomes. To help overcome this, some experiments used two researchers who independently wrote down the dice faces, and subsequently ensured that they matched up. Other experimenters preferred to take photographs of each dice trial in order to provide a fixed record.

[58] Tackling bias. What the analysis shows.
The 1991 Radin & Ferrari meta-analysis specifically looked into the dice bias problem. As discussed above, some die faces are lighter than others because they have more scoops taken out (compare a six with a one). In the 1991 report, a separate analysis was undertaken that looked into studies that used all six faces as targets in equal measure (what's known as a balanced protocol). This amounted to 69 studies, and results still confirmed that an apparent PK effect was present, ($p < 10^{-11}$. File drawer ratio of 20 to 1). The authors thus concluded that bias was not large enough to account for the overall results and suggested some other effect (e.g. psi) was present.

[59] Random Event Generators.
Background on randomness, and why it is useful.
Events, whether big or small, exist as probabilities. At the (big) macro level, which is the level you and I inhabit on a daily basis, the probability of something out-of-the ordinary happening is fairly limited. Taking a kitchen table as an example, the random activity of

all the billions of particles constituting the table average out, and the table stays where it is. That's why the world passes us by pretty much as expected; you don't get tables moving across the room of their own accord. In addition (and rather importantly for our world view), we can be fairly sure of our predictions for the table's behaviour at points in the future.

But when you get down to the atomic scale or 'quantum' level, where systems have far fewer (quantum) particles moving around in their random ways - the state of the system, at any one moment, becomes impossible to predict accurately. The state of the system at any moment can only really be considered in terms of probabilities (by a wave function that includes all potential states). Until you measure the system, you have to rely on a mathematical expectancy of what the system is likely, and for that matter unlikely, to be doing.

The randomness of these quantum systems is useful for parapsychologists. By measuring the system moment-to-moment, you can see if it starts to behave in a more predictable and ordered way (compared to the mathematical models) when people try to 'influence' it with consciousness. The underlying suggestion is that if a random system takes on greater bias (or order) when people try to influence it, the more confident you should be that some interaction is at work.

Random Event Generators.

Random Event Generators (also known as Random Number Generators) are the most popularly used means of measuring psychokinesis. One needs to clarify here the dichotomy between 'true' and 'pseudo' REGs. Pseudo REGs use a mathematical algorithm to generate an output, and this is a function of the algorithm and an initial starting value, known as the seed number. Although the output might look random, foreknowledge of the algorithm and seed number renders the output entirely predictable. True REGs typically utilise physical phenomena. Some REG systems, for example, use semiconductors as their source of randomness and sample the output currents from a pair of diodes to produce a data stream. These currents fluctuate moment-to-moment due to a number of factors including thermal and shot noise. In other words, the outputs are underpinned by quantum effects. True REGs are often used where proper randomness is imperative, such as with encryption software, and some computer based casinos.

Stochastic systems.

True REGs are an example of what's known as a stochastic system. In stochastic systems, the overall behaviour is predictable, but each event is not. If you take a perfectly balanced coin and toss it a thousand times, you can predict with some certainty that at the end, you will have a similar number of heads and tails – a number that falls within the parameters of chance expectancy. Heads and tails may not be entirely equal but they should be close enough to be explained by chance, say 492 heads and 508 tails. But if you take any single coin toss, you cannot predict in advance what the next toss will be; there is a 50/50 chance of either a head or a tail. This is the essence of a stochastic system.

Random Event Generators (continued).

Historically, REGs in parapsychology have tended to use either radioactive decay or quantum noise as their sources of randomness. These systems are useful for measuring PK because they are considered 'closed to influence'. With radioactive decay, for example, 'closed to influence' means that particle emission cannot be speeded up or slowed down by known techniques. Therefore, the appearance of any system bias is considered evidence by many that an anomalous mechanism (i.e. PK) is in operation. By combining the physical source with a measuring device (thus creating a Random Event Generator) certain measurement thresholds can be set where the physical process is converted into simple binary outputs (i.e. lots of ones and zeros).

Radioactive decay REGs.

REGs that used radioactive decay as their source of randomness were first employed in the early 1960s. Beloff & Evans (1961) were the first researchers to employ such systems, but it was Helmut Schmidt who really popularised their use (e.g. Schmidt 1969, 1970). The basic setup was to attach a Geiger counter to a timing device. Every so often, the Geiger counter would detect an emitted particle and register it. Rules were then applied such that - if an event happened during a certain period it was labelled a (1) or a (head), and if it happened during another equal length period it was a (0) or a (tail). These equal length periods flip-flopped between one another (e.g. every 100th of a second). Thus, you ended up with a stream of binary outcomes (1,0,0,0,1,0,1 etc...), that were synonymous with lots of coin tosses and wholly random.

Modern 'noise' based REGs.

Handling radioactive sources is not something you really want to do, as there is an obvious level of risk involved, and the rate of particle decay is relatively slow. Nowadays, one of the most common ways to derive a truly random data stream is by sampling Zener diodes. Basically, a combined output current (see above) from the diodes is sampled by a computer. By setting rules for the computer, (i.e. if the current is above 'x' it is a 0, if it is below 'x' it is a 1), the diodes can be used to generate the equivalent of lots of heads and tails. Modern REGs often use logic circuitry to overcome any potential biases in the devices, one way for example, is to invert every other bit (1=0 etc), preventing so called first-order bias. In using noise based REG equipment, masses of binary events can be generated (up to thousands per second) and outputs linked directly to storage files, thus limiting the chances of recording errors. These REGs are portable (about the size of a pack of cards), they are robust, and previous studies have suggested that environmental factors appear not to influence outputs (e.g. Nelson, Bradish & Dobyns, 1989). Under most experimental protocols, REGs will be sampled in 'control' conditions where no-one is trying to exert any influence. Data from these trials can then be compared against mathematical expectancy, and also against the data from trials where people are trying to influence them.

Some theory, please?

A number of theories have been proposed that try to explain whatever mechanism might underpin ESP and PK phenomena. Some theories speculate that there is an 'unknown' energy system through which psi is propagated. Others, that we transmit and receive conventional electromagnetic waves in some way (e.g. Kogan 1966), perhaps in Extremely Low Frequency form. Manyworld or Multiverse theories, on the other hand, hypothesize that all possible events occur somewhere, across an infinite number of universes, and that even highly unlikely events (including paranormal ones) happen as an inevitable matter of course.

One group of potential explanations, which have focussed attention across the years, are so called 'observation theories' that employ quantum mechanics as their explanatory backbones (see Walker 1975, Schmidt 1975, Houtkooper, 1977). These theories typically invoke the 'measurement problem' in quantum mechanics, where the act of measuring or observing a quantum system can influence its outcome. Prior to measurement, a quantum system is described in probabilistic terms, but following measurement a 'defined' state is applicable. "The act of observation by a motivated observer of an event with a quantum mechanically uncertain outcome influences that outcome." Houtkooper (2002, p 178). It is argued that once an event has been observed, it is fixed and cannot be changed no matter how many other observers try to influence it. Whilst it's clear how this might underpin PK (certainly in terms of REG experiments), how do observation theories relate to ESP phenomena? Here, it has been argued that quantum 'indeterminacy' in the brain is influenced, affecting neural processes which lead to the generation of ESP type perceptual experiences.

In all, there are a wide number of theories, some of which are more plausible than others. Explanatory justice cannot be done here, as we would end up with another book in its own right. So for an overview, the reader is directed to Stokes (1987).

[60] **What the REG database tells us.**
In the late eighties, a meta-analysis of the REG database was published (Radin & Nelson, 1989). The authors incorporated 152 articles relating to over 800 experimental and control studies, and found a small but robust effect (around 0.9% away from the expected 50/50 binary split) corresponding to a p value of 1.8×10^{-35}.

In 2003, Radin & Nelson updated their 1989 research to incorporate studies conducted between 1987 and 2000. The more recent studies, taken in conjunction with some newly uncovered pre-1987 experiments, added an extra 176 experiments to the analysis. The effect size across this expanded dataset remained small (equivalent to a 0.7% shift away from the expected 50/50 binary split), but there was a further increase in the p value ($p < 10^{-50}$). Results from these meta analyses provide strong support into the validity of PK/Mind-Matter Interactions.

Retro-PK.
Endnote 46 touched upon the idea that psi effects can operate across time, and one batch of supporting evidence comes from what are known as retroactive-psychokinesis (retro-PK) studies. In a typical retro-PK experiment, a participant is asked to influence an REG's output (i.e. produce more heads than tails etc.) whilst watching a computer screen that is showing them how they're doing, (e.g. they are provided with feedback, normally in the form of some graphical representations). But there's a twist. The participants are actually trying to influence a sequence of events that have already taken place.

Before the participant comes into the lab (and this can be any period of time – days, weeks, months, years) the REG is set up, as per normal. It is programmed to start running for a fixed period, and a camcorder is placed in front of the computer screen to record the feedback from the time. When the process has finished, the system shuts down and no-one is any the wiser as to what has happened. The only record of what has taken place is on the, as yet unwatched, camcorder tape. The tape is then locked away somewhere safe.

At some point afterwards, the participant is invited into the lab and according to a randomised protocol, asked to try and influence the system to produce either heads or tails. Multiple trials are conducted, each one using a different REG sequence and a different video taped recording. When we look at the results of these studies, it appears that the output of the REG system somehow conforms to what the participant was asked to achieve, even though the REG events technically took place in the past.

The explanations as to what is going on are quite interesting. As mentioned in the endnotes previously, quantum physics has shown how time has no direction when you get to the level of the very small. Events can go backwards and forwards. As such, some have argued that consciousness goes back to when the event was generated, influences it, and causes the quantum processes underpinning the randomness to collapse into a desired pattern. Others have suggested that since nobody has seen the tape, the REG events exist only as probabilities up to the moment the tape is watched, and the actual influencing is done (in real time) as people view the feedback. It's at that point that the REG events get fixed.

REGs as Field Measures.
REGs have also been used in environments where people don't actively seek to influence them. They sit in the background, being quietly sampled, and it is only afterwards that researchers look to see whether events in the environment correlate with bias in the devices (e.g. Nelson, Bradish, Dobyns, Dunne & Jahn, 1996; Nelson, Jahn, Dunne, Dobyns & Bradish, 1998; Radin, Rebman & Cross, 1996; Blasband, 2000). One experiment that is really putting this approach to the test is the Global Consciousness Project originally run out of Princeton University's engineering department. In the GCP, REGs all around the world (some sixty-five of them) are constantly sampled, sending their data back to the master computer. Researchers then examine whether events of global significance (e.g. elections, terrorism, global celebrations) correlate with departures from expectancy. Results so far have suggested that this may prove a fruitful avenue of study.
See: http://noosphere.princeton.edu

[61] **Violating the laws of the universe?**
Since the REG is only used for short periods, it need not violate chance expectancy overall to still be considered stable. As 'information transfer' is believed to be responsible for psi effects, no laws of thermodynamics are violated - energy is not being employed. Nonetheless, the 2nd law of thermodynamics, considered by many physicists to be an inviolable law, has also been held up as a reason to reject psi. Basically, the 2nd law states that entropy (disorder), increases as systems lose energy, and consciousness would have to oppose entropy (adding energy and imposing order to a system) which it is argued is impossible. Worldly observations suggest that such a view is correct, objects do not mysteriously heat themselves, they only get cooler. Entropy thus hands psi researchers a theoretical headache and has led some, such as Mattuck (1977) to suggest that rather than seeking ingenious workarounds, REG results may be due to a violation of the 2nd law of thermodynamics. Entropy also provides evidence for an arrow of time: entropy can only increase, therefore time must be uni-directional and we can only progress forwards through it. However, the quantum equations are bi-directional in nature; an influence could be exerted backwards through time as well as forwards. If an experiment could show that entropy does not always

increase and that under some circumstances it could decrease, then the 2nd law could not be used quite so readily to rebut psi.

Several years ago - Wang, Sevick, Mittag, Searles & Evans (2002) at the Australian National University published an article in Physics Review Letters showing that they had experimentally violated the 2nd law of thermodynamics. Under fluctuation theorem, the chances of the 2nd law being violated increase as things get smaller, thus researchers used a laser to electrically charge a tiny bead in a water container, trapping it. This container (which also held other uncharged beads) was moved very quickly side to side, and the system was found to take on order for periods of slightly less than one tenth of a second, implying that entropy decreased during that period. The point here is twofold; firstly there exist potential mechanisms which could facilitate psi should it hold quantum roots. Secondly, rejecting psi on theoretical grounds might not endure. 'Laws of the universe' arguments against psi may need to be revisited as our knowledge base grows.

[62] **Some of the techniques that Pseudo Psychics, also known as Cold Readers, may use.**

At this juncture, several key points should be considered.
-Psychic reading can be a highly lucrative business and repeat custom keeps the tills ringing. Therefore, it is in the cold reader's best interest to work effectively in retaining existing clients and gaining new ones.
-Clients tend to visit a psychic because they have issues or problems that they seek reassurance over, and these issues are unlikely to be inconsequential.
-As an imperative, the psychic must establish him/herself as credible, and this is typically done by providing information that the client can verify as true. Psychic predictions will then be accepted more readily.

So bearing in mind, that many pseudo psychics are not amateurs, but businesspeople running sustainable enterprises, let's set the scene:

A client telephones a psychic and asks to make an appointment. The psychic says "of course" and schedules a meeting. He/she also asks for a deposit, "send me a cheque", and a phone number in case the meeting needs to be cancelled.

Reconnaissance.
In some cases, reconnaissance is carried out before the psychic and client ever meet. By sending a deposit cheque, banking details are made available, and it only takes a small amount of digging into finances (easily outsourced) to throw up details of savings, investments, monies owed, income and employment. Bank statements and credit cards can also illustrate patterns of spending.

The client's phone number enables a backwards search to find the client's address and facilitate recon at the home. Even apparently minor things like the colour of the front door (*I'm seeing a blue front door*), or the level of upkeep (*I'm seeing a house, there's a broken gutter by the front window*), can be information that builds into a powerful experience when dropped into a reading. At the house, it is not unheard of for cold readers (or their agents) to root through rubbish - an excellent way of gathering data. Receipts, brochures, correspondence, even doodles on a notepad can all prove useful.

If the reading takes place at the client's home, environmental cues can be utilised. What decorative themes are there in the house? Are there lots of books, and if so what type? What about photographs on display? A psychic may excuse himself/herself and ask to use the bathroom, and those few moments of unsupervised privacy, enables them to look for further material. A calendar on the wall, sports equipment pushed into a corner, a note by a telephone. All good stuff.

Many people are referred to psychics through friends and word of mouth. The psychic may attempt to gather information about the new client, before they have even agreed to see them. A friend might ask (on behalf of the client) if the psychic will see them. *I'm very busy at the moment* the reader might say. *Oh* says the friend, *it's important, she/he is having some difficulties at home...family problems... and wants to know whether things will be all right.*

The reading begins...

Stereotyping.
Stereotyping can be highly effective in the early stages of any reading. Age, sex, regional accent, the type of clothes, the value of the jewellery, physical appearance, conscientiousness of appearance, body

language (e.g. confidence), pet hair on clothes – all factors that can lead to workable inferences.

Body language and Feedback.
The psychic can work out whether they are on the right track by picking up on the body language and verbal clues of how a client responds to the interaction. If an older lady comes in and sits there touching her wedding ring, the pseudo-psychic may start by subtly working on the idea of a deceased or ill husband. If it's a younger woman, marriage troubles would be more likely. In addition, attention will be paid to things such as eye blinks, body position, lip licking, openness of posture, hands touching the face, small nods, shakes of the head, and gaze direction.

Pre determined question areas.
You're here because you need questions answering. Important issues that I can help you with. You seem troubled, says the reader.
This is pretty likely as the vast majority of meetings are set up because there is a particular issue a client wants addressed. These typically revolve around love, children, marriage or money. Older people tend to worry more about health, and younger ones will be more concerned with relationships and careers. The reader will normally start by working on one of these topic areas, and use feedback to gauge whether they are on the right track.

Barnum statements.
One of the best ways to establish credibility is by providing insight into a person's character (which is perceived to be personal, and almost a secret, by many people). When doing this, Barnum statements are useful, for they are disclosures that appear to apply to the client, but could equally apply to almost any person.
You have a tendency to fret over important matters.
One of your big problems is that you can be very self-critical, can't you?

General chat.
In a further effort to establish credibility, the pseudo psychic may try to talk about some event the client previously experienced. Certain events are more likely than others - a strained relationship, the death of an older man (with heart trouble or cancer), recent sleeplessness

(especially relevant as people come to the psychic with a problem), someone they had a relationship with. *I'm seeing a man in your life with the letter J – does that make sense to you*? - in the UK, the letter J for men, and M for women, bumps up the chances of a hit. Often the cold reader will sit back and let the client fill in the gaps; nobody likes to sit in silence. *Yes, one of my best mates is called John/I have a brother called James.*

Setting up repeaters.
This involves the reader taking information from an early part of the reading without delving into it deeply, then reintroducing it later in the conversation as new information. Done skilfully, this looks like information that could only have been derived psychically.

Finishing people's sentences.
Although it might seem slightly implausible, finishing people's sentences (if done correctly) can make it seem like the cold reader is the one actually providing the information.
Reader: *I'm seeing your Grandfather, as he is right now, in a safe and tranquil place.* [pause]
Client: *Which one? Harry or Jona-*
Reader (louder than the client): *-Jonathan, his name is Jonathan. Is that correct?*

Reinterpreting information after it has been given.
Pseudo psychics should always try to make sure they have a 'get out'. If a psychic provides information that the client cannot see the veracity of, they can either say they will return to it (and not), try to rework it so that it becomes acceptable, or say they misunderstood the sign from the spirits. *Psychic reading is a little like weather forecasting, there's an element of uncertainty in it. It comes from a place where everything is not quite as cut and dry as it is here.* Cold Readers will talk of being guided through signs and metaphors.

Making predictions.
Life is difficult, be in no doubt. And, I'm not going to lie to you - there will be hard times ahead. But you have a strong character, much more than you sometimes give yourself credit for. You will be fine.
Such a statement is inherently meaningless. Everyone has hard times, and most people emerge from them in one piece. But delivered under

the auspices of a psychic reading, a statement such as this one will be interpreted as insightful and reassuring. *Yes. Excellent. I'll be okay in the long run.* The cold reader might then provide some additional affirmation: *I can see many occasions from your past where you have been your own worst enemy, and hindered yourself. This is not one of them – this is the time to be bold and courageous.*'

Boost accuracy by reducing specifics.
A good rule of thumb for the reader is to try to avoid specifics. Speak of 'possible' paths and outcomes that lie ahead. Avoid dates, but use months and years (e.g. in a few months, within the next couple of years). Assure a client that an event 'will' happen but make clear that timescales are not yet determined (in the grand cosmic plan). In reality, personal circumstances change all the time. Many events will come to pass naturally, if enough time is given.

People are usually pretty bad at discerning how accurate psychic predictions are. They remember the hits and not the misses, and often look to reinterpret misses as hits. Say you had a reading six months ago and were told that you would be facing a change in circumstances within the next half year. If you change job, or move house, break up with a partner, or even have to tighten the financial belt there's a good chance you will see that as a vindication of the reading. *Yes, my circumstances are different now.* But what if the event actually happens 10 months down the line? Most people will say the psychic was right about the event, just slightly out with the timing. It's all about interpretation.

Make a prediction, but let the client believe they must make a choice.
Imagine a situation where a pseudo psychic has worked out that the client is worried about their work-life. The psychic may then make a general prediction about the future: *I see a fork in the road for you on the career front. You will need to make a choice whether to continue on the same route or to change. But you must be warned - the change will not come to you on a plate. You must really want it. The new path will be very exciting and the rewards are by no means guaranteed. But with perseverance it will lead you to wonderful places.*

We make difficult decisions the whole time in our adult lives, and the psychic has made a prediction which basically says – if you're unhappy on the work front, it's up to you to make a change. Thus, the prediction may become self fulfilling.

You pays your money, you makes your choice.
Remember that there are plenty of charlatans out there. Sometimes, in moments of candour, they will admit: *look, I know I'm a fraud, but I'm performing a valuable service. I help people make life choices, and counsel those who might not seek professional help.* Someone goes to them with a problem, and they provide advice. Perhaps they help someone to move on with their lives after a bereavement or give someone the confidence to make a life changing decision. *We're cheaper than psychiatrists* some might argue.

It is worth remembering that as ESP can be demonstrated in the laboratory (albeit to a limited extent), it is not beyond the realms of imagination that it may occur in the real world. It may therefore be that there are individuals in the world, who represent themselves as mediums or psychics, and who are able to provide genuine information through ESP.

[63] **Kirlian photography.**
Semyon Kirlian discovered back in the late 1930s that if you photographed an object placed on a photographic film and subjected it to a powerful electric field, the developed image would often produce a 'halo' around that object. Some people believed that this halo represented a form of paranormal or supernatural energy, and even suggested that Kirlian photography was a window to the soul.

In reality, any object will give out an aura (caused by electrical/corona discharges around the object's edge) if placed in a high voltage field. This can be captured on photographic film that has been placed in contact with the object. The electric field pulls electrons from the object's surface (and any surface moisture) and pings them into the film emulsion, resulting (once the film is developed) in the appearance of unseen, additional imagery. Photographic film is not always required. A darkened room and the naked eye can sometimes suffice. The shape and relative moisture levels of the object being photographed will affect the shape and size of the aura produced, as will additional factors including environmental moisture, temperature and the voltage employed.

[64] **Synaesthesia and Auras.**
Psychics often report that they can see auras around their clients - coloured zones that sometimes get represented as a form of psychic energy. Recent research (Ward, 2004) has suggested that seeing auras might be attributed, under some circumstances, to a form of synaesthesia - an uncommon neurological condition where individuals involuntarily experience sensations in non-related modalities. For example, in what's known as lexical-gustatory synaesthesia, a person might hear a certain word (e.g. purple) which then evokes the sensation of a particular taste (e.g. the percipient then tastes vanilla). To all intents and purposes, the taste is as real as if they ate the food itself. It's worth pointing out that with this form of synaesthesia, the words do not *have* to link semantically (although they can), i.e. people do not necessarily have a taste experience that is citrus or sweet when they hear the word orange.

With aura reading, it has been suggested that a visual experience is fired, in relation to the emotion the reader is feeling at the time. If the reader looks at an individual and feels warm and happy, they might see a pink colour around the head/body of the client. If they feel uncomfortable with the client, the colour may be brown or blue (colours are personal and do not apply uniformly). It should be highlighted that any one theory is rarely able to explain all cases of a particular phenomenon.

[65] **Near Death Experiences.**
Near Death Experiences are somewhat more common than people might believe, and reports have suggested that incidence levels may be as high as one in three (See Ring, 1984; Greyson, 1998). Others (van Lommel, van Wees, Meyers & Elfferich, 2001) have posited that between 10 and 15% of the population may experience an episode at some point in their lives.

As the name implies, Near Death Experiences are episodes when people 'believe' or 'perceive' themselves to be dying (Gabbard & Twemlow, 1991). Ring (1980) has pointed out that NDEs do not have to entail accompanying Out of Body Experiences.

It is claimed that NDEs often share characteristics across cultures and ages, which suggests that they may be at least partially ingrained -

involving perceptual and cognitive functioning at some deep rooted level. Young children who have NDEs have reported similar experiences to adults. At other times, the NDE can be quite culture specific, implying that certain elements may be 'learned'. Christians, for example, may see Jesus Christ during an experience, whilst those from other faiths see figures relevant to their own religion (Osis & Haraldsson, 1977; Gabbard & Twemlow, 1984).

Three main theories have been put forward to explain NDEs.
-That experiences are due to oxygen deprivation.
-They represent a psychological response to the perception of oncoming death.
-They are genuine, and experiences of heaven (etc.) show there really is an afterlife.

In 2002, Parnia and Fenwick examined a batch of blood samples from patients who had experienced NDEs during heart attacks; they found elevated oxygen levels in the samples rather than a lack thereof. In turn, heightened salt levels (such as potassium and sodium) which can be linked to delusional episodes were not found. Could the resuscitation process have sparked NDEs? It seems unlikely; conventional resuscitation drugs (e.g. adrenaline) were employed which do not precipitate hallucinations.

[66] **Tunnel of Light phenomenon.**
Some people report that during their NDEs, they find themselves moving down a tunnel towards a point of light. Blackmore & Troscianko (1988) proposed that the tunnel of light phenomenon is a product of the visual cortex's architecture. More cells are in the centre (as opposed to the periphery) and thus anoxia (an absence of oxygen) causes these to fire producing a stronger effect in the centre of the visual field (relatively light) than at the edges (relatively dark).

[67] **Is the tunnel of light a re-experiencing of birth?**
One idea that seems to have caught the popular imagination is the tunnel of light as a re-experiencing of birth. It was proposed by Grof & Halifax (1978) who suggested that it was a re-visiting of the unborn child's journey down the birth canal towards the new world.

The obvious way to test the hypothesis is to examine whether individuals who were born by caesarean section had the tunnel of light experience during their NDEs. Whilst investigating Out of Body Experiences (which are not the same thing as NDEs, but relevant here) Blackmore (1982) found that 36% of people born conventionally had the tunnel of light experience, whilst 29% born by c-section also had, dealing a serious blow to the Grof & Halifax theory.

[68] **Evidence for the afterlife.**
Tests that examine whether the afterlife is real are not easy. The traditional approach has been to pre-arrange some form of sign to be delivered from the 'other side', by the deceased person to show that they remain existent. In one such attempt, Robert Thouless (who was a member of the Society for Psychical Research) set out his 'cipher test' back in 1946. Thouless enciphered a phrase that read as: "CBFTM HGRIO TSTAU FSBDN WGNIS BRVEF BQTAB QRPEF BKSDG MNRPS RFBSU TTDMF EMA BIM". The phrase could be deciphered by the use of a 'keyword' and Thouless wrote: "I have not communicated and shall not communicate this key-word to any other person while I am still in this world, and I destroyed all papers used in enciphering as soon as I had finished. My intention is to see whether after my death I can give evidence of my continued existence by communicating the key necessary for the passage to be deciphered." (p254).

When Thouless finally died (in 1984), the Society for Psychical Research asked people to 'crack' the code by providing the key. Thouless also set a combination lock where the numbers needed to open it corresponded to the first six letters of the 'key', (the letters were converted into numbers according to a pre-determined table).

It was not until 1996 that success arrived (see Stevenson 1996) when the key words 'Black Beauty' revealed the cipher to read: "This is a cipher which will not be read unless I give the keyword." So who was the psychic who provided the information? It was computer expert James Gillogly who had decrypted it using computer software. In all, attempts to establish a channel of verifiable communication from beyond the grave have not been successful, but at the same time it is worth remembering that failure in itself 'proves' nothing.

[69] **The Super Psi/ESP hypothesis.**
Under conventional ESP tests, agents know where, what or whom, their source is. In a clairvoyance experiment, for example, the receiver normally knows *where* they are supposed to be looking for information; in a telepathy experiment, the receiver typically knows *who* the source person is.

But with psychic readings where information is to be provided from an unknown point or person (which is what many readings that purport to communicate with spirits are), it is argued that a higher level of ESP would be required. In turn, the so called Super ESP (or Super psi) hypothesis has been proposed (Gauld, 1961; Braude 1989, 1992) which basically says - a psychic operator need not know the location or identity of any source in order to access relevant information because psi can locate the information anyway. Neither the Super psi hypothesis nor the survival hypothesis have any real primacy over each other, as it is the information that is considered key, not the source.

[70] **Evidence to suggest that consciousness is indeed capable of affecting other biological systems.**
DMILS (Direct Mental Interaction with Living Systems) is basically research that examines whether a person can exert influence over the physiological functioning of a spatially separated organism. See endnote 76.

A meta-analysis by Braud & Schlitz (1991) looking into whether consciousness and intention could remotely influence biological systems proved highly significant $p = 2.58 \times 10^{-14}$, and suggested that consciousness was indeed capable of remotely influencing biological systems. A later review by Stefan Schmidt (2003) that incorporated 24 experiments and 636 experimental sessions concluded that there was evidence to support the idea that remote intention could affect a removed biological system (albeit with a smallish effect size), and that these effects were of a similar magnitude irrespective of study size.

[71] **Research with bacteria.**
In a typical study, bacteria are set up on agar plates, and healers asked to either speed up, or slow down their growth. Various controls are implemented to prevent unwanted factors influencing the results.

These often include preventing healers from getting too close to the plates (in case their body heat affected them), and making sure that any plate handling is conducted by people unaware of which were control plates and which were target plates (i.e. those to be healed). Nash (1984) provides an example of such bacterial growth research. On the plates where healers tried to retard the growth of the bacteria, the micro-organisms grew significantly slower than those on control plates.

It is important to note that 'healing' is not necessarily about special powers in the hands, or unusual physiological qualities in the healer. It is typically about volition - using mental effort to 'will' organisms to get better, or inhibit undesirable conditions.

[72] **Healing with mice.**
A variety of experiments have been conducted on mice. In one batch of trials, non life-threatening goitres were induced through an iodine deficient diet, and a healer subsequently asked to slow the rate of growth. Once again, care was taken to minimise confounding factors. For example, concern that heat from the healer's hands might impact on the study outcome (rather than healing per se) saw electrical heating tapes used in control trials to simulate the warmth from the healer's hands. In another condition, the healer worked with bobs of cotton wool that were then placed in the animals' cages, so that he did not interact with the animals directly. At the end of the experiment, mice groups that had been attended to by the healer experienced significantly slower goitre growth. In another study that used mice, tissue samples were taken to prompt skin regrowth. When the rate of regrowth was measured, it was substantially faster in the mice than had been 'healed' than those in the control groups.
See: Grad (1976) for a review.

n.b. *Sceptical researchers inhibit recovery.*
One DMILS study worth highlighting showed that sceptical medical students (i.e. those who felt that volition could not affect recovery rates) appeared to inhibit the recovery rate of mice with surgically induced wounds.
See: Grad (1976).

[73] **Salamander tail regrowth.**
See: Wirth, Johnson, Horvarth & MacGregor (1992).

[74] **Is there a causal effect?**
With alternative healing approaches, whatever they may be, people often report feeling better post-treatment. Thus, we need to consider what is actually happening. Is the effect due to some process bringing about physical change, or is it the heightened expectation of success (in the healee) that facilitates self healing?

When people go see a healer, they typically have a positive anticipation that the healing will be of benefit. Many report subjective feelings of increased wellbeing following treatment, and it may be that treatment produces psychosomatic effects. This heightened wellbeing may reduce stress levels and prompt heightened self-healing (perhaps through an auto-immune response).

Sometimes recovery from a terminal illness is considered proof that alternative healing works. It is worth remembering that spontaneous recovery can occur naturally, but that people obviously look for a causal explanation post-remission. Some might attribute any recovery to God and miracles, others to psychic healing, whilst others might simply say they were damned lucky. Their explanation will centre on the activities and beliefs they held prior to remission.

[75] **The haemolysis rate of blood.**
The rate at which red blood cells get broken down by the body.

[76] **Using the nervous system as a measure of psi.**
One line of experimentation is to look at how the nervous system can be affected by volition. Fundamentally, a participant's physiology is measured whilst someone remotely tries to influence it by trying to increase and decrease a level of physiological arousal, according to a randomised and balanced (i.e. equal numbers of increase and decrease periods) protocol. Whilst the target participant knows the purpose of the experiment, they don't know moment-to-moment whether it is an active or calm condition. In turn, target participants are not asked to influence themselves actively, rather to remain passive.

The influencing agent conducts the experiment from a completely separate area, and there is no means of communication between him/her and the receiver. The experimenter running the trial doesn't know, at the time of measurement, whether an active or calm condition is being attempted. It's only when the experiment is finished, and the measurements are compared with the instructions, that we can see what happened.

[77] **The nervous system shifts in accordance with the experimental manipulation.**
Explanations for how the receiver's nervous system shifts in accordance with volition vary. Some argue that there is a direct causal effect (similar to a force like mechanism) that comes from the sender and acts on the target's physiology. Others suggest there may be communication between the influencer and the receiver that prompts the receiver to alter their own physiology subconsciously. Alternatively, the receiver may be using his/her own ESP to remotely monitor the instructions provided to the sender, once again leading to a subconscious self-adjustment of physiology.

[78] **Other DMILS experiments.**
Charles Tart, in the 1960s, examined whether the receiver in a sender/receiver pair would react to electric shocks administered to the sender, as measured by changes in skin conductance and heart rate. Tart himself acted as sender and received mild but painful shocks. All in all it was found that the receivers responded when Tart was shocked, even though they were in a separate room and unaware of the shock schedule.
See: Tart (1963).

Current research is focussing on measuring brain waves, and whether there are changes in pattern during periods of remote influence. The Electroencephalograph is used in science and medicine to examine brain function and abnormality, and uses electrodes on the scalp to measure the level of activity in regions beneath the skull. As an interesting historical side note, the EEG device was actually invented, by Hans Berger in 1929, in an attempt to measure telepathy.

[79] **Could somebody cause another person to have a heart attack through thought alone?**
Laboratory conditions aren't the same as the street. As participants in an experiment, individuals are amenable to the experimental interaction. In turn, the psychokinetic effects seen in the laboratory are typically small. Whether PK (if it is a force like phenomenon) could be 'ramped up' to induce a heart attack in a target individual seems unlikely under our current understanding.

As a footnote to this however, it is worth considering the story of Nina Kulagina. Kulagina was a housewife from Stalingrad, Russia and an alleged star psychic. It was reported that she was once able to stop a frog's heart from beating (whilst under the supervision of experimenters), separate the yolk from the albumen in an egg, and cause a compass to deviate from its regular north bearing.

Kulagina was tested (although not under proper laboratory conditions) by both Soviet and Western scientists and at the time there was no evidence of cheating. Indeed, by all accounts she seemed like an everyday person who seemed somewhat bemused by her abilities. When Kulagina's physiology was measured during her psi episodes, she was found to be in a state akin to rage. She is reported to have had two heart attacks during testing, and on medical advice retired soon after the second.

Caveat: Kulagina's alleged exploits should not be held up as proof of psi, as test conditions cannot be considered tight enough, and trials took place during the Cold War when there may have been a perceived benefit in promoting psychic abilities beyond the iron curtain. Nonetheless, it may be that certain individuals do have abilities above and beyond the levels that most other others hold.
See: Ullman (1974).

[80] **Remote healing studies, with human targets.**
This is a particularly controversial area of paranormal research which looks at whether religious or intercessory prayer (on behalf of another) can affect the health of remote human targets.

It is controversial for two primary reasons – firstly because it sits uneasily with the modern medical point of view, and secondly because it has associations with religion. "Prayer" is a label heavy with casual implication, and perhaps a misleading one. Prayer suggests a supernatural cause and effect - you pray to God, who then helps the patient. It may be more relevant to think of prayer as an attempt by consciousness to "influence" other biological systems, a mechanism that does not require outside assistance. Fierce debate has often followed the reporting of positive studies, and as yet there is no universal accord on what protocols experimenters need apply, or what outcome measures need to taken. In turn, speculation has surrounded whether certain types of medical condition respond better to remote healing than others.

One well known study, used here to illustrate the remote healing approach, was conducted by a doctor in California by the name of Randolph Byrd (1988). He carried out research that looked at whether 'prayer' could speed up the recovery of coronary patients.

In Byrd's study, patients in coronary care units were randomly chosen, and some basic details such as first name and diagnosis were given to members of various church groups. These church group members then tried to assist the recovery rates of said patients by asking for/willing them to get better. Neither the patients nor their attending physicians knew that they were being prayed for, and thus placebo or psychosomatic effects should be considered inappropriate. The full identities of the patients and where they were based were not given out, preventing accidental or deliberate contact between the church groups and the patients.

At the end of the study, the patients who were remotely willed to recover were less likely to require drugs during their recovery, and less likely to suffer oedemas or require respiratory assistance. However, the actual length of recovery time did not vary significantly between groups.

Two of the criticisms to this study were: Byrd's failure to investigate whether patients in the control group were 'prayed for' by people outside the study, and no verification as to whether people in the prayer groups actually carried out their tasks.

In further experiments that looked at groups healed from a distance, Harris (1999) reported another coronary care study with 990 patients that uncovered some positive results. Sicher, Targ, Moore & Smith (1998) investigated AIDS patients and found fewer, and less acute, new associated illnesses. Greyson (1996) found no effect with patients being treated for depression, whilst Harkness, Abbot & Ernst (2000) found no effect for individuals undergoing treatment for warts. Thus, whilst there have been positive study outcomes, there have also been apparent failures. There have been differences in the symptoms and illnesses investigated, the relative quality of the approaches undertaken, and the level of effect (or lack thereof) uncovered.

In 2000, Astin, Harkness & Ernst looked at 23 previously conducted healing studies and found positive effects in over half of them. Latterly, Astin (2004) reviewed 14 research trials that were considered to be the most methodologically sound, and reported that six showed positive outcomes on at least one health measure. Aside from a call for more large-scale research to be conducted, Astin concluded: "…there is at present moderate scientific evidence supporting the efficacy of various distant healing/intercessory prayer approaches in medicine." (p21).

Benor (2000) has suggested that the scale of distance between healers and healees does not have an inhibitory effect on outcomes, and that positive outcomes are as likely in the absence of religious overtones, as those stemming from a religious context (e.g. prayer to God).

[81] **Measuring healing using Random Event Generators.**
See Radin, Taft & Young (2004); Lumsden-Cook, Thwala & Edwards (2006).

[82] **PK experiments with animals.**
Cockroaches: Schmidt (1970a) set up an experiment to test whether cockroaches were able to use psychokinesis to prevent themselves from being electrically shocked. He found significant but unexpected results - the cockroaches were being shocked *more often* than they should by chance. This outcome prompted Schmidt to have a good think about the nature of psi, and ultimately led him to hypothesise that the experimenter may have a substantial effect upon the study

outcome - using his or her psi to influence matters without consciously realising it (i.e. the test animals were not responsible).
Baby Chicks: See Schmidt (1970b).
Cats and ESP: See Osis & Foster (1953).
Lizards: Watkins (1971).
Gerbils: Parker (1974).
Rats: Craig & Treurniet (1974).

[83] **Occurrence of OBEs.**
According to two surveys by Susan Blackmore (1982, 1996), up to one fifth of the population will experience an OBE during their lifetime. Conversely, Alvarado (2000) has suggested that 10% of the general population might experience an OBE, a figure that rises to 25% for university students. Alvarado (1986) found that once people have an OBE, 67% of them go on to have at least one other.
Also see: Twemlow, Gabbard & Jones (1982).

[84] **OBEs induced by drug use.**
There may be a link between OBEs and marijuana use (Tart, 1971) and the use of psychedelic drugs such as LSD and mescaline (Blackmore & Harris, 1983), and possibly ketamine.

[85] **Meditation can lead to OBEs.**
Some researchers have found that meditation, or more accurately - the length of time spent practising meditation, correlates positively with OBEs.
See: Myers, Austrin, Grisso & Nickeson (1983), Kohr (1980).

[86] **Induced OBEs.**
See: Osis & Mitchell (1977), Morris, Harary, Janis, Hartwell & Roll (1978), Gabbard & Twemlow (1984).

Aside from trying to induce OBEs through willpower, there are also reports that the feelings associated with an OBE can be artificially produced by stimulating certain parts of the brain (in a similar vein to the surgical methods detailed in endnote 34). Some argue that having the feeling of an OBE can't be considered the same as having one, especially when experients having spontaneous episodes are able to provide information that should not be available to them (i.e. psychically derived).

Recent research has shed light on what might be happening during some Out of Body Experiences, where effects are due to a mix up in the brain's processing of sensory information. Ehrrson (2007) filmed participants with two closely placed cameras that simulated the 3D viewpoint of a 'virtual' person seated behind them. The feed from each camera was shown, via video screen goggles, to the participant (i.e. one feed went to one eye, the other feed went to the other eye) providing a stereoscopic image of their back.

Then a researcher moved a plastic rod to a point just below the cameras (as though it was poking the virtual chest), and touched the participant's actual chest at the same time. Participants were not able to see this. This synchronous multi-sensory activity prompted an out-of-body experience where participants reported that they felt as though they were physically seated behind their real bodies (in the virtual space) observing them.

[87] **Cord connecting the physical body and the 'astral' body.**
Crookall (1964) estimated that 20% of OBE cases involved a cord, although Alavarado (2000) re-categorised Crookall's data and reduced this figure to 11%.

[88] **Some out-of-body experients feel a shock when returning to the body.**
See: Alvarado & Zingrone (1997).

Final Comments.

The paranormal. It continues to divide opinion, both professionally and across society in general. There are those who want to believe that psychic abilities exist, those who vehemently oppose such a view, and those who couldn't care less. There are those who believe they have had a psychic episode, and those who think there *must* be a rational explanation for any such event.

For sceptics and advocates alike, this book illustrates that our understanding of the paranormal is nowhere near complete. Phenomena (if they are real) are often elusive, complex, and difficult to investigate. It is unlikely there will be a definitive experiment any time soon.

Moving forwards, it seems clear that more research is needed. Experiments must be conducted objectively, deliberately and fairly. In the meantime, we should not be bowled over by those who shout the loudest or talk the smoothest - no matter how sure they seem.

References:

Alvarado, C.S. (1986). Research on spontaneous out-of-body experiences: A review of modern developments, 1960-1984. In B. Shapin & L. Coly (Eds.), *Current trends in psi research* (pp. 140-167). New York: Parapsychological Foundation.

Alvarado, C.S. (2000). Out-of-body experiences. In E. Cardena, S.J. Lynn & S. Krippner (Eds.), *Varieties of Anomalous Experience* (pp. 183–218). Washington D.C.: American Psychological Association.

Alvarado, C.S., & Zingrone, N.L. (1997). Out-of-body experiences and sensations of 'shocks' to the body. *Journal of the Society for Psychical Research, 61*, 304-313.

Astin, J.A. (2004). Intercessory prayer and healing prayer. In W.B. Jonas & C.C. Crawford (Eds.), *Healing Intention and Energy Medicine* (pp. 13-22). London: Churchill Livingstone.

Astin, J.A., Harkness, E., & Ernst, E. (2000). The efficacy of 'distant healing': a systematic review of randomized trials. *Annals of Internal Medicine, 132,* 903-910.

Batcheldor, K.J. (1984). Contributions to the theory of PK induction from sitter-group work. *Journal of the American Society for Psychical Research, 78,* 105-122.

Beloff, J., & Evans, L. (1961). A radioactivity test for PK. *Journal of the Society for Psychical Research, 41,* 41-46.

Bem, D.J., & Honorton, C. (1994). Does psi exist? Replicable evidence for an anomalous process of information transfer. *Psychological Bulletin, 115,* 4-18.

Bem, D.J., Palmer, J., & Broughton, R.S. (2001). Updating the ganzfeld database: A victim of its own success? *Journal of Parapsychology, 65*(3), 207-218.

Benor, D.J. (2000). Distant healing. *Subtle Energies and Energy Medicine, 11*(3), 349-364.

Bierman, D.J., & Radin, D. (1997). Anomalous anticipatory responses on randomized future conditions. *Perceptual and Motor Skills, 84,* 689-690.

Blackmore, S.J. (1982). *Beyond the Body: An investigation of out-of-the-body experiences.* London: Heinemann.

Blackmore, S.J. (1996). Out-of-body experiences. In G Stein (Ed.), *Encyclopaedia of the Paranormal* (pp. 471-483). Buffalo, NY: Prometheus.

Blackmore, S.J., & Harris, B. (1983). OBEs and perceptual distortions in schizophrenic patients and students. In W.G. Roll, J. Beloff & R.A. White (Eds.), *Research in Parapsychology 1982* (pp. 232-234). Metuchen, NJ: Scarecrow Press.

Blackmore, S.J., & Troscianko, T. (1988). The physiology of the tunnel. *Journal of Near Death Studies, 17,* 111-120.

Blanke, O., Landis, T., & Seeck, M. (2000). Electrical cortical stimulation of the human prefrontal cortex evokes complex visual hallucinations. *Epilepsy & Behavior, 1*(5), 356-361.

Blasband, R.A. (2000). The ordering of random events by emotional expression. *Journal of Scientific Exploration, 14*(2), 195-216.

Braud, W.G. (1978). Allobiofeedback: Immediate feedback for a psychokinetic influence upon another person's physiology. In W.G. Roll (Ed.), *Research in Parapsychology 1977* (pp. 123-134). Metuchen, NJ: Scarecrow Press.

Braud, W.G., & Hartgrove, J. (1976). Clairvoyance and psychokinesis in transcendental meditators and matched control subjects: a preliminary study. *European Journal of Parapsychology, 1*(3), 6-16.

Braud, W. G., & Schlitz, M. J. (1991). Consciousness interactions with remote biological systems: Anomalous intentionality effects. *Subtle Energies: An Interdisciplinary Journal of Energetic and Informational Interactions, 2,* 1-46.

Braude, S.E. (1989). Evaluating the Super ESP hypothesis. In G.K. Zollschan, J.F. Schumaker & G.F. Walsh (Eds.), *Exploring the paranormal: Perspectives on belief and experience* (pp. 25-38). Bridport, UK: Prism Press.

Braude, S.E. (1992). Survival or Super Psi? *Journal of Scientific Exploration, 6,* 127-144.

Byrd, R.C. (1988). Positive therapeutic effects of intercessory prayer in a coronary care population. *Southern Medical Journal, 81*(7), 826-829.

Camp, B.H. (1937). Statement in notes section. *Journal of Parapsychology, 1,* 305.

Child, I.L. (1985). Psychology and anomalous observations: The question of ESP in dreams. *American Psychologist, 40,* 1219-1230.

Clarke, D. (1995). Experience and other reasons given for belief and disbelief in paranormal and religious phenomena. *Journal of the Society for Psychical Research, 60,* 371-384.

Craig, J.G., & Treurniet, W. (1974). Precognition in rats as a function of shock and death. In W.G. Roll, R.L. Morris & J.D. Morris (Eds.), *Research in Parapsychology 1973* (pp. 75-78). Metuchen, NJ: Scarecrow Press.

Crookall, R. (1964). *More astral projections: Analyses of case histories.* London: Aquarian Press.

Dalton, K. (1997). Exploring the links: Creativity and psi in the ganzfeld. In *The Parapsychological Association 40th Annual Convention: Proceedings of Presented Papers* (pp. 119-134). Durham, NC: Parapsychological Association.

Dalton, K., Steinkamp, F., & Sherwood, S.J. (1999). A dream GESP experiment using dynamic targets and consensus vote. *Journal of the American Society for Psychical Research, 93*(2), 145-166.

Debes, J., & Morris, R.L. (1982). Comparison of striving and non-striving instructional sets in a PK study. *Journal of Parapsychology, 46,* 297-312.

Delanoy, D. L. (1997). Important psi-conducive practices and issues: Impressions from six parapsychological laboratories. *European Journal of Parapsychology, 13,* 63-70.

Druckman, D., & Swets, J.A. (Eds.). (1988). *Enhancing human performance: Issues, theories and techniques.* Washington, DC: National Academy Press.

Ehrsson, H.H. (2007). The experimental induction of out-of-body experiences. *Science, 317*(5841), 1048.

Gabbard, G.O., & Twemlow, S.W. (1984). *With the eyes of the mind: An empirical analysis of out-of-body states.* New York: Praeger Scientific.

Gabbard, G.O., & Twemlow, S.W. (1991). Do "near-death experiences" occur only near death? – Revisited. *Journal of Near-Death Studies, 10,* 41-47.

Gardener, M. (1983). *The whys of a philosophical scrivener.* New York: Quill.

Gauld, A. (1961). The "Super-ESP" hypothesis. *Proceedings of the Society for Psychical Research, 53,* 226-246.

Gauld, A., & Cornell, A.D., (1979). *Poltergeists.* London: Routledge & Kegan Paul.

Gissurarson, L.R. (1992). Studies of methods of enhancing and potentially training psychokinesis: A review. *Journal of the American Society for Psychical Research, 86*(4), 303-346.

Gissurarson, L.R., & Morris, R.L. (1991). Examination of six questionnaires as predictors of psychokinesis performance. *Journal of Parapsychology, 55,* 119-145.

Good, I.J. (1997). Where has the billion trillion gone? *Nature, 389,* 806-807.

Grad, B.R. (1976). The biological effects of the "laying on of hands" on animals and plants: Implications for biology. In G.R. Schmeidler (Ed.), *Parapsychology: Its relation to physics, biology, psychology, and psychiatry* (pp. 76-89). Metuchen, NJ: Scarecrow Press.

Granqvist, P., Fredrikson, M., Unge, P., Hagenfeldt, A., Valind, S., Larhammar, D., & Larsson, M. (2005). Sensed presence and mystical experiences are predicted by suggestibility, not by the application of weak complex transcranial magnetic fields. *Neuroscience Letters, 379,* 1-6.

Greeley, A.M. (1987). Mysticism goes mainstream. *American Health, 6*(1), 47-49.

Green, C.E. (1960). Analysis of spontaneous cases. *Proceedings of the Society for Psychical Research, 53,* 97-161.

Green, C.E. (1966). Extra-sensory perception and the Maudsley Personality Inventory. *Journal of the Society for Psychical Research, 43,* 285-286.

Greyson, B. (1996). Distance healing of patients with major depression. *Journal of Scientific Exploration, 10,* 447-465.

Greyson, B. (1998). The incidence of near-death experiences. *Medicine and Psychiatry, 1,* 92-99.

Grof, S., & Halifax, J. (1978). *The human encounter with death.* London: Souvenir Press.

Hamani, C., McAndrews, M.P., Cohn, M., Oh, M., Zumsteg, D., Shapiro, C.M., Wennberg, R.A., & Lozano, A.M. (2008). Memory enhancement induced by hypothalamic/fornix deep brain stimulation. *Annals of Neurology, 63*, 119-123.

Hansel, C.E.M. (1966). *ESP: A scientific evaluation.* New York: Scribners.

Hansel, C.E.M. (1980). *ESP and parapsychology: A critical re-evaluation.* Buffalo, NY: Prometheus.

Hansel, C.E.M. (1989). *The search for psychic power: ESP and parapsychology revisited.* Buffalo, NY: Prometheus.

Haraldsson, E. (1985). Representative national surveys of psychic phenomena: Iceland, Great Britain, Sweden, USA and Gallup's multinational survey. *Journal of the American Society for Psychical Research, 53,* 145-158.

Haraldsson, E. (1994). Apparitions of the dead: Analysis of a new collection of 350 reports. In E.W. Cook & D.L. Delanoy (Eds.), *Research in Parapsychology 1991* (pp. 1-6). Metuchen, NJ: Scarecrow Press.

Haraldsson, E., & Houtkooper, J.M. (1991). Psychic experiences in the Multinational Human Values Study: Who reports them? *Journal of the American Society for Psychical Research, 85,* 145-165.

Harkness, E.F., Abbot, N.C., & Ernst, E. (2000). A randomized clinical trial of distant healing for skin warts. *American Journal of Medicine, 108,* 448-452.

Harris, W.S. (1999). A randomized, controlled trial of the effects of remote intercessory prayer on outcomes in patients admitted to the coronary care unit. *Archives of Internal Medicine, 159,* 2273-2278.

Harris, M. J., & Rosenthal, R. (1988). *Human performance research: An overview.* Washington, DC: National Academy Press.

Harris, M. J., & Rosenthal, R. (1988a). *Postscript to "Human performance research: An overview.".* Washington, DC: National Academy Press.

Hearne, K.M. (1981). The effect on the subject (in waking, SWS and REM states) of electric shocks to the agent: An "ESP" experiment. *Journal of the Society for Psychical Research, 51*, 87-92.

Hearne, K.M., & Worsley, A. (1977). An experiment in telepathic phobic fear and REM sleep. *Journal of the Society for Psychical Research, 49*, 434-439.

Honorton, C. (1977). Effects of meditation and feedback on psychokinetic performance: a pilot study with an instructor of transcendental meditation. In J.D. Morris, W.G. Roll, & R.L. Morris (Eds.), *Handbook of parapsychology 1976* (pp. 435-472). New York: Von Nostrand Reinhold.

Honorton, C. (1983). Response to Hyman's critique of psi ganzfeld studies. In W.G. Roll, J. Beloff & R.A. White (Eds.), *Research in Parapsychology 1982* (pp. 23-26). Metuchen, NJ: Scarecrow Press.

Honorton, C. (1985). Meta-analysis of psi ganzfeld research: A response to Hyman. *Journal of Parapsychology, 49,* 51-91.

Honorton, C. (1993). Rhetoric over substance: The impoverished state of scepticism. *Journal of Parapsychology, 57,* 191-214.

Honorton, C., Berger, R.E., Varvoglis, M.P., Quant, M., Derr, P., Schechter, E.I., & Ferrari, D.C. (1990). Psi communication in the ganzfeld: Experiments with an automated testing system and a comparison with a meta-analysis of earlier studies. *Journal of Parapsychology, 54,* 99-139.

Honorton, C., & Ferrari, D.C. (1989). Meta-analysis of forced-choice precognition experiments 1935 - 1987. *Journal of Parapsychology, 53,* 281-308.

Honorton, C., Ferrari, D.C., & Bem, D.J. (1998). Extraversion and ESP performance: a meta-analysis and a new confirmation. *Journal of Parapsychology, 62,* 255-276.

Houtkooper, J. M. (1977). A study of repeated retroactive psychokinesis in relation to direct and random PK effects. *European Journal of Parapsychology, 1*(4), 1-20.

Houtkooper, J.M. (2002). Arguing for an observational theory of paranormal phenomena. *Journal of Scientific Exploration, 16,* 171-185.

Huesmann, M., & Schriever, F. (1989). Steckbrief des spuks. Darstellung und diskussion einer sammlung von 54 RSPK-berichten des FreiburgerInstituts für Grenzgebiete der Psychologie und Psychohygiene aus denJahren 1947-1986 [Wanted: The poltergeist. Description and discussion of a collection of 54 RSPK reports from the years 1947-1986, collected by the Freiburg IGPP]. *Zeitschrift für Parapsychologie und Grenzgebiete der Psychologie, 31,* 52-107.

Humphrey, B.M. (1951). Introversion-extraversion ratings in relation to scores in ESP tests. *Journal of Parapsychology, 15,* 252-262.

Hyman, R. (1983). Does the ganzfeld experiment answer the critics' objections? In W.G. Roll, J. Beloff & R.A. White (Eds.), *Research in Parapsychology 1982* (pp. 21-23). Metuchen, NJ: Scarecrow Press.

Hyman, R. (1985). The ganzfeld psi experiment: A critical appraisal. *Journal of Parapsychology, 49,* 3-49.

Hyman, R., & Honorton, C. (1986). A joint communiqué: The psi ganzfeld controversy. *Journal of Parapsychology, 50,* 351-364.

Irwin, H. (2004). *An introduction to parapsychology: Fourth Edition.* London: McFarland & Company.

Isaacs, J. (1981). A mass screening technique for locating PKMB agents. *Psychoenergetics, 4,* 125-158.

Josephson, B.D. http://www.tcm.phy.cam.ac.uk/~bdj10/psi/doubtsregood.html, retrieved 1 February 2008.

Josephson, B.D., & Pallikari-Viras, F. (1991). Biological utilisation of quantum nonlocality. *Foundations of Physics, 21,* 197-207.

Kogan, I.M. (1966). Is telepathy possible? *Telecommunication and Radio Engineering, 21*(1), 75-81.

Kohr, R.L. (1980). A survey of psi experiences among members of a special population. *Journal of the American Society for Psychical Research, 74,* 395-411.

Krippner, S., Honorton, C., & Ullman, M. (1972). Telepathic transmission of art prints in sleep under two conditions. *Proceedings of the 80th Annual Convention of the American Psychological Association, 7,* 319-320.

Kubis, J.F., & Rouke, F.L. (1937). An experimental investigation of telepathic phenomena in twins. *Journal of Parapsychology, 1*(3), 163-171.

Lawrence, T. (1993). Gathering in the sheep and goats, a meta-analysis of forced choice sheep-goat studies 1947-1993. *Proceedings of the 36th Annual Convention of the Parapsychological Association,* 75-86.

Lumsden-Cook, J.J., Thwala, J., & Edwards, S.D. (2006). The effects of traditional Zulu healing upon a Random Event Generator. *Journal of the Society for Psychical Research, 70*(3), 129-137.

Mangan, G.L. (1954). A PK experiment with thirty dice released for high and low face targets. *Journal of Parapsychology, 18,* 209-218.

Martinez-Taboas, A. (1984). An appraisal of the role of aggression and the central nervous system in RSPK agents. *Journal of the American Society for Psychical Research, 78,* 55-69.

Matas, F., & Pantas, L. (1972). A PK experiment comparing meditating versus non-meditating subjects. In W.G. Roll, R.L. Morris, & J.D. Morris (Eds.), *Proceedings of Parapsychology Association 1971* (pp. 12-13).

Mattuck, R.D. (1977). Random fluctuation theory of psychokinesis: Thermal noise model. In J.D. Morris, W.G. Roll & R.L. Morris (Eds.), *Research in Parapsychology 1976* (pp. 191-195). Metuchen NJ: Scarecrow Press.

McClenon, J., Roig, M., Smith, M. D., & Ferrier, G. (2003). Coverage of parapsychology in introductory psychology textbooks: 1980-2002. *Journal of Parapsychology, 67,* 167-179.

Meletti, S., Tassi, L., Mai, R., Fini, N., Tassinari, C.A., & Russo, G.L. (2006). Emotions induced by intracerebral electrical stimulation of the temporal lobe, *Epilepsia, 47*(5), 47-51.

Milton, J., & Wiseman, R. (1999). Does psi exist? Lack of replication of an anomalous process of information transfer. *Psychological Bulletin, 125,* 378-391.

Morris, R.L., Harary, S.B., Janis, J., Hartwell, J., & Roll W.G. (1978). Studies of communication during out-of-body experiences. *Journal of the American Society for Psychical Research, 72,* 1-21.

Myers, S.A., Austrin, H.R., Grisso, J.T., & Nickeson, R.C. (1983). Personality characteristics as related to the out-of-body experience. *Journal of Parapsychology, 47,* 131-144.

Nash, C.B. (1981). Simultaneous high and low aim in the same roll of dice. *Journal of the American Society for Psychical Research, 75*(3), 259-266.

Nash, C.B. (1984). Test of psychokinetic control of bacterial mutation. *Journal of the American Society for Psychical Research, 78*(2), 145-152.

Nelson, R.D., Bradish, G.J. & Dobyns, Y.H. (1989). Random Event Generator qualification, calibration and analysis. *Technical Note PEAR 89001*, Princeton Engineering Anomalies Research, Princeton University, School of Engineering/Applied Science.

Nelson, R.D., Bradish, G.J., Dobyns, Y.H., Dunne, B.J., & Jahn, R.G. (1996). FieldREG anomalies in group situations. *Journal of Scientific Exploration, 10*(1), 111-141.

Nelson, R.D., Jahn, R.G., Dunne, B.J., Dobyns, Y.H., & Bradish, G.J. (1998). FieldREG II: Consciousness field effects: Replications and explorations. *Journal of Scientific Exploration, 12*(3), 425-454.

Nichols, A., & Roll, W.G. (1999). Discovery of electromagnetic anomalies at two reputedly haunted castles in Scandinavia. *Proceedings of presented papers: The Parapsychological Association 41st Annual Conference,* 97-107.

Orme, J.E. (1974). Precognition and time. *Journal of the Society for Psychical Research, 47,* 351-365.

Osis, K., & Foster, E.B. (1953). A test of ESP in cats. *Journal of Parapsychology, 17,* 168-186.

Osis, K., & Haraldsson, E. (1977). *At the hour of death.* New York: Avon.

Osis, K., & Mitchell, J.L. (1977). Physiological correlates of reported out-of-body experiences. *Journal of the Society for Psychical Research, 49,* 525-536.

Palmer, J. (1971). Scoring in ESP tests as a function of belief in ESP: I. The sheep-goat effect. *Journal of the American Society for Psychical Research, 65*(4), 373-408.

Palmer, J. (1979). A community mail survey of psychic experiences. *Journal of the American Society for Psychical Research, 73,* 221-251.

Palmer, J.A., Honorton, C., & Utts, J. (1989). Reply to the National Research Council study on parapsychology. *Journal of the American Association for Psychical Research, 83*, 31-49.

Parker, A. (1974). ESP in gerbils using positive reinforcement. *Journal of Parapsychology, 38,* 301-311.

Parnia, S., & Fenwick, P. (2002). Near death experiences in cardiac arrest: visions of a dying brain or visions of a new science of consciousness. *Resuscitation, 52,* 5-11.

Persinger, M.A. (2003). The sensed presence within experimental settings: Implications for the male and female concept of self. *Journal of Psychology, 137*(1), 5-16.

Persinger, M.A., & Healey, F. (2002). Experimental facilitation of the sensed presence: Possible intercalation between the hemispheres induced by complex magnetic fields. *Journal of Nervous and Mental Disease, 190*(8), 533-541.

Pratt, J.G., & Roll, W.G. (1958). The Seaford Disturbances. *Journal of Parapsychology, 22,* 79-124.

Pratt, J.G., Rhine, J.B., Smith, B.M., Stuart, C.E., & Greenwood, J.A. (1966). *Extrasensory perception after sixty years.* Boston: Bruce Humphries.

Radin, D. I. (1997). *The conscious universe: The scientific truth of psychic phenomena.* San Francisco: HarperEdge.

Radin, D. I. (1997a). Unconscious perception of future emotions: An experiment in presentiment. *Journal of Scientific Exploration, 11*(2), 163-180.

Radin, D.I., & Ferrari, D.C. (1991). Effects of consciousness on the fall of dice: A meta-analysis. *Journal of Scientific Exploration, 5*(1), 61-85.

Radin, D.I., & Nelson, R.D. (1989). Evidence for consciousness related anomalies in random physical systems. *Foundations of Physics, 19,* 1499-1514.

Radin, D.I., & Nelson, R.D. (2003). Meta-analysis of mind-matter interaction experiments: 1959 to 2000. In W.B. Jonas & C.C. Crawford (Eds.), *Healing, Intention, and Energy Medicine: Science, Research Methods and Clinical Implications* (pp. 39 – 48). London: Churchill Livingstone.

Radin, D.I., Rebman, J.M., & Cross, M.P. (1996). Anomalous organisation of anomalous events by group consciousness: Two exploratory experiments. *Journal of Scientific Exploration, 10*(1), 143-168.

Radin, D.I., Taft, R., & Young, G. (2004). Possible effects of healing intention on cell cultures and truly random events. *Journal of Alternative and Complementary Medicine, 10,* 103-112.

Ratte, R.J. (1960). Comparison of game and standard PK testing techniques under competitive and non-competitive conditions. *Journal of Parapsychology, 24,* 235-245.

Rhine, J.B. (1934). *Extrasensory Perception.* Boston: Boston Society for Psychical Research.

Rhine, J.B. (1943). Dice thrown by cup and machine in PK tests. *Journal of Parapsychology, 7,* 207-217.

Rhine, J.B. (1969). Position effects in psi test results. *Journal of Parapsychology, 33,* 136-157.

Rhine, J.B., & Humphrey, B.M. (1944). PK tests with six, twelve, and twenty-four dice per throw. *Journal of Parapsychology, 8,* 139-157.

Rhine, J.B., & Humphrey, B.M. (1944b). The PK effect: special evidence from hit patterns, I, Quarter distributions of the page. *Journal of Parapsychology, 8,* 18-60.

Rhine, J.B., & Pratt, J.G. (1954). A review of the Pearce-Pratt distance series of ESP tests. *Journal of Parapsychology, 18,* 165-177.

Rhine, J.B., & Pratt, J.G. (1962). *Parapsychology: Frontier science of the mind, (Revised Edition).* Springfield, Illinois: Charles Thomas.

Rhine, L.E. (1953). Subjective forms of spontaneous psi experiences. *Journal of Parapsychology, 17,* 77-114.

Rhine, L.E. (1956). The relationship of agent and percipient in spontaneous telepathy. *Journal of Parapsychology, 20,* 1-32.

Rhine, L.E. (1961). *Hidden channels of the mind.* New York: William Sloane Associates.

Rhine, L.E. (1962). Psychological processes in ESP experiences. Part 1. Waking experiences. *Journal of Parapsychology, 26,* 88-111.

Ring, K. (1980). *Life at Death.* New York: Coward, McCann & Geoghegan.

Ring, K. (1984). *Heading toward omega: In search of the meaning of the near-death experience.* New York: Morrow.

Roe, C.A., Sherwood, S.J., Luke, D.P., & Farrell, L.M. (2002). An exploratory investigation of dream GESP using consensus judging and dynamic targets. *Journal of the Society for Psychical Research, 66*(3), 225-238.

Roig, M., Icochea, H., & Cuzzucoli, A. (1991). Coverage of parapsychology in introductory psychology textbooks. *Teaching of Psychology, 18*(3), 157-160.

Roll, W.G. (1969). The Newark disturbances. *Journal of the American Society for Psychical Research, 63,* 123-174.

Roll, W.G. (1977). Poltergeists. In B.B. Wolman (Ed.), *Handbook of Parapsychology* (pp. 382-413). New York: Von Nostrand Reinhold.

Roll, W.G., & Pratt, J.G. (1971). The Miami disturbances. *Journal of the American Society for Psychical Research, 65,* 409-454.

Rubin, L., & Honorton, C. (1972). Separating the yins from the yangs: an experiment with the I-ching. *Proceedings of the Parapsychological Association 1972*, 6-7.

Sannwald, G. (1963). On the psychology of spontaneous paranormal phenomena. *International Journal of Parapsychology, 5,* 274-292.

Schmeidler, G.R. (1943). Predicting good and bad scores in a clairvoyance experiment: A preliminary report. *Journal of the American Society for Psychical Research, 37,* 103-110.

Schmidt, H. (1969). Precognition of a quantum process. *Journal of Parapsychology, 33,* 99-108.

Schmidt, H. (1970). A PK test with electronic equipment. *Journal of Parapsychology, 34*(3), 175-181.

Schmidt, H. (1970a). PK experiments with animals. *Journal of Parapsychology, 36,* 282-283.

Schmidt, H. (1970b). PK experiments involving animals. *Journal of Parapsychology, 36,* 302-303.

Schmidt, H. (1975). Toward a mathematical theory of psi. *Journal of the American Society for Psychical Research, 69,* 301-309.

Schmidt, H. (1976). PK effect on pre-recorded targets. *Journal of the American Society for Psychical Research, 70,* 267-291.

Schmidt, H. (1984). Comparison of a Teleological Model with a Quantum Collapse Model of Psi. *Journal of Parapsychology, 48,* 261-276.

Schmidt, H., Morris, R., & Rudolph, L. (1986). Channeling evidence for a psychokinetic effect to independent observers. *Journal of Parapsychology, 50,* 1-15.

Schmidt, H., & Schlitz, M.J. (1989). A large scale pilot PK experiment with pre-recorded random events. In L.A. Henkel & R.E. Berger (Eds.), *Research in Parapsychology 1988* (pp. 6-10). Metuchen, NJ: Scarecrow Press.

Schmidt, S. (2003). Direct mental interactions with living systems (DMILS). In W. Jonas & C. Crawford. (Eds.), *Healing, intention and energy medicine: Science, research methods and clinical implications* (pp. 23-38). London: Churchill Livingstone.

Schouten, S.A. (1981). Analysing spontaneous cases: A replication based on the Sannwald collection. *European Journal of Parapsychology, 4,* 9-48.

Schouten, S.A. (1982). Analysing spontaneous cases: A replication based on the Rhine collection. *European Journal of Parapsychology, 4,* 113-158.

Sherwood, S.J., Roe C.A., Simmonds, C.A., & Biles, C. (2002). An exploratory investigation of dream precognition using consensus judging and static targets. *Journal of the Society for Psychical Research, 66*(1), 22-28.

Shrager, E.F. (1978). The effects of sender-receiver relationship and associated personality variables on ESP scores. *Journal of the American Society for Psychical Research, 72,* 35-47.

Sicher, F., Targ, E., Moore, D., & Smith, H.S. (1998). A randomised double-blind study of the effects of distant healing in a population with advanced AIDS. *Western Journal of Medicine, 169*, 356-363.

Simon-Buller, S., Christopherson, V.A., & Jones, R.A. (1988). Correlates of sensing the presence of a deceased spouse. *Omega, 19,* 21-30.

Smith, M.D. (2003). The role of the experimenter in parapsychological research. *Journal of Consciousness Studies, 10,* 69-84.

Stanford, R. G., & Thompson, G. (1974). Unconscious psi-mediated instrumental response and its relation to conscious ESP performance. In W. G. Roll, R. L. Morris, & J. D. Morris (Eds.), *Research in Parapsychology 1973.* (pp. 99-103) Metuchen, NJ: Scarecrow Press.

Steilberg, B.J. (1975). "Conscious concentration" versus "visualisation" in PK tests. *Journal of Parapsychology, 39*(1), 12-20.

Steinkamp, F. (2000). Acting on the future: A survey of precognitive experiences. *Journal of the American Society for Psychical Research, 94,* 37-59.

Stevens, P. (2001). Effects of 5 s exposures to a 50μT, 20 Hz magnetic field on skin conductance and ratings of affect and arousal. *Bioelectromagnetics*, 22, 219-223.

Stevenson, I. (1967). An antagonist's view of parapsychology, *Journal of the American Society for Psychical Research, 61,* 254-267.

Stevenson, I. (1996). The opening of Robert Thouless's combination lock. *Journal of the Society for Psychical Research, 61,* 114-115.

Stokes, D.M. (1987). Theoretical parapsychology. In S. Krippner (Ed.), *Advances in Parapsychological Research, volume 5* (pp. 77-189). Jefferson, NC: McFarland.

Tandy, V., & Lawrence, T.R. (1998). The ghost in the machine. *Journal of the Society for Psychical Research, 62,* 360-364.

Tart, C.T. (1963). Physiological correlates of psi cognition. *International Journal of Parapsychology, 5,* 375-386.

Tart, C.T. (1971). *On being stoned: A psychological study of marijuana intoxication.* Palo Alto, CA: Science and behaviour books

Thalbourne, M.A., & Jungkuntz, J.H. (1983). Extraverted sheep versus introverted goats: Experiments VII and VIII. *Journal of Parapsychology, 47,* 49-51.

The Steering Committee of the Physicians' Health Study Research Group. (1988). Preliminary report: Findings from the aspirin component of the ongoing physicians' health study. *New England Journal of Medicine, 318*(4), 262–264.

Thouless, R.H. (1942). "Experiments on paranormal guessing". *British Journal of Psychology, 33,* 15-27.

Thouless, R.H. (1946). A test of survival. *Proceedings of the Society for Psychical Research, 48,* 253-263.

Twemlow, S.W., Gabbard, G.O., & Jones, F.C. (1982). The out-of-body experience: a phenomenological typology based on questionnaire responses. *American Journal of Psychiatry, 139,* 450-455.

Ullman, M. (1974). Symposium: Psychokinesis on stable systems: Work in progress, PK in the Soviet Union. In W.G. Roll, R.L. Morris & J.D. Morris (Eds.), *Research in Parapsychology 1973* (pp. 121-155). Metuchen, NJ; Scarecrow.

Ullman, M., Krippner, S., & Vaughan, A. (1986). *Dream Telepathy.* New York: Macmillan.

Utts, J. (1995). An assessment of the evidence for psychic functioning. *Journal of Parapsychology, 59,* 289-320.

van Lommel, P., van Wees, R., Meyers, V., & Elfferich, I. (2001). Near-death experience in survivors of cardiac arrest: A prospective study in the Netherlands. *The Lancet, 358,* 2039-2045.

Vassy, Z. (1978). Method of measuring the probability of 1-bit extransensory information transfer between living organisms. *Journal of Parapsychology, 43*(2), 158-160.

Virtanen, L. (1990). *That must have been ESP! An examination of psychic experiences.* (Translated by J. Atkinson & T. Dubois), Bloomington, IN: Indiana University Press.

Walker, E.H. (1975). Foundations of paraphysical and parapsychological phenomena. In L. Oteri (Ed.), *Quantum Physics and Parapsychology* (pp. 1-53). New York: Parapsychology Foundation.

Wang, G.M., Sevick, E.M., Mittag, E., Searles, D.J., & Evans, D.J. (2002). Experimental demonstration of violations of the second law of thermodynamics for small systems and short time scales. *Physical Letters Review, 89*(5), 050601/1-4.

Ward, J. (2004). Emotionally mediated synaesthesia. *Cognitive Neuropsychology, 21(7)*, 761-772.

Watkins, G.K. (1971). Possible PK in the lizard Anolis sagrei. *Proceedings of the Parapsychological Association, 8,* 23-25.

Watkins, G.K., Watkins, A.M., & Wells, R.A. (1973). Further studies on the resuscitation of anesthetized mice, In J.D. Morris, W.G. Roll & R.L. Morris (Eds.), *Research in Parapsychology 1972* (pp. 157-159). Metuchen, NJ: Scarecrow Press.

Watt, C., & Ramakers, P. (2003). Experimenter effects with a remote facilitation of attention focusing task: A study with multiple believer and disbeliever experimenters. *Journal of Parapsychology, 67,* 99-116.

Weiner, D. (1982). The effects of preferred cognitive mode and goal conceptualisation in an intentional PK task. *Journal of Parapsychology, 46,* 56-57.

Wirth, D.P., Johnson, C.A., Horvarth, J.S., & MacGregor, J.D. (1992). The effect of alternative healing therapy on the regeneration rate of salamander forelimbs. *Journal of Scientific Exploration, 6,* 375-390.

Wiseman, R., & Schlitz, M. (1997). Experimenter effects and the remote detection of staring. *Journal of Parapsychology, 61,* 197–207.

Wiseman, R., & Schlitz, M. (1999). Experimenter effects and the remote detection of staring: An attempted replication. *Proceedings of Presented Papers: The Parapsychological Association 42nd Annual Convention,* 471–479.

Wiseman, R., Watt, C., Stevens, P., Greening, E., & O'Keeffe, C. (2003). An investigation into alleged 'hauntings'. *The British Journal of Psychology, 94,* 195-211.

www.ingramcontent.com/pod-product-compliance
Lightning Source LLC
Chambersburg PA
CBHW021216090426
42740CB00006B/243
* 9 7 8 0 9 5 5 9 1 1 4 1 5 *